MW00648113

THE NEW HUMAN REVOLUTION

VOLUME 8

THE NEW HUMAN REVOLUTION

VOLUME 8

DAISAKU IKEDA

ILLUSTRATIONS BY
KENICHIRO UCHIDA

World Tribune
—*Press*—

Published by World Tribune Press
606 Wilshire Boulevard
Santa Monica, California 90401

Complete Set   ISBN 978-0-915678-32-7
Volume 8   ISBN 978-0-915678-40-2

Interior and cover designed by Gopa & Ted2

10   9   8   7   6   5   4   3

Contents

Editor's Note

The citations most commonly used in this book have been abbreviated as follows:

◆ GZ refers to the *Gosho Zenshu*, the Japanese-language compilation of letters, treatises, essays and oral teachings of Nichiren Daishonin.

◆ LS refers to *The Lotus Sutra*, translated by Burton Watson (New York: Columbia University Press, 1993). The citation usually appears as (LSXX,xx), where XX refers to the chapter number and xx is the page number.

◆ WND refers to *The Writings of Nichiren Daishonin,* vol. 1 (WND-1) (Tokyo: Soka Gakkai, 1999) and vol. 2 (WND-2) (Tokyo: Soka Gakkai, 2006).

Securing
the Foundation

EVERY RIVER has a source. Nichiren Daishonin writes, "The farther the source, the longer the stream" (WND, 940). The Soka Gakkai, likewise, has a brilliant spiritual source: the oneness of mentor and disciple. This was set forth by the Soka Gakkai's first and second presidents, Tsunesaburo Makiguchi and Josei Toda, and is the eternal way. As long as this spirit remains alive, the stream of kosen-rufu will continue to nourish the world.

Makiguchi was arrested by the oppressive militarist

government in Japan and died in prison at age seventy-three. He died during the cold of late autumn, on November 18, 1944. Makiguchi gave his life to achieve peace and happiness for all humankind. He upheld the great philosophy of Buddhism and fought against authoritarianism to the very end. His was a noble death.

Toda was arrested along with Makiguchi. While in his prison cell he steadfastly prayed for his elderly mentor: "Please allow me to bear the brunt of blame, and let Makiguchi go home as soon as possible." His beloved mentor, however, was not to leave prison alive.

When Toda learned of Makiguchi's death, he shook with rage. When he was finally released from prison, this indomitable champion of the Mystic Law swore revenge against unjust authority.

Toda resolved to prove his mentor's cause and inherit Makiguchi's will to create a flow of kosen-rufu as broad and powerful as a great river. He wanted to eradicate misery from the world and create an age in which power was restored to the people. The strength of the human spirit would triumph over authority, military might and violence, and establish a lasting global peace.

Embracing his mentor's heart, Toda vowed to devote himself to spreading the Daishonin's teachings. Both his mentor who died in prison, and he, the disciple who emerged from prison alive, were lions prepared to stake everything for the spread of the Mystic Law.

The way of the lion is the way of mentor and disciple — a life dedicated to truth and justice. It is the way of the courageous who stand alone, afraid of nothing. It is the path of victory in which all evil and injustice are defeated. Moreover, it is the way of compassion in which one gives oneself completely to championing the cause of the people.

The Soka Gakkai is a gathering of lions, an alliance of people who share Josei Toda's spirit and create indestructible happiness and peace.

Many who joined the organization in the beginning were grappling with problems like illness, poverty and family discord. By challenging their karma, they awakened to their mission as Bodhisattvas of the Earth—their true mission as human beings—and began working to improve society. Herein lies the greatness of the Soka Gakkai's kosen-rufu movement and the essence of Mahayana Buddhism.

MAY 3, the day of the Twenty-Fifth Headquarters General Meeting, would mark the third anniversary of Shin'ichi Yamamoto's presidency. With this occasion approaching, Shin'ichi gave much thought about his next move. This May 3 marked the final year leading up to the first milestone he had set—the seventh memorial (sixth anniversary) of Josei Toda's death on April 2.

Each goal he made upon becoming president to achieve by this milestone was being realized. The membership goal of three million households was reached five months earlier, with the membership now standing at more than 3.3 million households.

Work on the Grand Reception Hall at the head temple, which the Soka Gakkai built and donated to the priesthood, was moving smoothly toward its scheduled completion the following spring. In addition, the new

Soka Gakkai Headquarters would be finished in August, and a ceremony to celebrate its completion was slated for early September.

The Komei Political Federation, with the Soka Gakkai as its main supporting body, was also making great progress. Its representation in local government assemblies now surpassed one thousand officials. It was steadily developing into a substantial force for restoring government to the people and creating a society in which the people played a leading role.

Since Shin'ichi's inauguration, the Soka Gakkai had clearly grown and advanced by leaps and bounds. This made him more aware that in order to take the next big step, it was necessary to reorganize and secure the foundations of the headquarters and general chapters in each area.

Shin'ichi also keenly perceived an even more important task — to preserve for all eternity the spirit of his predecessors, Makiguchi and Toda. Unafraid of even death, they dedicated their lives to achieving peace and happiness for all humankind. Shin'ichi was concerned that this spirit was gradually weakening among the Soka Gakkai leadership as the organization continued to develop.

He was beginning to notice leaders who were taking advantage of the Soka Gakkai now that it was well established. Rather than considering what they could do for kosen-rufu and the Soka Gakkai, they were expecting the Soka Gakkai to do something for them.

Some leaders mistakenly believed that acquiring a high position in the organization was a sign of success. Preoccupied with becoming important, they were elated when appointed to a higher position and disheartened if they were not.

If people obsessed with fame and personal profit who exploit the Soka Gakkai for their own benefit become leaders, the members will suffer. Inevitably, this leads to the decay of the entire organization and its collapse from within.

For the future advancement of the Soka Gakkai, Shin'ichi silently pledged to cut these tendencies off at the root. He would begin by causing the Soka Gakkai spirit to shine within each leader's heart.

THE TWENTY-FIFTH Headquarters General Meeting took place on May 3. The weather that morning in Tokyo was the same as on the day of the Headquarters general meeting three years before when Shin'ichi Yamamoto was inaugurated as the third Soka Gakkai president.

Though the participants did not need to assemble at the Nihon University Auditorium in Ryogoku until 9:00 A.M., many began arriving hours earlier. When overseas members from the America General Chapter and Southeast Asia General Chapter entered the auditorium at 7:00 A.M., they heard cheers from the already full venue.

The overseas members strode happily and proudly into the auditorium carrying banners: Los Angeles Chapter, Hong Kong Chapter, Bangkok Chapter, Saigon Chapter and Jakarta District. This gave the Japanese members a stronger sense of the international scope of the kosen-rufu movement. In the two-and-a-half years since President Yamamoto's first overseas trip, the dream of the worldwide propagation of Nichiren Dai-shonin's Buddhism had become a reality before their very eyes.

The meeting officially began at 9:45 A.M., and President Yamamoto entered the auditorium led by the Soka Gakkai Headquarters flag and a grand chorus of "Song of Innovation."

After opening words, Vice General Director and Guidance Division Leader Hisao Seki reported on the Soka Gakkai's activities over the past year. Remarkable growth was achieved in every area. The previous May, the membership stood at 2.6 million households; there were now more than 3.3 million, an increase of more than seven hundred thousand in just one year.

On the organizational front, four new headquarters, twenty-one general chapters and one hundred and thirty-five chapters were established. Overseas growth was particularly outstanding, with two general chapters created in South America and Europe and nine new chapters started in Saigon, Rangoon, Peru, Bolivia, Hawaii, West Germany, New York, Paris and Seattle. A new community center also was opened in Los Angeles. In addition, the Soka Gakkai built and donated fifteen new temples to Nichiren Shoshu. The Academic and Arts Department of the Culture Bureau was dissolved and reformed into two independent departments.

Hearing that all of this was accomplished in a single year inspired the participants. Each year was like a new dawn, with the movement of kosen-rufu advancing by unprecedented leaps and bounds.

The Soka Gakkai's momentum was building. The joy

of one victory led to another, becoming the energy and force behind even greater victories.

NEXT CAME the appointment of new leaders. Eight new directors were named, increasing the Soka Gakkai's board of directors to one hundred and twenty-seven. Kyushu Headquarters was divided into three, and the leaders of each new headquarters were announced. The Soka Gakkai Young Women's Leader, Tokie Tani, moved to the women's division, and Michiyo Watari, previously the young women's planning department leader, was appointed in her place. Overseas, Chou Chi Kong was made the leader of the Hong Kong Chapter to replace Ikuyo Oka, who had returned to Japan.

Michiyo Watari, the new young women's leader, was married to Goro Watari, head of the student division. Both of them were young leaders whom Shin'ichi Yamamoto had personally raised.

Michiyo was born in 1932 in Iri, Korea. She was thirteen and living in Seoul when World War II ended. Her father worked for the railways and could not leave Korea immediately. It was decided that the rest of the family — herself, her two grandparents, her pregnant mother and her two siblings — would return to Japan.

It was not an easy journey. When they arrived at Shimonoseki, a port city on the southwestern tip of Honshu, Japan's main island, the family boarded a packed train and began making their way toward Chichibu in Saitama Prefecture, central Japan, where they would live with relatives.

At one point, the train stopped in the middle of a burned-out expanse that had once been a city. It was

Hiroshima. This horrific image of her home country was etched into young Michiyo's mind forever.

From Hiroshima, they transferred to a coal-carrying freight train. The roofless cars overflowed with passengers. Along the way, rain began to fall. Raindrops mixed with the tears running down Michiyo's cheeks.

Life in Chichibu thus began. The family of six lived in an old cowshed which had flooring installed. To help make ends meet, Michiyo worked while attending school, carrying bundles of firewood down from the mountains to the road. At times her heavy load cut into her shoulders until they bled. In winter, she continued to labor in this way, dragging along on chilblained feet.

Eventually her father returned to Japan and the family moved to neighboring Kumagaya City. Michiyo decided that she wanted to attend college, but the family could not afford to send her.

She managed to pay for her high school expenses herself by working part time. When her family moved to Omiya, a city east of Kumagaya, they happened to be close to a middle school. Taking advantage of this opportunity, Michiyo borrowed some money from her father and turned the front of their house into a school-supply shop. Through this business, she saved enough money for her university tuition and entered the Law Department of Waseda University.

MICHIYO WATARI became involved in the socialist movement during her high school days. She wanted to build a peaceful nation and find a solution to the contradictions of society that ignored the plight of the poor and the weak. She was disheartened to find how the other activists who sacrificed their happiness for their cause, ultimately wound up in despair.

Realizing there were problems that social reform alone could not resolve, such as incurable disease and family discord, Michiyo felt that the socialist movement had its limitations. Around this time, she learned about the Soka Gakkai from Seiichiro Koyama, a young man who delivered milk to her home. His assertion that Nichiren Daishonin's Buddhism aimed to achieve both social prosperity and individual happiness inspired her to take faith.

Michiyo joined the Soka Gakkai in November 1952 while she was a university student. She intended to give it her all for one year — but if she did not get the results she was looking for by then, she would quit.

Determined to get something out of her efforts, Michiyo exerted herself diligently in her Buddhist practice. She visited the Soka Gakkai Headquarters branch office in Ichigaya, Tokyo, almost every day and even sought guidance on occasion from President Toda. Eventually, she realized that only the Daishonin's Buddhism had the power to liberate people from their suffering.

When a year had passed, Michiyo strengthened her resolve to live out her life with the Soka Gakkai. After graduating from college, she began working for the Headquarters as a *Seikyo Shimbun* correspondent. She was the first woman to hold such a position.

As a reporter, she placed great importance on the social perspective of any story she covered. When she reported on the experience of someone who overcame an illness through faith, for example, she would visit the attending doctor and find out how he or she viewed the recovery from a medical standpoint. She made a conscious effort to write articles that were free of dogma and that would convince others of the power of Buddhism.

She also called upon noted editors of magazines or other publications and asked their opinion of the *Seikyo Shimbun*. Her desire for self-improvement was strong, and she always strove for perfection in her work. Our personal growth depends to a large degree on whether we possess such a desire for self-improvement.

Michiyo became the head of the planning department in the young women's division under the leadership of Young Women's Leader Tokie Tani, and demonstrated enormous ability. She was full of fresh ideas, yet her seniors in the women's and young women's divisions did not always accept them. Frustrated, she often went to Shin'ichi Yamamoto for guidance.

SHIN'ICHI wanted Michiyo fully to utilize her talents to benefit young women. For this reason, he was sometimes strict with her.

Once, when Michiyo came to him disheartened because her proposal was rejected, Shin'ichi said to her: "Kosen-rufu is a bloodless revolution to create happiness and peace for all people. Even socialist revolutionaries have fought with their lives, enduring one persecution after another without compromising their ideals. Those who become discouraged just because others do not accept their ideas are not qualified to work for kosen-rufu."

Michiyo renewed her resolve and threw herself back into activities — so much so that she neglected her physical appearance. Seeing this, Shin'ichi said to her: "As a leader of young women, it is important to pay attention to how you look and dress, and to always try to be neat and presentable. Women at the top of their fields throughout the world are attentive to this. No one will follow a leader who lacks such composure."

On another occasion he said: "If you are always trying to do everything yourself according to how you want it, your members will not grow. It is important to think about how to enable each member to joyfully make the most of her potential and to put the spotlight on others, not on yourself.

"It is also vital to listen carefully to what others have to say and be warm and accepting. A leader who is cold and mechanical will only end up rejected by everyone. Always remember that the purpose of faith is to polish our humanity."

Michiyo steadily developed her capacity as a young women's leader.

In May 1959, the year after President Toda's death, she married Goro Watari. He was also a *Seikyo Shimbun* reporter, and the two had fallen in love.

When they came to tell Shin'ichi that they were to be married, he said: "Is that so? Congratulations! I know that if Mr. Toda were still alive, he would be very happy."

President Toda had once told Shin'ichi that he would like to see the two young people get together because he thought they would make a charming couple, and Shin'ichi had never forgotten this.

Michiyo continued to work for the *Seikyo Shimbun* after marriage and after giving birth, quite unusual for the time. She also continued to fulfill her responsibilities as the head of the young women's division planning department. Her mind was set on carrying out her mission without retreating a single step, no matter how her circumstances might change.

AFTER THE LEADERSHIP appointments, the former Hong Kong Chapter leader, Ikuyo Oka, returned the chapter flag to President Yamamoto. He, in turn, presented it to the new chapter leader. Flags were also presented to the Hawaii and Seattle chapters, both established in January.

Vice General Director Eisuke Akizuki then announced the organization's activities and goals toward the seventh memorial (sixth anniversary) of President Toda's death. This was followed by determinations from representatives of each division.

First, Student Division Leader Goro Watari pledged to increase the division's membership to twenty-thousand and to unite the membership under its crimson and navy flag.

Newly appointed Young Women's Leader Michiyo Watari took the podium next and began speaking energetically of her hopes and goals: "I have been entrusted with the great responsibility of leading the young women on this auspicious occasion commemorating the third anniversary of President Yamamoto's inauguration. This is a time for fresh advancement. I am determined to muster all my strength and devote myself entirely to kosen-rufu!"

She next introduced the first of two new mottoes for the young women: "Establish unshakable faith."

A life without roots is like a floating weed being tossed about on the waves; it is easily swayed by the trends of the times and by personal weaknesses. A person who lives this way will be daunted when faced with harsh trials. Faith, Michiyo stressed, is the very root that grounds us. It begins and ends with chanting daimoku.

She then introduced the second motto: "Lifelong learning."

There is no growth or progress for those who do not strive to cultivate their minds. As a saying goes, "A life without learning is base." In particular, for those who aim to become leaders of the next generation, study is not only a right but also the greatest duty.

Michiyo further expressed her hope that young women would especially pour their energies into studying the teachings of Nichiren Daishonin—the basic foundation for life—and adopt the Buddhist philosophy of life.

The next speaker was Kenshiro Ishikawa, the young men's leader. He reported on the first European young men's general meeting held in Paris in April. He also spoke of a new surge in the spread of the Daishonin's Buddhism around the world, powered by youth. Emphasizing the need for many more capable young people to bolster this progress, he voiced his hope that young men would do their best to raise such youth in many fields.

In closing, Ishikawa said: "The Soka Gakkai is the body from which capable individuals are fostered. It is a vast ocean of people, and only by diving in and getting actively involved can we develop ourselves into individuals as strong as orca whales.

"We, the young men, will build a solid organization. We will stand at the front lines of our activities for kosen-rufu and become pillars of support to all members while waging a great struggle to rebuild society."

FOLLOWING the resolutions by youth representatives, Katsu Kiyohara addressed the gathering on behalf of the women's division members.

She began speaking proudly of their energetic efforts: "I wish to affirm that women are the motivating power and driving force of the Soka Gakkai's activities to build a peaceful society. Has it not been women who introduced the Daishonin's Buddhism to those suffering from illness who were abandoned even by their doctors? Have they not gone time and time again to visit families suffering in poverty to teach them about Buddhism?

"In their own families, they give courage to their husbands who are worn out from working to put food on the table. They are also the ones raising their children to be capable individuals who will shoulder the Soka Gakkai's movement in the future.

"Mr. Toda used to say that kosen-rufu would be accomplished by the efforts of women. The fact that more than half of the entire Soka Gakkai membership is women is clear proof of his conviction.

"That is why, I believe, President Yamamoto treasures the women's division members, and why he wrote the editorial 'To the Women's Division' for the March issue of *The Daibyakurenge.*"

Touching on Shin'ichi's message, Kiyohara called on the women to open a road leading to the revitalization of society. As pioneers of true women's liberation, she hoped that they would excel in their chosen fields—in the media, arts, education or any other area.

Shin'ichi was pleased and reassured to see the members of each division pledging their commitment to fresh progress while utilizing their own unique capabilities, each division burning with strong determination for the realization of kosen-rufu.

Next came greetings from a vice general director and other leaders, followed by President Yamamoto's speech.

The members applauded enthusiastically in anticipation of Shin'ichi's impassioned words. His speech would mark a fresh start on this significant third anniversary of taking the Soka Gakkai's helm.

Shin'ichi's voice resonated clearly throughout the auditorium: "It is through the kind help and support of the board of directors, the other leaders and the members that, despite my inexperience, I am able to bring our movement to where it is today. I am striving in accord with the Daishonin's teaching 'Life is limited; we must not begrudge it. What we should ultimately aspire to is the Buddha land' (WND, 214). I thank you from the bottom of my heart."

Joyful applause filled the hall.

Shin'ichi continued: "Now I engrave in my heart once again the following words of the Daishonin: 'This I will state. Let the gods forsake me. Let all persecutions assail me. Still I will give my life for the sake of the Law' (WND, 280).

"With your support, I will continue taking the lead in the next step in our efforts for kosen-rufu, aiming toward April 2 next year—the seventh memorial of Mr. Toda's death—as well as next May 3."

Shin'ichi's call for further advancement was like a lion's roar. Once again, the Nihon University Auditorium erupted in applause, and it did not subside for some time.

SHIN'ICHI wanted to take the opportunity at the May 3 general meeting to answer clearly a question that some political analysts and journalists focused on during the nationwide local elections in April: Is the Soka Gakkai conservative or progressive?

Shin'ichi was looking for a way to separate the activities of the Soka Gakkai and the Komei Political Federation into distinct realms—religious and political. Although both shared the same fundamental ideals, each would have its own administration and would function in an independent way.

Many analysts seemed to think that the Soka Gakkai was aiming for a union of government and religion, and that the two groups were really one and the same. That is why they questioned whether the Soka Gakkai, and not the Komei Political Federation, was conservative or progressive.

Shin'ichi addressed this topic at smaller gatherings, but he decided at the general meeting to articulate the official Soka Gakkai stance: "Regardless of how much the Soka Gakkai has contributed to society, rather than being praised, we have been exposed to constant criticism.

"If we look for a basis for such criticism, however, we find only the vaguest suspicions. For example, because our youth uses such titles as corps leader and company leader, and because we are united and well organized, some irresponsibly assert that we are militaristic.

"This same thinking has led to speculation and rumor over the Soka Gakkai's political leanings. Some contend that, because the Komei Political Federation supported the rightist Liberal Democratic Party's candidate in the Tokyo gubernatorial race, the Soka Gakkai is an arm of that conservative party—and therefore must be conservative. There are those who claim, on the other hand, that because we have spoken of a new form of socialism based on humanistic ideals, we are allied with the socialist party and must be seeking reform.

"Another argument states that since the Soka Gakkai is based on the teachings of Nichiren Daishonin's Buddhism, which dates back to Japan's Medieval Period, it must be a conservative body. Others say we are progressive because we have many youthful members who aim to improve society. Still others say that within the organization, older members are conservative while younger ones are progressive.

"So people are eager to label the Soka Gakkai as either conservative or progressive, but the truth is that they cannot decide which one it should be. In my opinion, the need to pigeonhole things represents an extremely conservative way of thinking. It means stagnation even for those who claim to be progressive, and it will lead nowhere."

SHIN'ICHI expanded on the basic stance of the Soka Gakkai: "A sutra states, 'Immeasurable meanings are born from a single Law.' The Soka Gakkai aims to bring happiness to all humanity and build lasting peace based on the Law of Nam-myoho-renge-kyo and the Gohonzon, and the Daishonin's philosophy of life. From the standpoint of life's eternity, therefore, it is our mission to show all people, regardless of their political position, the way to genuine happiness.

"Without fundamental guidelines on which people can base their lives, even a free-market society will deteriorate into corruption and chaos. The law of the jungle, the survival of the fittest, will rule. Without an internal revolution in the lives of individuals, socialism will only produce a coldhearted, oppressive system. We of the Soka Gakkai live by a profound, powerful philosophy that is capable of guiding liberalism and socialism, both conservatives and progressives alike.

"In that sense, if the Soka Gakkai must be called progressive, I think it is so in the truest sense of the word. This is different from being a progressive political force, as some now view us.

"The Daishonin's Buddhism is a great teaching of enduring, eternal happiness that enables all people to attain Buddhahood in this lifetime. The power of the Gohonzon is as limitless and vast as the universe.

"We have spread this philosophy to more than three million households nationwide, showing them the way to true happiness. With the conviction that our movement is giving people a means to revitalize their lives based on human revolution, let us boldly push forward along the path of our mission, never getting caught up in such narrow-minded political labeling as whether something is conservative or progressive."

Enthusiastic applause filled the hall.

Shin'ichi worried that some members might be led astray by the attempts of outside critics to tag the Soka Gakkai as a political force and thus lose sight of the important path of faith.

"With your support," Shin'ichi continued, "the Komei Political Federation has made tremendous progress. I am worried, however, that we will now see the emergence of people who wish to use the Soka Gakkai as a stepping-stone into the political arena, people who will try to take advantage of the Soka Gakkai in the elections. We must look for any such tendencies and continue to advance while always putting faith first."

SHIN'ICHI ended his speech on the subject of human happiness.

"What makes our lives truly shine?" he asked. "It is not wealth or power. It is when we, as disciples of Nichiren Daishonin and emissaries of the Buddha, become allies to those who are suffering.

"When we devote ourselves to that mission, we can savor a life of ultimate radiance and joy. It is the internal flame of our passion toward this mission that causes our lives to shine eternally with the unfading light of humanity.

"Let us therefore continue to carry out faith that flows

like water. Let's also advance together along the great path of mission and honor, striving to grow as individuals and build happy, harmonious families."

On this third anniversary of his inauguration as Soka Gakkai president, Shin'ichi's words signaled a new beginning.

Sharing the same resolve, the audience's applause echoed throughout the auditorium.

Vice General Director Takeo Konishi then led the members in "Song of the New Century."

When the song finished, Shin'ichi removed his jacket, took a folding fan in his hand and stood up. "Now I'll lead a song," he announced. "What shall we sing?"

"Song of Progress," a voice immediately called out.

"That's a good choice," said Shin'ichi, "since the Soka Gakkai is progressive in the truest sense."

The Brass Band and Fife and Drum Corps played the melody while the members clapped to the music.

Shin'ichi began to move with all the power and dignity of a mighty eagle soaring in the sky. The twenty-thousand leaders present sang enthusiastically in tempo with Shin'ichi's lead. Their voices rang with a renewed resolve toward the seventh memorial (sixth anniversary) of their mentor Josei Toda's death.

Shin'ichi's movements embodied the strong determination he had spoken of that day—to take the lead in the next stage of the kosen-rufu movement. His movements also signified the rhythm of fresh advancement, an introduction to a new period of development.

With this day as the starting point, Shin'ichi stood in the vanguard of the Soka Gakkai's activities once again.

The next day, May 4, he visited the head temple, and on May 5 he participated in the completion ceremony for the new Fuji Community Center in Fuji City, Shizuoka Prefecture. On May 6, he attended the monthly young men's leaders meeting at the Taito Gymnasium in Tokyo. On May 9, he delivered a lecture on *The Three-fold Secret Teachings*[1] to young women's leaders, and the following day he attended another young women's leaders meeting signifying the division's fresh start with new leadership at the Hibiya Civic Hall in Tokyo.

Shin'ichi was determined to set an example of the true Soka Gakkai spirit and the way leaders should behave through his actions.

AFTER the headquarters general meeting, Shin'ichi met with some of the Soka Gakkai directors to discuss activities leading up to the seventh memorial service for Josei Toda.

Hiroshi Yamagiwa, head of the organizational statistics department, handed out charts showing the rate of membership growth broken down by chapter and general chapter, giving a clear picture of the real condition of the organization.

Using these charts as a reference, the leaders began to discuss the situation of each chapter. One vice general director commented under his breath: "According to this, the gap is widening between the areas experiencing growth and those that are stagnating. Overall, it seems that the urban areas are growing while the outlying areas are lagging behind."

Another vice general director added: "That's partly

because old customs have a stronger hold in the countryside, making it more difficult to introduce people to the Daishonin's Buddhism. But the real problem lies with the chapter leaders. When the chapter leader is slack, the organization simply will not grow."

Hearing this input, Shin'ichi looked at the two vice general directors and asked sharply: "And what have you, in your capacities, done to help those chapters?"

Surprised by his strict tone, they sat in silence looking embarrassed.

"Even in his advanced years," Shinichi continued, "Mr. Makiguchi would go anywhere in Japan to visit even one member. Wherever he went, he would introduce people to Buddhism.

"This is the true spirit and behavior of a Soka Gakkai leader. All across Japan, the men's and women's leaders on both the chapter and district levels are doing their very best. They are constantly wracking their brains and exerting themselves wholeheartedly in their activities.

"Senior leaders who sit back and do nothing while members struggle — commentating on which chapters are strong and which are weak as if watching a baseball game — are no more than cheap critics. Those who make no effort themselves but look down on others from on high while making irresponsible comments, have been poisoned by bureaucracy. They have started toward their own downfall, though they do not realize it.

"I will resolutely challenge any such leader. If I do not, the members will suffer. As we enter the final phase of completing our goals toward the seventh memorial of Mr. Toda's death, we must first revive within each of our hearts the true Soka Gakkai spirit, the spirit of the early days of our organization.

"On February 11, in the year he died, Mr. Toda held a banquet to celebrate his recovery from illness as well as his birthday. Do you remember what he said then?" Shin'ichi's eyes swept the faces of everyone in the room, but no one answered.

"MR. TODA expressed his concern that the leaders' encouragement had not produced the expected results. He said this was not the fault of the members but a lack of faith and personal growth on the part of the leadership who were the core of the organization.

"He also said: 'I, as president, must first be diligent on this point if the Soka Gakkai is to develop. I realize that I must educate and refine myself.' He advised us that leaders on every level of the organization should similarly be vigilant in their efforts to improve themselves.

"Mr. Toda was stressing the importance of self-improvement for himself as well as other leaders. This is his legacy to us. One cannot be called a true leader unless one continuously strives for self-improvement. I feel the same way as Mr. Toda and share the same determination.

"Every day, I study and self-reflect. I challenge myself and strive for personal growth. All of the Soka Gakkai's affairs are my responsibility. They are my concern. It is because of this firm awareness that I absolutely cannot sit idly by and make careless remarks like an uninvolved critic or spectator.

"I hope each of you, as directors and vice general

directors, will have the same commitment I do. Otherwise, kosen-rufu will never progress, no matter how many directors we have. In fact, our movement will only be slowed down."

Shin'ichi feared the degeneration of the true spirit of leadership more than anything. This was because, as the Soka Gakkai grew and developed, he could see that there were leaders who, rather than trying to contribute to the Soka Gakkai, were instead becoming dependent on it, almost as if they were living off it.

"When Mr. Toda became president," Shin'ichi continued, "the Soka Gakkai consisted of twelve chapters, and all twelve chapter leaders were resolved to give their very lives to carrying out the widespread propagation of Nichiren Daishonin's Buddhism together with Mr. Toda. None of them cared the least for social status, recognition or wealth. Their only thought was advancing kosen-rufu and carrying out their mission in this lifetime. This is the Soka Gakkai spirit, the spirit that kept us going from the beginning.

"The resolve of these pioneers became the driving force for kosen-rufu. Some of you here today were the very leaders I am talking about, and all of you have been leaders from the outset. I therefore hope that you will revive and reawaken that firm resolve within you.

"I hope all of us in this room will start by returning to the original Soka Gakkai spirit—the spirit of those early days."

DETERMINATION shone in everyone's eyes. Shin'ichi looked intently at each leader as he continued: "With the seventh memorial service for Mr. Toda as our target, I want all of the vice general directors, including General Director Harayama, to take responsibility for each local organization as headquarters leaders.[2] In doing so, I hope that each of you as a leader of this organization will embody the spirit prevalent in the pioneering days of our movement.

"Without a clear outline of one's responsibilities it is easy to lose touch with the organization. This gives rise to a careless attitude. I wish to completely eliminate this tendency from the Soka Gakkai. Your new leadership appointments will be announced at this month's Headquarters leaders meeting.

"Of course, what I am saying does not only apply to you. As president, I will also work much harder than before. I will exert myself fully in serving our members, the children of the Buddha. Just watch me."

In fact, Shin'ichi always looked for those working hard for kosen-rufu behind the scenes, doing whatever he could to encourage them. That is why, prior to the headquarters general meeting earlier that day, he proposed that "Seniors Gatherings" be held for the Soka Gakkai's elderly members. On May 12 and 14, every regional organization would put on events where these members could gather and enjoy performances of music, song, dance or theater. Shin'ichi wanted to take the opportunity of the Soka Gakkai's fresh start to recognize and show appreciation to the pioneer members.

When Shin'ichi saw a Soka Gakkai leader taking action on all fronts, he always thought about those who were supporting that leader in the shadows. He knew that, just as the tip of an iceberg is all one sees above the surface of the water, there is always a multitude of people supporting a leader working in the limelight.

Whenever Shin'ichi looked for those supporters, inevitably he would find elderly members. Some were experts at giving personal guidance, striving to enable their juniors to participate joyfully in Soka Gakkai activities. Paying close attention to the needs of those younger members, the elderly members would visit them in their homes regularly and listen to their troubles, encouraging them based on their rich experiences in faith. Many would also look after their grandchildren and help with household chores, while their daughters-in-law, with whom they usually lived, were out exerting themselves on the frontlines of the organization.

The Buddhist law of cause and effect applies equally to all people. The Buddha will absolutely praise and protect those doing their best to advance kosen-rufu, even if no one else takes notice. The efforts of such people will turn without fail into great fortune and benefit.

Nevertheless, as Soka Gakkai president, Shin'ichi wanted to do something extra to recognize and reward those hardworking members.

IT IS A LEADER'S DUTY to be considerate to those working behind the scenes. Nichiren Daishonin always took care to express his appreciation to such people. Throughout his writings, the Daishonin offers kind words of gratitude to those followers he could not meet regularly, particularly the wives and elderly parents of his active followers.

His profound compassion toward the elderly is especially moving. For example, he once received a gift of an unlined summer robe from Toki Jonin, a leading follower in the Shimousa³ region. Jonin's ninety-year-old mother had apparently made it for her son, sewing each stitch with great love and care. Perhaps because he felt it inadequate to repay his mother's kindness and sincerity simply by using the robe himself, Jonin presented it as an offering to the Daishonin, thinking that it would most please her.

Jonin's mother was advanced in age. No doubt she put tremendous effort into sewing the kimono, struggling with failing eyesight and unsteady fingers. The Daishonin makes a special point of mentioning this in his reply to Jonin, saying, "She must have strained her eyes and expended her very life to make it" (GZ, 968).

The Daishonin goes on to say that he, too, would find it difficult to repay his debt of gratitude to her, but since it would not be proper to return the robe, he would wear it and report about it in detail to the god of the sun.

He cherished the noble spirit of such elderly mothers and fathers, crying with them, rejoicing with them and offering them comfort and hope. The Daishonin assured them he would always be with them, so they had nothing to worry about. Warmly embraced by the Daishonin's compassion, they must have put the finishing touches on their lives without any fear.

Shin'ichi Yamamoto always reminded himself that he must take action with the Daishonin's spirit.

On May 14, Shin'ichi attended a Seniors Gathering at the Kyoritsu Auditorium in Kanda, Tokyo. The festivities began at 1:00 P.M. with a rendition of "The Spring Sea" by the young women's Fife and Drum Corps. This was followed by various other performances, including songs by the young women's chorus, a skit by young women from the student division, songs and dances by arts division members, and a performance by the young men's Brass Band.

Often the older Soka Gakkai members stayed at home to look after the house, while their family went to kosen-rufu activities. So for many, it was the first time to hear the Fife and Drum Corps and Brass Band perform. This only added to their joy, and when a song was played that they knew, they sat forward in their seats, swaying and clapping their hands in time, and even singing along.

A T THE END of the meeting, Shin'ichi shared his feelings: "I am very happy to see all of you looking so well and thoroughly enjoying today's event. Thank you very much for coming. I know I am from the same generation as many of your children. Having inherited Mr. Toda's legacy and having become the Soka Gakkai president, however, I am determined to do my best to serve all of you, my fellow members, with utmost sincerity.

"While living in this defiled, corrupt world of ours, you have embraced the Gohonzon and practiced your faith diligently, enduring all manner of obstacles along the way. No matter how you were attacked or ridiculed, you persisted in spreading the Daishonin's Buddhism to help those who are suffering. You also supported and protected your family members from behind the scenes, as they participated in Soka Gakkai activities.

"I pledge to fulfill my mission to support and protect all of you, whom I deeply respect, so that you may practice faith with great pride, living your lives with dignity and savoring boundless happiness and joy."

Hearing Shin'ichi's declaration, many of the members' eyes filled with tears.

"By the way," Shin'ichi went on, "there is something for which I must apologize. At first, I proposed calling this event the Golden-Agers Gathering, but one of our elderly members scolded me, saying: 'There are no golden-agers among those of us who have faith in the Daishonin's teachings! We practice with a spirit as vibrant as the young women and men!'

"That is certainly true. Realizing that my initial suggestion was inappropriate, I immediately changed the sign for the meeting to 'Seniors Gathering.'

"In my defense, however, I meant that you are all enjoying the golden age of perpetual youth, just as the Daishonin promises when he says, 'We will find perpetual youth and eternal life before our eyes!' (WND, 413). I hope you will accept my apology!"

Laughter and applause filled the venue.

Shin'ichi continued with great conviction: "The Daishonin declares that 'There is no doubt, however, that in my present life I am the votary of the Lotus Sutra, and that in the future I will therefore reach the seat of enlightenment without fail. Judging the past from this point of view, I must have been at the Ceremony in the Air. There can be no discontinuity between the three existences of past, present, and future' (WND, 386).

"The fact that all of you are enjoying lives filled with happiness as a result of your daily efforts to chant daimoku and promote worldwide kosen-rufu is clear proof that you will absolutely attain Buddhahood again in the future."

EMOTION FILLED Shin'ichi Yamamoto's voice as he concluded his speech at the Seniors Gathering: "There are young people who are old and older people who are young. The key to staying young is to possess a flexible mind that constantly strives for self-improvement. At the same time, how we live our final years determines our ultimate happiness in life. No matter how wonderful and happy our lives may have been in the past, nothing could be more tragic than ending up miserable, bitter and full of complaint.

"Happiness is not a matter of wealth, nor is it determined by social status or fame. Rather, our happiness is determined by whether we live always with a sense of purpose and mission, regardless of our age.

"That each of you, our seniors in life, practice faith wholeheartedly and live each day in high spirits, with tremendous energy and hope, is the greatest proof of the validity of Nichiren Daishonin's Buddhism. I close my remarks today with sincere prayers for your continued health and longevity."

The Seniors Gathering thus concluded.

Shin'ichi was scheduled next to meet with the Soka Gakkai directors at the Soka Gakkai Headquarters. Upon leaving the stage, however, he headed directly for the main entrance of the auditorium to greet and encourage the elderly members exiting the building.

No one lives forever. Realizing that there were members present whom he might never have the chance to meet again, Shin'ichi seized the opportunity to speak with every person he could.

Grasping the hand of one elderly woman, he said: "Thank you for coming today. May I ask how old you are?"

"I'm eighty-three," she replied.

"I cannot believe it! You look so young. Please take good care of yourself!"

Beautiful smiles lit the members' faces as they reached

out to squeeze Shin'ichi's hand. Some were so happy that their eyes filled with tears.

Words are like light. A single kind word can shine a ray of hope into a person's heart. Shin'ichi put all his energy into speaking with the members, showering them with words of inspiration, praise and courage.

Later that month, on May 24, the Soka Gakkai was officially recognized as a religious corporation in the United States, becoming the first Soka Gakkai organization overseas to gain such legal status. In accord with Shin'ichi's vision of the worldwide propagation of the Daishonin's teachings, a pioneering step was taken — a solid foundation for the future of the Soka Gakkai in America was secured.

THE MAY Headquarters leaders meeting was held on the twenty-fifth at the Nihon University Auditorium in Ryogoku, Tokyo. New organizational units were established on a large scale. Two new headquarters were formed—the second Chubu Headquarters and Hyogo Headquarters—along with twenty-nine general chapters and sixty-nine chapters nationwide. Now the Soka Gakkai consisted of twenty headquarters, eighty-seven general chapters and four hundred and sixty-three chapters.

All vice general directors, starting with General Director Koichi Harayama, were appointed as headquarters leaders. This meant that the top-ranking leaders would now stand at the forefront of the organization and take the lead in Soka Gakkai activities. Kazumasa Morikawa and Yukio Ishikawa were also appointed as new vice general directors.

Furthermore, an Institute of Asian Culture was established in Kansai to parallel the Institute of Oriental Studies in Tokyo, and Yoshihiko Ohya was made its head.

President Yamamoto's decision to carry out such a major expansion of the organization came from his determination to begin a full-fledged stage of advancement in the spread of the Daishonin's Buddhism toward the seventh memorial (sixth anniversary) of Josei Toda's death. Shin'ichi keenly sensed that he must build a strong foundation for worldwide kosen-rufu during his lifetime. If he did not, the wonderful opportunity to teach others of the Daishonin's philosophy—that now presented itself some seven hundred years after the time of the Daishonin—would be lost forever. That is why he resolved to forge ahead valiantly, using every ounce of his strength.

No one, not even the top leaders, understood Shin'ichi's profound determination. They were simply astonished at the remarkable progress made since he became president. Some were even satisfied in thinking that the Soka Gakkai had grown large enough. Shin'ichi had accepted the Daishonin's will for the widespread propagation of Buddhism as his personal mission and devoted his entire life to it, but a wide gap was starting to form between his attitude and that of the leaders who lacked such dedication.

As he surveyed the newly appointed leaders at the Headquarters leaders meeting, Shin'ichi vowed in his heart that he would raise them to become true comrades in faith who shared his commitment and awareness.

The success of kosen-rufu depends entirely on people. The Daishonin writes: "The Law does not spread by itself. Because the people spread it, both the people and the Law are worthy of respect" (GZ, 856).

Essential to the transmission of the Law are people of conviction who are selflessly dedicated to serving others while basing themselves entirely on that Law, not on self-centered desires. It requires people of integrity, justice, courage, sincerity, wisdom and firm resolve.

SHIN'ICHI'S speech that day was brief and to the point. First he announced that leaders at the chapter level and above—those who comprised the organization's core leadership—now numbered about three thousand, and that a strong foundation was thus in place for the widespread propagation of Nichiren Daishonin's Buddhism.

"When Mr. Toda died," he said, "only about two hundred people held the positions of chapter leader and higher. When I became president, I determined to increase that number to three thousand toward expanding and strengthening the organization. Now we have reached that goal, and I am confident that with this many leaders taking responsibility as central figures on the chapter level, we have secured a solid foundation that nothing can disturb.

"I assure you that, if these leaders advance together in iron unity, an eternal current of kosen-rufu will definitely be set in motion. As our first step in that direction, let us set as our targets Mr. Toda's seventh memorial on April 2 and the headquarters general meeting on May 3 next year, and begin to move toward victory with dignity, joy and the courage of a lion."

Along with the organizational expansion announced at the Headquarters leaders meeting, major personnel changes were also made in the young men's and young women's divisions. After speaking at a women's division leaders meeting on the afternoon of May 27, Shin'ichi attended a young men's division leaders meeting that evening and then one for the young women's division the following day. He celebrated together with these young people the fresh start they were making.

On May 30, Shin'ichi moved to Kansai, attending leaders meetings at each headquarters in the region. The Kyoto Headquarters leaders meeting took place on May 30 in the Ojiyama Gymnasium of Otsu City, Shiga[4]

Prefecture. Until then, Goro Watari, who was also the nationwide student division chief, had been the leader of Kyoto Headquarters. With the formation of the new Hyogo Headquarters, Watari was made Hyogo Headquarters chief. To replace him, Tatsuzo Oyama, a dentist, was appointed as the new Kyoto Headquarters chief.

Shin'ichi wanted to attend the Kyoto Headquarters leaders meeting because he felt it was his responsibility as a top leader to ensure that the members understood and were comfortable with the new personnel changes and were prepared to work together. He therefore introduced Oyama at the meeting, spoke about his character and clearly explained the reasons behind the latest changes.

Laying the groundwork for kosen-rufu is not simply a matter of forming new headquarters and chapters and appointing new leaders. The key is fostering an awareness in new leaders of their missions and, at the same time, inspiring each member, arousing in them a determination to start afresh.

IT WAS A HOT DAY, and many members were crowded into the gymnasium for the Kyoto Headquarters leaders meeting in Otsu City. Despite the heat, Shin'ichi Yamamoto had given his all to encouraging the members, and now he was dripping with sweat. After the meeting, he returned to Kyoto where he invited several leaders to join him for a public bath.

Towels in hand, they went out in search of an open bathhouse. Finally, after walking around for some time, they found one.

As they sat soaking in the tub, one of the Kyoto leaders

said, "You know, we have a bathtub at the community center. It was not necessary to walk all this way just to take a bath." Laughing, Shin'ichi replied, "I know that, but I thought going to a public bath[5] together would help us get to know each other better. Sometimes leaders need to think of such things for the members' sake. It's important for leaders to do things with their members, rather than act as if they were above them.

"Also, offering guidance, encouraging and inspiring others to stand up in faith do not have to happen only at meetings—they can take place in the public bath, for example, or over dinner."

Shin'ichi then turned to Goro Watari, the new Hyogo Headquarters chief, and said, "Watari, your center of activities will move from Kyoto to Hyogo. Please become friends with the members there. You're young, so I hope you will always be careful to listen to and respect the opinions of your elders. I'm sure it will be easier to surround yourself with people of your own generation and work more closely with them, but that will only upset the balance of the organization, and you'll end up alienated from everyone.

"At the same time, older leaders should surround themselves with youth and value their opinions. The Soka Gakkai's membership is made up of young and old alike. The true power of the Soka Gakkai can only be revealed when each member uses his or her full potential and all work together in harmony and unity."

On the way back from the bath, Shin'ichi and the others ate ice cream and talked about the future prospects for kosen-rufu. Shin'ichi wanted to eliminate formalism

from the Soka Gakkai as much as possible. He was completely natural at all times, and this had always been the
way he lived.

On May 31, the day after the Kyoto Headquarters
leaders meeting, Shin'ichi attended the Kansai Headquarters leaders meeting held that afternoon at the Osaka
Prefectural Gymnasium. That night, he attended the
Hyogo Headquarters leaders meeting at the Amagasaki
City Municipal Gymnasium. In June, leaders meetings
marking a new start for each headquarters in the Tokyo
and Kanto[6] regions awaited him.

THE TOKYO NO. 1 Headquarters leaders meeting
took place on June 3 in the Taito Gymnasium, kick-
ing off a string of such meetings in the Tokyo and Kanto
regions. The newly appointed headquarters leader of
Tokyo No. 1 Headquarters was General Director Koichi
Harayama.

Members attended despite the rain, and many vice
general directors came to congratulate them and offer a
few words. Since each was appointed the leader of
another headquarters, their speeches reflected a spirit of
healthy competition.

Katsu Kiyohara, leader of Tokyo No. 5 Headquarters,
declared: "Please be aware that your biggest rival from
now on will be Tokyo No. 5. We do not intend to lose!"
Eisuke Akizuki, the newly appointed head of Tokyo No.
4 Headquarters, said, "I came here to challenge Tokyo
No. 1 to a contest of propagation." Kiyoshi Jujo, head of
Tokyo No. 2 Headquarters, remarked, "I hope that Tokyo
No. 1 will always be the best in the Soka Gakkai, but I

want you to understand that we of Tokyo No. 2 intend to be even better!"

Each of these challenges was greeted by a wave of applause and smiles that were fueled by the members' fighting spirit. Healthy and enjoyable competition is an important factor in activities for kosen-rufu. A friendly rivalry motivates the individual as well as the organization as a whole.

Shin'ichi was happy to see that these new headquarters leaders each wanted to make their headquarters the best. He felt that Mr. Toda was, without a doubt, looking warmly on this "contest of goodwill" that his disciples were engaged in while aiming for the seventh memorial service (the sixth anniversary).

Shin'ichi spoke next, his tone humorous: "General Director Harayama has just been made leader of Tokyo No. 1 Headquarters, but it looks like all the vice general directors now in charge of the other headquarters are plotting to bring his headquarters down!

"As president, it would not be right for me to get behind any one headquarters, but today I am here as a member of Tokyo No. 1. Therefore, I'd like to declare just for today that Tokyo No. 1 will become the top runner in the race for kosen-rufu not only in Tokyo, not only in Japan, but in the entire world!

"Please build a tradition of winning every challenge you take on. In whatever struggle, coming out a winner makes you happy. When we succeed in our activities, we experience boundless vitality and joy, which becomes a great source of hope and energy. If we lose, however, that joy and energy does not well forth from our lives."

SHIN'ICHI next explained why it is important for the individual to win in activities for kosen-rufu: "Whether in our efforts to share Buddhism with others or to increase the number of members attending meetings, if we want to win, we need to first set a goal, muster our determination and chant daimoku in earnest. We must then bring forth our wisdom and bravely face the challenge while taking resolute action.

"Each obstacle we overcome brings us wonderful benefit and good fortune. It is through this process that we learn the formula for triumphing in life. Moreover, the tremendous conviction in faith we gain by exerting ourselves in our activities endows us with the strength to surmount any difficulty or hardship we encounter in life.

"Nichiren Daishonin writes, 'Buddhism primarily concerns itself with victory or defeat' (WND, 835). This is because kosen-rufu is a struggle against the devil king of the sixth heaven, the negative function that destroys life. In fact, human existence is itself a struggle. Realizing genuine happiness begins with challenging and winning over our own cowardice and laziness. Human revolution means to overcome the negative aspects of the self, and our Soka Gakkai activities are the arena in which we can do so.

"I am not really concerned with the short-term results of our propagation activities; what matters most is that each of you exerts yourself wholeheartedly in faith, enjoys great benefit and an enriched life, and attains a boundless state of life overflowing with joy. I hope you will always remember that this is the reason we share the Daishonin's Buddhism with others and why we engage in Soka Gakkai activities."

After this, Shin'ichi attended headquarters leaders meetings held successively in the Tokyo and Kanto regions, giving his all to encouraging the members. With the new organizational changes and personnel assignments announced, Shin'ichi wished to secure a strong spiritual foundation for kosen-rufu in each member's heart.

At almost every meeting, Shin'ichi personally led the members in singing Soka Gakkai songs. His shoulders were stiff from swinging his fan, and his exhaustion mounted, but he was determined to do anything necessary to encourage and inspire his precious fellow members and serve them to the end. He was also trying to be an example of the essential attitude of a leader.

The series of headquarters leaders meetings that took place throughout the Tokyo and Kanto regions ended on June 14 with the Santama Headquarters leaders meeting in a suburb of Tokyo. The wheels of fresh advancement were thus set in motion.

Late that night, a big news story began to circulate around the globe.

TV AND RADIO NEWS announced that at 3:00 P.M. on June 14, 1963, the Soviet spacecraft *Vostok 5*, piloted by cosmonaut Valery F. Bykovsky, had entered earth's orbit.

The first piloted space flight had taken place two years earlier, in April 1961, when Soviet cosmonaut Yuri A. Gagarin had successfully orbited the earth aboard *Vostok 1*, so the launching of *Vostok 5* in itself did not astonish the world. But with the news about Lieutenant Colonel

Bykovsky also came word that the Soviets would soon send a woman into space for the first time. This stirred the world's interest.

Then, two days later, another news flash circled the globe: at 12:30 A.M. on June 16, the Soviet spacecraft *Vostok 6* was launched with a female cosmonaut on board. Her name was Valentina Vladimirovna Tereshkova, and she was a twenty-six-year-old second lieutenant.

"It is I, Seagull!" Her bright and cheerful voice reached earth from outer space. Moscow television showed the interior of the cabin of *Vostok 6* and an image of a young woman floating in zero gravity to people's television screens. Her face, with its lovely smile and determined expression, became known around the world.

"It is I, Seagull! I see the horizon. A light blue, a beautiful band. This is the earth. How beautiful it is! All goes well!" "Seagull" was the call sign she used for contacting earth. Lieutenant Colonel Bykovsky, who had begun his flight two days earlier aboard *Vostok 5,* used the call sign "Hawk." The purpose of these two flights was to compare the effects of long-term space flight on men and women.

Seagull and Hawk both held parallel orbits around planet earth. *Vostok 6* completed forty-eight orbits in seventy-one hours. It landed safely on June 19, at 11:20 A.M. *Vostok 5* made a new record for time in orbit, completing eighty-one orbits in one hundred nineteen hours and six minutes. It returned safely to earth on June 19 as well, at 2:06 in the afternoon.

THE WORLD applauded the achievement of Soviet cosmonaut Valentina Tereshkova, who had soared into the vast skies of freedom.

She was an ordinary working woman. Her father, a skilled tractor driver, was killed in the World War II when she was a child. Her mother worked hard in a textile mill, doing her best to raise three children. Growing up watching her mother work dauntlessly in spite of their many hardships, Valentina went to work at a tire factory in Yaroslav on the banks of the Volga when she was seventeen. Later, she got a job in the same textile mill where her mother worked.

Her dream of becoming a cosmonaut began when she heard the news of the successful first piloted space flight of cosmonaut Yuri A. Gagarin in *Vostok 1*. The thought of flying into space excited her. It became her grand dream. It was a dream shared by many young people around the world in those days.

Every young person has a dream. Having dreams and ideals is one of the privileges of youth. Far too few, however, actually realize their dreams. Once the opposing winds of difficulty begin to buffet them, many sink as quickly as a leaky boat. Only by pursuing a dream in the face of such realities, by continuing to pursue it until the very end, will that dream be realized.

At the time the *Vostok 1* mission succeeded, Valentina was a member of the state aviation club and a skilled amateur parachutist. The young textile-mill worker was already beginning to weave her dream of flight. Her original reason for joining the aviation club was that she wanted to see her hometown from the sky. Her first jump took place during a rainstorm. No doubt she felt anxious and afraid. But she challenged herself and took flight, breaking through the dark clouds of fear that loomed in her heart.

From that time on, she grew more and more fascinated with the sky. It was then she learned of Major Gagarin's space flight. Less than one year later, she was selected for the Soviet space program.

The training for cosmonauts turned out to be far tougher than she anticipated. Of course the physical training was difficult; but she also needed to study many specialized subjects, including rocket science. Each day she underwent continuous, intensive training that challenged the physical and mental limits of her being.

IMMEDIATE DIFFICULTIES often severely diminish a person's dreams. But Valentina refused to give up. She spent her free time studying, staying up late night after night. She persistently questioned her instructors and seniors in the program about points she did not understand until she grasped them to her satisfaction. Without uttering a complaint, she tenaciously kept pace with the strict cosmonaut training. Even Major Gagarin, who made that first historic flight into space aboard *Vostok 1*, was impressed and moved by her diligence.

Valentina was a thoughtful and loving person who, despite her demanding routine, managed to send money and letters to her mother on a regular basis. Her kindness and flexibility were accompanied by an iron will.

Just as a flower blossoms after enduring the bitter cold of winter, a dream can be realized only if one is willing to endure the accompanying trials and put forth the necessary effort. The bright smile that Valentina showed the world from inside the cabin of *Vostok 6* surely expressed her genuine satisfaction at dedicating herself to achieving her chosen goal.

Valentina was a subject of great interest among the Soka Gakkai's young women's division members. At a meeting between Shin'ichi Yamamoto and YWD leaders at the *Seikyo Shimbun* offices, the conversation turned to the first female cosmonaut.

"Ms. Tereshkova has shown the women of the world that a woman is capable of piloting a spacecraft," said Shin'ichi. "She has helped usher in a new age in which women will play the leading roles in society.

"Japan is still a male-dominated society—but Japan,

too, will need to change eventually. It will be women who make that happen by refusing to accept the traditional role that Japanese society has placed on them.

"Indeed, there are many problems with the way men treat women, but I believe that if women wish to improve their status in society, they must be prepared to do their absolute best at any given job, working even harder than men.

"Toward this end, it is crucial to have a solid perspective on life, a firm philosophy on how to live."

To this, Michiyo Watari, the Soka Gakkai YWD leader, responded: "I hope you will consider establishing guidelines for the YWD in this regard. Until now, we have used the youth division guidelines set forth by President Toda, 'Precepts for Youth' and 'Youth, Be Patriotic!' Of course, the fundamental spirit of these is the same for both men and women, but I think guidelines that specifically address the way young women should live would be very useful."

"I see," Shin'ichi said. "I agree; such guidelines are needed. Let me think about it. I will introduce something new when the time is right."

Two months later, the September issue of *The Daibyakurenge* magazine carried an editorial Shin'ichi had written titled "To the Young Women's Division," outlining the sort of guidelines that Watari had suggested.

O N JUNE 20, Shin'ichi Yamamoto flew to Kagoshima and Miyazaki Prefectures in Kyushu[7] to encourage the members there. That afternoon he attended a groundbreaking ceremony for the Kagoshima

Community Center, to be built in the Kamoike-cho district of Kagoshima City. At 7:00 P.M., he attended the Kagoshima General Chapter leaders meeting held at the Municipal Central Public Hall. The next day, June 21, he headed for the island Amami Oshima.[8] His main goal on this trip to Kyushu was to encourage the members living in the Amami group of islands.

Shin'ichi was very concerned for his fellow members striving to practice Buddhism in this isolated archipelago. Not only were their means of transportation limited, but some of the islands were without medical care or even electricity. Their livelihoods were also at the mercy of the weather; typhoons or other storms could cut them off from life's essentials. Long spells of dry heat would leave many of the islands without drinking water.

Old customs and traditions were strongly rooted there so trying to spread Nichiren Daishonin's Buddhism under these circumstances proved quite a challenge.

Shin'ichi wanted to visit and encourage members living on remote islands since becoming president. He firmly believed that it was his mission to offer encouragement, support and praise to the members who had suffered the most. There were many things he had to take care of, however, and as the days and months passed he only became busier. Still, he managed to squeeze some time out of his schedule and plan a trip to Amami Oshima.

Outside of the large main islands of the Japanese archipelago, Amami Oshima was the third largest island after the islands of Okinawa and Sado. It was also the largest in the Amami island chain. In Japan's medieval period, the

Amami Islands were part of the Ryukyu Kingdom,[9] but at the beginning of the seventeenth century after the defeat of the Ryukyus by Shimazu Iehisa,[10] they fell under the control of the Satsuma domain.[11]

Toward the end of the Edo Period, in particular, these islands were subject to severe oppression under feudal rule, and their inhabitants were forced to grow sugar cane and process sugar as tribute. The heavy taxes and hard labor caused them to suffer terribly.

During the Pacific War, Amami Oshima was the target of intense bombings by U.S. forces, and some ninety percent of the island's capital of Naze was reduced to ashes. After Japan's defeat, Amami Oshima came under U.S. military rule. Okinawa, also under U.S. rule, had become a U.S. protectorate and military bases covering vast areas of land were built there because of its strategic location. Amami Oshima, however, was left on its own, lacking sufficient investment to aid in its post-war reconstruction.

With its trade severely stifled, the production of local products such as sugar and Oshima *tsumugi* (pongee, a soft thin cloth woven from raw silk) declined, and the island's economy fell into a severe recession. It was against this backdrop that a movement to return the islands to Japan began to grow among the residents.

THE AMAMI ISLANDS were returned to Japan on December 25, 1953, eight years after World War II. The seeds of Nichiren Daishonin's Buddhism were first planted there in 1955, and they sprouted with the appearance of new practitioners on the islands of Kikaijima,

Kakeromajima, Amami Oshima, Okinoerabujima, Yoron-jima and Tokunoshima. In July 1961, the Soka Gakkai's Amami Oshima Chapter was established. By the time Shin'ichi Yamamoto visited in 1963, the membership had grown to more than 6,000 households.

When Shin'ichi recalled the bitter history and perseverance of the people of the Amami archipelago, he was happy to see such progress toward kosen-rufu being made there. Though he intended to visit all of the remote islands throughout the country where members were living, he decided to start with Amami Oshima. He wanted to encourage and support the members of Amami Oshima Chapter, who struggled so hard to get where they were.

Shin'ichi's plane departed from Kagoshima at 1:00 P.M. on June 21, heading first for Tokunoshima. The small propeller plane, a De Havilland Heron, carried only a dozen passengers. There was no airport yet in Amami Oshima, so it was decided he would fly to Tokunoshima and make the trip to Amami Oshima by boat.

He arrived at the Tokunoshima Airport, located on the north side of the island, at around 3:00 P.M. From there he was to travel to Kametoku Harbor on the island's south side in a car arranged for by the local members.

Shin'ichi began encouraging members the moment he landed at Tokunoshima Airport. When he saw a group waiting for him, almost hidden in the shade of some trees, he went immediately over to them, expressing his gratitude and offering words of encouragement. Brilliant smiles adorned their suntanned faces.

The road to the harbor was unpaved, and the car

stirred up great clouds of dust as it went. Still, the scenery from the window was breathtaking. The island was densely forested with screw pines and palms, and red hibiscus flowers bloomed in all their glory. Many of the houses had thatched roofs.

Again and again, whenever Shin'ichi spotted people along the road who looked as if they were members waiting to greet him, he stopped the car to speak with them and shake hands.

After about an hour's drive, they arrived at Kametoku Harbor. Moored there was the ship that would transport Shin'ichi to Amami Oshima, a four-hundred-ton vessel called the *Akebonomaru*. A large crowd stood on the pier. The local members had chartered the ship for those attending the chapter meeting on Amami Oshima, and the crowd on the pier was all Soka Gakkai members.

THE MEMBERS gathered at the harbor to welcome Shin'ichi and his party, and all were waiting anxiously for their cars to arrive.

"Thank you for all your trouble!" he said, stepping from the car. Waving his hands high in greeting, he made his way toward the group of friends.

How praiseworthy were the efforts of the members living on the Amami Islands—they had worked to increase their membership to more than 6,000 households in just seven or eight years! Spoken ill of for trying to share Buddhism with others, they were sometimes even shouted at or cursed. The other villagers shunned them—a matter of life and death on an isolated island. Yet they held back their tears of frustration, gritted their teeth and continued to devote themselves to kosen-rufu. Their most fervent wish was that President Yamamoto would visit their islands.

"I finally made it here to see you!" Shin'ichi continued. "There are so many members here on Tokunoshima! How wonderful!" As Shin'ichi spoke, some of the members could be heard sobbing, unable to hold back tears of joy.

Shin'ichi deeply understood their feelings. He spoke to one person after another. To a mother holding her infant daughter he said: "What a beautiful baby! Please raise her to be a fine successor," and he patted the child on the head. To a young men's division member, he said: "I am counting on you to take care of Tokunoshima! Let's stand up and fight together!"

He met a woman whose leg had been disabled after she was bitten by a poisonous snake that inhabited the islands. "Faith guarantees that we will become happy no matter what. Please don't worry," he said, shaking her hand firmly yet tenderly.

In the limited time he had, Shin'ichi poured his whole life into encouraging each member. When it was time to go, he said: "I must be off now. I will be waiting for you over there. Let's meet again!" With that, he boarded the ship.

Some eighty members were with Shin'ichi on the ship, which made its way to Naze, the main city on Amami Oshima. The ship was to shuttle back and forth between Tokunoshima and Amami Oshima three times in order to transport all the members who would be attending the chapter meeting. Shin'ichi was in the second group.

The journey to Amami Oshima took about five or six hours. The local members remarked that the sea was very calm, but the leaders from Tokyo who had accompanied Shin'ichi were unaccustomed to ocean travel, and to them the waters seemed rough and choppy. Soon after they left the harbor, all but Shin'ichi were seasick. Their faces pale, they sat slumped against the back of their seats.

EVEN ON THE SHIP, there was no time for Shin'ichi to rest. After greeting the ship's captain and taking a brief tour of the engine room, he met with the local leaders on board and discussed plans for expanding kosen-rufu on the Amami Islands.

The twilight hue of the sea was soon overtaken by the veil of night, and stars filled the sky. The faint outline of an island became visible far in the distance. It was Amami Oshima. It would be another two hours, though, before they docked at Naze, the island's main city.

Shin'ichi turned to the leaders accompanying him from Tokyo and said: "Has your seasickness subsided? I hope so, because there's no getting off the ship just yet! Actually, the same can be said of kosen-rufu and of faith. Once we've set sail, no matter what storm may hit, there's no turning back." He spoke these words casually, but he felt them deeply.

The *Akebonomaru* landed at Naze around 10:00 P.M. The dock was crowded with members waiting to greet Shin'ichi. When he stepped onto the deck and waved, a great welcoming roar erupted from the crowd. Even though the members had heard that President Yamamoto would be visiting the island, many did not actually believe it until they saw him with their own eyes.

Just before Shin'ichi's departure from Kagoshima,[12] the sea was rough due to the effects of Typhoon No. 4, and the regular passenger ships scheduled from Kagoshima had been canceled. There was concern that airline flights would also be delayed or canceled. When they saw that President Yamamoto had really come, the members could not contain their joy.

"Thank you, everyone, thank you!" Shin'ichi shouted again and again, responding to the warm welcome.

Shin'ichi and his party were driven to the newly completed Amami Oshima Community Center. It was a chalk-white, two-story building made of reinforced concrete, with a large, seventy-tatami mat meeting room on the ground floor, and was the first Soka Gakkai center in the Amami Islands. The completion ceremony for the new building was scheduled for the following day.

After arriving at the center and chanting daimoku three times, the leaders traveling with Shin'ichi stretched out their legs and made themselves comfortable. The journey had worn them out.

General Director Koichi Harayama muttered, "Amami is so far! And the rocking of the ship really got to me." Hearing this, Shin'ichi quickly remarked: "We've finally made it to Amami. Having come this far, I'm determined to really accomplish something. While we're here, let's put out five years worth of effort to secure the development of our movement in Amami!"

SHIN'ICHI'S rousing words transformed the spirits of the leaders accompanying him. Vice General Director Yukio Ishikawa said: "It certainly would be a waste if we made the long trip here to Amami and did not put out our best effort. I'm going to pour my life into giving guidance on faith to our members here."

Shin'ichi smiled and replied: "Ishikawa, let's not think of it as giving guidance; instead let's learn all we can about faith from the members here in Amami. Every month, the local chapter men's and women's division leaders travel all the way to Tokyo from these remote islands to attend the Headquarters leaders meeting. The entire trip takes them a whole week. During that time, they have to put their work on hold, and their absence must be hard on their families.

"They also travel from island to island to encourage and support their fellow members, giving their all to forge a way for the spread of Buddhism. They could not have accomplished what they have without making sacrifices in their private lives. Each one has made tremendous contributions to our movement.

"Just because one leader has a higher position within the organization than another does not mean his faith is necessarily stronger or that he is more important. I'm sure you are all better at talking and you probably know more about Buddhist principles, but that in itself does not amount to faith.

"What matters is what you have actually done for the sake of kosen-rufu. How many people have you enabled to practice, how much have you inspired your fellow members to take action, to what extent have you taken action yourself and how much blood, sweat and tears have you put into your efforts?

"Yes, Amami is far from Tokyo, but the hearts of our Amami members are closest to mine. They are with me. There are leaders who work at the Soka Gakkai Head-quarters but whose hearts are very distant from mine. When it comes to the heart, it's not where you are that counts.

"I brought you all here to Amami because I wanted you to have contact with our Amami members and see what true faith, true struggle and true effort are."

Looking around the room at each of his companions, Shin'ichi continued: "I propose that we establish a general chapter here in the Amami Islands. Amami is a place with a painful past. It has suffered various kinds of cruel oppression. During the Edo Period, it was subject to the harsh rule of the Satsuma clan. After the war, it endured a period of U.S. military rule. To transform that bitter karma, to make Amami strong and independent, I want to establish a general chapter here, even though the membership is still quite small. This is the conclusion I have reached after long, hard consideration. Let's talk about ideas for the organization and leadership of the general chapter."

The discussions began, with Shin'ichi taking the lead. It was nearly 11:00 at night, but Shin'ichi's internal engine for advancing kosen-rufu in Amami had begun to roar.

SHIN'ICHI YAMAMOTO and the other leaders talked until the early morning, deciding finally to call the new organization Amami General Chapter and that it would consist of the chapters Amami Oshima, Naze and Koniya. It was also decided to appoint Takashi Nogawa, until then the leader of Amami Oshima Chapter, as the new general chapter leader, and Haru Fujisawa, the current chapter women's division leader, as the general chapter women's division leader.

Nogawa ran a general store on Amami Oshima. An earnest-looking man in his late thirties, he was straightforward and honest. Upon returning home after serving in the army during the war, his life on Amami Oshima under U.S. military rule was very difficult, and he lived day after day in desperate poverty.

Eventually he opened the general store and married, but just as business seemed to be taking off, he contracted tuberculosis. Both of his parents had died when he was a child, and his sister died at sixteen. Sensing that his entire family was fated to die young, Nogawa began to fear his own demise.

He grew thin from the disease, and his face became so pale that he needed rouge when he went into the store to meet with customers. It was around this time that he first heard about Nichiren Daishonin's Buddhism. He was so moved by the confidence of the Soka Gakkai members who came to talk to him that he and his family decided to join in the hopes that the practice would cure him. They received Gohonzon in May 1957.

Determined to beat his illness, Nogawa devoted himself enthusiastically to Buddhist practice. Day by day, he began to feel better, and when he had an X-ray taken about a year later, not a trace of shadow was found on his lungs. The doctor was astonished. This experience gave

Nogawa tremendous confidence in his faith, and he began to put even more energy into Soka Gakkai activities. He experienced the power of Buddhist practice to change karma.

Three years after he had joined the Soka Gakkai, in October 1960, Koniya District of Kagoshima Chapter was formed, and Nogawa was appointed district leader. Ten months later, in July 1961, with the establishment of Amami Oshima Chapter, he was asked to become the chapter leader. He was troubled about whether he should accept the appointment. Though he would be head of Amami Oshima Chapter, in addition to his home island of Amami Oshima, the chapter included Kikaijima, Kakeromajima, Tokunoshima, Okinoerabujima and Yoronjima — all of the Amami Islands.

He knew full well that it would be impossible to fulfill his responsibilities as chapter leader unless he devoted himself entirely, day and night, to the happiness of the chapter members.

AT THE TIME, the roads on Amami Oshima were in extremely poor condition. Furthermore, the only way to travel to the other islands was by boat, which often involved many transfers from one passenger ship to another, or making one's way in a small fishing vessel while being tossed about by the waves. It took thirteen-and-a-half hours by regular passenger boat to get from Naze on Amami Oshima to Chabana on Yoronjima, if all went according to schedule. The return trip took eighteen-and-a-half hours.

A chapter leader in those early days of the Gakkai's

activities in the Amami Islands would have to cut back on working hours to visit all the members. Nogawa knew this and was therefore hesitant to accept the position of head of Amami Oshima Chapter. His wife Yoshimi was also well aware of the weight of responsibility that came with the post. If her husband accepted it, she knew he would be virtually unable to work in the general store or contribute to taking care of the household. But she also understood that to transform the tragic karma of the Amami Islands and bring happiness to all of the people there, someone had to take on that task, and so she made up her mind.

"We can do it. I'll take care of the store!" she told her husband. These words enabled Mr. Nogawa to make his decision. He felt that he owed his very life to his faith and it was therefore only right that he should devote that life to the spread of the Daishonin's Buddhism.

He was appointed as chapter leader at the Headquarters leaders meeting in Tokyo, and on that day he met President Yamamoto for the first time at the Soka Gakkai Headquarters. Shin'ichi sincerely congratulated Nogawa on this new start for Amami Oshima Chapter, and expressed high hopes for him in meeting the bold challenges ahead.

After his appointment, Nogawa gave himself wholeheartedly to helping the members practice and to spreading the Daishonin's teachings throughout the Amami archipelago. It turned out to be just as challenging as he anticipated—in fact, even more so.

Visiting the islands often kept Nogawa away from home for a week or two at a time. When he left his house, he'd say, "See you soon!" without mentioning when he might return. He simply could not say, mostly due to the unpredictability of the weather.

Some of the islands had no regular passenger ship service and the only way to reach them at all was on a fishing boat or by rowboat. When he went to Tokunoshima, the second largest of the Amami Islands, he would take a motorbike with him and use that to get around the island.

Nogawa was rarely able to sleep in his own bed. He always carried a raincoat on his travels, and when he became tired, he would put it on and sleep under the stars. While traveling very late one night, he was suddenly overcome with fatigue. He stopped his bike and lay down by the roadside. He awoke to the feel of something on his stomach. He opened his eyes and gulped. It was a *habu,* a poisonous snake native to the southern Japanese islands.

NOGAWA FROZE in terror. He knew that if he shouted or moved, he was likely to get bitten; so he held his breath and lay as still as he could, chanting furiously in his mind.

The snake slowly made its way across Nogawa's abdomen and slithered away. The whole incident had lasted only about ten seconds, but it seemed like hours.

There was always a risk of encountering these snakes on the islands of Amami Oshima and Tokunoshima. They are nocturnal, so night travel was especially dangerous — but since Nogawa needed to travel at night, he often chanted as he went. He was constantly praying under his breath, whether on his bike or on foot.

When traveling by ship, he would voraciously read Soka

Gakkai publications and Nichiren Daishonin's writings. He would express his attitude toward study as follows: "I only attended elementary school, and I'm not very smart, so unless I study very hard I cannot keep up with other people. When you're working to propagate Buddhism, you need to have the ability to convince others. To get that ability, I have to study twice as much as anyone else."

The more he traveled from island to island and the harder he exerted himself, the more strain it put on his family budget. His wife Yoshimi scrimped and saved, barely making ends meet. But when her husband asked her if she could afford to give him some money, she always smiled reassuringly and said, "Yes," and handed him what he needed, even if it left her without enough to buy food.

She knew her husband was working for the happiness of the people of the Amami Islands, and she was determined to at least take care of the household in his absence. That was her personal vow. They both felt it was their mission and a great honor to dedicate their lives to the lofty goal of helping others become happy and realizing peace based on the Daishonin's Buddhism.

Haru Fujisawa, who was to be appointed Amami Oshima General Chapter women's division leader, was a wise, kindhearted woman in her fifties. Her husband Keisuke was a high school teacher and a scholar of local history. They both were born in the Amami Islands, but they married in Tokyo. Later they went to Manchuria, and there saw the end of World War II. After the war, they returned to Amami.

Haru had always been physically weak, which kept her

in bed sick for most of each month. Her greatest wish was to be healthy. She experienced several miscarriages and stillbirths and three of her children died early, leaving her with one surviving daughter.

HARU JOINED the Soka Gakkai in December 1956.

Her daughter Chizuko was accepted to a high school in Kagoshima City in southern Kyushu, and Haru went to live there with her while her husband remained on Amami. In Kagoshima City, Haru's nephew Saburo Shigehara came for a visit and began to talk to Chizuko about Buddhism. Shigehara once had tuberculosis, in those days considered an incurable disease, and had overcome it through the power of faith.

At first, Chizuko was not interested in what her cousin said about Buddhism, but eventually she was struck by his complete conviction that through Buddhist faith and practice all of her prayers would be answered. She then decided to join. She wrote a letter to her father asking his permission, and he wrote back saying that if she thought she was doing the right thing, he had no objections.

Haru, however, was skeptical about religion in general, and did not want her daughter to get caught up in something strange. So she decided to join the Soka Gakkai herself in order to keep a close eye on her daughter and protect her.

Chizuko graduated from high school and entered a pharmaceutical college in Shizuoka Prefecture, and Haru returned to Amami. Though she was now a Soka Gakkai member, Haru was not particularly active or involved.

The turning point came when, at the strong encouragement of another member, she decided to take the Study Department entrance examination. A leader would come all the way from the Kagoshima mainland every week to help the members study for the exam. Haru was deeply moved by the commitment of this leader, who would voluntarily travel some twenty hours by ship at her own expense to come and teach them.

Furthermore, as she studied Buddhism and read the Daishonin's writings, Haru's impression that all religions were mere superstitions and not to be trusted had changed. She realized that among religious teachings there were right and wrong, profound and shallow, and that the Daishonin's Buddhism was a solid and correct philosophy.

Haru gained confidence in her practice and, after passing the examination, enthusiastically involved herself in Soka Gakkai activities. Seeing her vibrant example, her husband Keisuke also joined and began supporting his wife's Buddhist activities.

Haru had chronic liver and kidney problems, and suffered also from sciatica and high blood pressure but as she practiced, her ailments began to subside. Her faith grew deeper as a result, and she gradually became an enthusiastic advocate of Buddhism. When Amami Oshima Chapter was founded, she was appointed the chapter women's division leader.

AFTER BEING appointed as the chapter women's leader, Haru Fujisawa traveled from island to island igniting the flame of the Mystic Law.

Her journeys did not always go smoothly. If a storm hit, the beautiful blue sea would turn into a swarm of angry waves, and her way would be blocked. She once found herself stranded offshore for seven hours, her boat unable to dock due to the high swells. On another occasion, she slipped and fell while transferring from a ferry to a small boat that would take her to shore. On the islands, she often spent two or three hours each night walking from place to place visiting members but this exposed her to the danger of being bitten by the poisonous *habu* snake.

Sometimes people even threw salt[13] at her and her fellow members who came to talk with them about Nichiren Daishonin's Buddhism. Watching the salt scatter around her like falling snow, Haru continually vowed to herself: "I will not give up! Whatever happens, I will spread the Daishonin's Buddhism throughout the Amami Islands faster than any other part of Japan and make this the happiest place in the entire country!"

Takashi Nogawa, the Amami Oshima Chapter leader, shared this conviction with Haru, as did all the Amami members.

Folk religion was still deeply rooted in the Amami Islands, and people worshipped the female priests who conducted local shaman rituals as well as those believed to be faith healers who could communicate with and speak for the gods. Anyone who opposed such traditions was thought to be cursed.

Amid these circumstances, the Soka Gakkai members proudly strove to teach people about Buddhism. They broke ties with the old customs and proclaimed to others the difference between correct and false teachings. This caused great anxiety among the islanders, and their reactions to the Soka Gakkai members' efforts were often quite severe.

Saburo Shigehara, for example, began sharing Buddhism with people on his home island of Kakeromajima. Some twenty local households out of the nearly one hundred in his area decided to join the Soka Gakkai, but just around that time, Saburo's eighty-five-year-old grandmother died. Then, in a three-month period, his cousin, aunt, younger brother and father also died.

A rumor spread that anyone who joined the Soka Gakkai would die. It was a curse, people said. Criticism of the Soka Gakkai flared violently, and even members began to have doubts.

It was true that Shigehara's family members had died after taking faith, but this did not shake his confidence at all. He had seen their faces at the time of their deaths, and each had looked completely different than at any time before. Their complexions were rosy and they seemed to be smiling. They looked totally at peace. This fact served to convince Shigehara even further that he was practicing a correct religion.

Shigehara told fellow members: "If I, a member of the Shigehara family, am not disturbed by these deaths, why should anyone else be? This faith is tremendous!" His firm conviction allayed the members' fears.

THE SUN ROSE high above the vast ocean. The long-awaited day of a new beginning had dawned. Early on June 22, Shin'ichi stepped into the garden of the Amami Oshima Community Center and looked at the sun rising in the sky. The night's blackness vanished like a dream, and a brilliant, beautiful world of light enveloped him. It was a wonderful and majestic morning, a golden dawn. Green papaya trees, banana trees, date palms and cycads growing in the center's garden glistened in the sunlight under a cloudless sky.

"If there is a sun shining in our hearts," thought Shin'ichi, "we can dispel all inner darkness and without fail arrive at a glorious morning of victory. If we want to transform the community in which we live, we must ask ourselves: Does our heart burn with a fighting spirit and are we truly committed to spreading the Daishonin's teachings?"

A fighting spirit like a majestic sun burned brightly in Shin'ichi's heart. For him, each day was supremely important. He lived each moment of his life as if it were the last. Such is the determination of one who strives to create a new history.

The eagerly anticipated completion ceremony for the Amami Oshima Community Center began just before 10:00 A.M. Some 500 members packed the building, and the crowd overflowed into the grounds. Their joy-filled faces turned the center into a garden of smiles. Seeing the members so happy wiped away Shin'ichi's fatigue from his long journey.

After gongyo, there was a progress report and words from a number of leaders, and then Shin'ichi spoke of the tremendous power of the Gohonzon. He hoped that the members of the Amami Islands would enjoy wonderful benefit from their practice.

"The Gohonzon is a mandala, which means 'cluster of blessings' and 'perfectly endowed,'" he said. "In other words, it contains the benefits of all Buddhas and all teachings or laws without exception. The strength of our faith and the strength of our practice are what draw forth the power of the Buddha and the Law from the Gohonzon. At the same time, our strong faith and practice manifest themselves as the powers of the Buddha and the Law."

Shin'ichi spoke next of the importance of chanting daimoku, and finished by saying: "This community center is a castle of the Law for all of you to use freely for spreading the Daishonin's teachings. I hope that your unity and courage will give rise to a great surge of propagation that will flow from this castle, which is the southernmost of our community centers in Japan. I am counting on you to achieve kosen-rufu here in the Amami Islands in my place."

The Amami members listened deeply, absorbing each of Shin'ichi's words.

AFTER THE COMPLETION ceremony, interviews wereconducted with the proposed leaders of Amami Oshima General Chapter on the second floor of the new building.

This was the first that any of the members heard about the formation of a general chapter, and they were very surprised. Takashi Nogawa, who was a candidate for the post of general chapter leader, was thinking of turning down the position. He felt that he had been unable to carry out his duties fully as chapter leader, and that he would not be able to handle the even heavier responsibilities of general chapter leader.

When time for his interview came, he expressed this concern to Shin'ichi Yamamoto, who said: "It is true that the Amami Oshima General Chapter will cover a lot of territory and the responsibilities of that leader will be great. But that does not mean you cannot do it.

"At age thirty-two, I took on the entire world. The Amami Islands may be spread out, but they're not that wide!"

Nogawa could say nothing in response to this. He thought of the personal vow he made to devote himself to working for kosen-rufu alongside President Yamamoto and decided to challenge himself to the very end.

At about this time, members were gathering at Shiohama Beach, an area of reclaimed land that faced Naze Harbor, where a large meeting was to be held that day. A covered stage was set up against the mountain backdrop, and a banner with "Soka Gakkai Amami Oshima Chapter Meeting" written in bold strokes stretched across the stage. At the last minute, the meeting was changed to an inaugural meeting for Amami Oshima General Chapter, but there was no time to redo the banner.

Six thousand members filled the beach by 11:00 A.M. They sat on straw mats and ate picnic lunches as they waited for the meeting to start at 1:00. When President Yamamoto and the other leaders stepped onto the stage at 12:45, a roar of applause erupted and the meeting began.

After several Soka Gakkai songs, Vice General Director Kiyoshi Jujo announced the formation of Amami

Oshima General Chapter and introduced the new leadership. This was greeted by a wave of joyous applause that seemed to go on forever.

Next, the new general chapter leader, Nogawa, took the podium and shared his determination with the audience. "Today," he said, "Amami Oshima General Chapter is established. It is a new beginning for all of us. Seven or eight years ago, there were almost no members in the Amami Islands. I believe that the establishment of this general chapter is a sign of the triumph of our faith and proof that we really can achieve kosen-rufu."

NOGAWA called out at the top of his voice: "The karma of the Amami Islands is deep. Not only do we have a painful past, but also each year typhoons inflict great damage, causing our fellow citizens terrible hardship.

"We are the ones who can change all that. I am determined to devote every ounce of my strength to turning these islands into a Buddha land. President Yamamoto once said that the more a region suffers and the more misfortune it encounters, the stronger the organization will grow there. Let's work together and make our general chapter the best in all Japan! Let's stand up together once again!"

The members signaled their agreement by raising their fists high into the air. Their response was immediate and came with a force that seemed to shake the heavens.

After Nogawa, Young Women's Leader Michiyo Watari, Director Ryoichi Sawada, and Vice General Directors Yukio Ishikawa, Katsu Kiyohara and Eisuke

Akizuki each delivered greetings, followed by General Director Koichi Harayama. Finally, Shin'ichi expressed his deep appreciation to the members for their hard work and began his speech with a bright smile on his now-sun-tanned face.

Declaring that Nichiren Daishonin's Buddhism is the ultimate teaching from both a documentary and theoretical perspective, Shin'ichi stated that the benefits gained from its practice are primarily inconspicuous in the way they are manifested. "There are two kinds of benefits from our prayers," he said, "those that are immediately apparent, or 'conspicuous,' and those that we cannot see right away, or 'inconspicuous.' Inconspicuous benefit is the focus of the Daishonin's Buddhism, for it is what brings real happiness.

"There are cases in which a person's illness is cured soon after taking faith, but true benefit does not appear in this manner — nor is it anything like beginning to practice and coming into a large some of money. If the real benefits of faith came in the form of unexpected windfalls without any effort on our part, we'd become lazy and spoiled.

"So what is inconspicuous benefit? It can be likened to the growth of a tree. You can spend day after day watching a tree, and nothing will seem to change. But if you observe it after five, ten, twenty years have passed, you will see that it has grown large and tall. In the same way, if you keep practicing this faith for five, ten or twenty years, your negative karma will disappear and you will change your destiny, accumulate good fortune and gain tremendous benefit. This is what is meant by inconspicuous benefit, and it is the true benefit of the Daishonin's Buddhism."

MANY MEMBERS thought of benefit only in the conspicuous sense, and so what Shin'ichi Yamamoto was saying at the inaugural meeting surprised some. His purpose, however, was to confirm for them the correct attitude in faith.

He continued: "Inconspicuous benefit can be described as how, through practicing the Daishonin's Buddhism, we manifest infinite life-force and wisdom, forge our character, accomplish human revolution and build indestructible happiness.

"I therefore hope that all of you will live out your lives with the Soka Gakkai, always striving to spread Nichiren Daishonin's teachings, and polishing and developing yourselves just as a tree patiently and persistently sends its roots deep into the earth and grows tall and strong. Then, ten, twenty or thirty years down the line, you will find that you have attained a state of happiness you never dreamed of."

"The Soka Gakkai's second president, Josei Toda," Shin'ichi said, "established three guidelines for our faith: 1) faith for a harmonious family, 2) faith to enable each person to become happy, and 3) faith to surmount obstacles. The family is a microcosm of kosen-rufu. To create a family in which all get along joyfully, a family that people look to in admiration, is to prove the power of your Buddhist practice.

"The purpose of faith is for each of us to say with confidence, 'I am truly happy!' Ultimately, our activities for kosen-rufu and our Buddhist practice are for our own happiness.

"The only way to achieve such happiness is by overcoming obstacles. They will arise without fail to impede the spread of this true teaching. When we struggle against wrong, we will face challenges as a matter of course. Just as a kite needs the resistance of wind to rise into the air, however, we need struggle and opposition to bring our lives to shine with increasing brilliance. The noblest life is one lived challenging injustice without giving in to obstacles. The boundless life-force and sense of mission this brings forth will allow us to soar into the vast skies of genuine happiness.

"Other people cannot make us happy. Neither can science or government. We can only attain real happiness through strong determination and a lofty devotion to faith, by which we elevate and open our lives. I conclude today's speech with my hopes that all of you, as champions of faith standing in the vanguard of the times, will pave the way to a life of supreme happiness."

The earth and heavens seemed to shake with thunderous applause.

THE MEETING ended with a resounding chorus of "Song of Kosen-rufu in Asia."

A meeting of this scale on Amami Oshima was big news, even to the public. All the local papers reported it. The next day, on June 23, *The South Sea Daily News* ran a detailed story with a photograph. A column in the *Oshima News* read: "Members numbering more than seven thousand, from every village and town on Amami

Oshima as well as from the islands of Kikaijima and Tokunoshima, attended the Soka Gakkai Amami Oshima General Chapter Meeting. They seemed to fill Shiohama Beach, fully reclaiming that reclaimed stretch of land. The one road leading to Shiohama, which runs along the foot of Mount Benten, was packed with people and their vehicles. A group of young men wearing Soka Gakkai armbands deftly guided traffic, leaving the local police with nothing to do but stand around at the main intersection and watch all the activity."

Despite the article's sarcastic undertones, it was true that the people living in the neighborhood were surprised at just how well organized the event had been.

After the meeting, guidance sessions for each division's leaders were held. Shin'ichi would join the meeting for men's leaders. In the time between the two meetings, Shin'ichi and his party took the opportunity to see Naze City with the newly appointed Amami Oshima General Chapter Leader Takashi Nogawa and other leaders. On the way, they stopped and took a stroll at Akasaki Point. To the right they could see the houses of Naze beyond the harbor, and to the left was the clear blue East China Sea. A pleasant breeze came off the ocean.

As they looked out at the water, Shin'ichi asked Nogawa, "What is the biggest problem facing the people of the Amami Islands?"

"*Habu* snakes," he replied. "Last year alone as many as two hundred and twenty people were bitten, and this year it's already been about fifty. *Habu* bites must be cut open and drained of the poison and the victim must receive medical treatment immediately. But some areas on the islands have no doctors, in which case these bites can be fatal."

"Since this is a life-threatening problem," Shin'ichi said, "the national government should find a good way to deal with it. Why aren't any of your representatives in parliament addressing this?"

"Because the population of our islands is small and our few votes mean little to them," Nogawa replied.

"*Habu* bites, then, are a problem caused by human negligence," said Shin'ichi.

SHIN'ICHI turned to General Director Koichi Harayama, who was also serving as a member of the Upper House of the Japanese parliament, and said: "Do you not think that politicians should listen closely to such problems and wrack their brains to come up with good solutions? Representatives of the Clean Government Group in particular should never overlook even a single cry for help from among the people." Shin'ichi then asked Takashi Nogawa, the Amami Oshima general chapter leader, "Are there any other problems besides *habu* snakes?"

"Yes," replied Nogawa. "Typhoons. So many typhoons hit Amami that it is called Typhoon Alley. We suffer enormous damage every year."

"This is also an area where the government should think of various ways to assure the public's safety and security," Shin'ichi said. "But the fundamental solution to these problems lies in the members' determined prayers.

"Buddhism teaches that the mind encompasses the entire universe. When we change our innermost state of mind, our whole being changes, and this affects the world in which we live. This is the teaching of the oneness of life and its environment, and the principle of a single life-moment possessing three thousand realms. This means that if more and more people start chanting with determined prayer, even the most difficult of situations will change.

"Everything starts with a strong determination. Such determination may inspire us to research ways of protecting the home or find out what crops are most likely to survive a typhoon, for example. This determination also can move the government. Our duty, our mission, is to make the place we live a Land of Eternally Tranquil Light, a realm of happiness and peace. I hope the members here in the Amami Islands will be pioneers in this endeavor."

After sightseeing, Shin'ichi headed for Ryuan-ji, the temple where the men's division group leaders meeting was to be held. It was built and donated to Nichiren Shoshu by the Soka Gakkai in December 1959, when there were only a few members living in the Amami Islands. Believing it would be a great source of strength for future kosen-rufu activities, Shin'ichi had proposed its establishment. The Soka Gakkai had always given the construction of temples and the growth of Nichiren Shoshu top priority, even if it meant delaying the construction of Soka Gakkai facilities.

The priesthood later took advantage of the Soka Gakkai's sincerity and, intending to exploit the membership, excommunicated Shin'ichi, their staunchest supporter, setting into motion a contemptible plot to disband the organization. The offense committed by these priests will never be erased. Thus, decades after its establishment,

Ryuan-ji became a stronghold for the attempted destruction of Nichiren Daishonin's Buddhism in the Amami Islands.

Such malice is like a cancer. The longer it is left untreated, the farther it will spread, until it finally destroys life. That is why it is so important to challenge injustice and wrongdoing. It is the only way to protect the realm of good and secure the correct path of faith.

A T THE MEN'S division group leaders meeting, Shin'ichi spoke of the sense of commitment and responsibility required of leaders. He was profoundly aware of the hardships faced by the Amami Islands' inhabitants, and he knew how difficult it was for the members there to do Soka Gakkai activities. Yet, without the continuous spread of the Daishonin's teachings, the fate of Amami would not be changed and happiness for the people could not be realized. That is why Shin'ichi chose to talk about the attitude of those taking the lead in activities for kosen-rufu.

"Thank you for your hard work every day. The challenges you face geographically, economically, and in trying to share the Daishonin's Buddhism amid deep-seated local traditions must be overwhelming. As you know, the Daishonin states that we voluntarily choose to be born in evil circumstances so that we may help others (see WND, 243). In other words, we deliberately chose to be born into this defiled age so that we could help all living beings become truly happy.

"Buddhism teaches that we appeared in the Latter Day of the Law to propagate the Daishonin's Buddhism as

Bodhisattvas of the Earth. This means that all of you volunteered to be born here in the Amami Islands. Well aware that this place is frequently struck by typhoons, has poisonous snakes, is difficult to get around and suffers economically, you accepted the karmic burden and appeared here as Bodhisattvas of the Earth with a vow to work for kosen-rufu.

"If you are complaining that these circumstances are not what you expected, that they are more than you bargained for, then you are not yet demonstrating the real essence of your mission. You will in that case be unable to manifest your innate power and wisdom, which means you will not break through your problems. Only when you have a firm awareness of your mission to accomplish kosen-rufu are you a true Bodhisattva of the Earth. Then, as you strive to fulfill your mission, your eternal self will take over and boundless strength and wisdom will well forth, enabling you to surmount all obstacles."

The men's division group leaders listened intently as Shin'ichi spoke. Looking directly at each person, he continued: "Today I want to talk about what will prevent our achievement of kosen-rufu. It is not the harshness of our circumstances or our environment but the complacency of leaders and their willingness to give up. When leaders start thinking: 'My area has accomplished so much. There is nothing more we can do,' or 'We set a goal, but if we cannot reach it, then so be it,' then they have already lost the battle.

"A strong determination is the driving force for victory. If that is lost, defeat is the only outcome."

THE HEAT of the summer and the Amami members' excitement filled the hall at the men's division group leaders meeting. Beads of sweat trickled down their faces as they listened intently to President Shin'ichi Yamamoto. "Propagation is the lifeblood of religion, and kosen-rufu is the spread of the True Law," he said. "If this Law does not spread, happiness for all people will not be realized. Naturally, the means of propagation differs according to time and place, but without steady growth, our movement will stagnate.

"Some people believe that because the Soka Gakkai has reached a total membership of three million households, it will probably not grow any larger, but that is completely unfounded. We must develop and expand our movement for kosen-rufu throughout our lives. If we consistently act with the determination to spread Nichiren Daishonin's Buddhism and to dedicate our lives to promoting this great cause, no matter what anyone says, even if we have to do it alone, there will be no limit to the Soka Gakkai's development.

"Our movement has made incredible progress in a very short time in the Amami Islands. That is because all of you have worked diligently to tell as many people as you can here about this Buddhism, without fearing any obstacle.

"That is the Soka Gakkai spirit. If we can keep this spirit burning forever, passing it on from member to member, to our children and our grandchildren, we will achieve kosen-rufu without fail. Please remember that leader is another name for those who are responsible for kosen-rufu. It is important that you always ask yourself how much you, as one of the central figures of our organization, have contributed to this movement.

"Amami is the Hawaii of Japan. I love these islands. Your friends in nearby Okinawa have written a song, 'Heroes of Okinawa,' and are singing it proudly as they advance. Why don't you write a song of your own and call it 'Heroes of Amami'? You can sing it together as you go forward in high spirits and friendship, with 'unity first' as your motto.

"You are the only ones who can realize kosen-rufu of the Amami Islands. I hope that you, taking my spirit and determination as your own, will begin to advance anew." Shin'ichi's words moved and inspired the members.

As Shin'ichi climbed into the car after the meeting, a wave of dizziness swept over him. In addition to being unaccustomed to the heat, he was suffering from exhaustion and lack of sleep.

When he arrived back at the community center, some two hundred and sixty-nine members from Okinoerabujima and Yoronjima were waiting for him in the main hall. Their ferry to Amami Oshima was delayed, causing them to miss the inaugural meeting for Amami Oshima General Chapter.

SHIN'ICHI called energetically to the members waiting for him: "Thank you for coming! How nice to see you! How long did it take you to get here?" One of the members from Yoronjima answered cheerfully, "The sea was rough, so it took thirty-eight hours."

"That is a long time!" Shin'ichi responded. "You must

be tired. This center belongs to all of you, so please relax and make yourselves at home."

Shin'ichi then encouraged the members, praising their strong seeking spirit. He said that he hoped all would persist in their faith, never forgetting the great joy of encountering the supreme teaching of Buddhism, and that they would continue to transform their lives to the point where they could say they attained a state of unsurpassable happiness.

He then addressed each member individually, exchanging firm handshakes. To an elderly woman he said: "Please live very long. Being healthy and happy in itself is proof of the power of Buddhism." To a young man he said: "The future belongs to your generation. Please develop your strength and ability and become a great leader! A great leader of Okinoerabu!" One men's division member shared his determination with Shin'ichi as they shook hands, and another woman told him with tears in her eyes of the tremendous joy she felt through her faith.

Superficial words do not touch other people's lives. Shin'ichi poured his entire being into each word and each handshake as he wholeheartedly encouraged the members. After twenty minutes of shaking hands and exchanging greetings, his right hand was numb.

Following dinner, he met with the leaders of Amami Oshima General Chapter. He then sat down to inscribe copies of Mr. Toda's poems to present to members as gifts:

No matter how painful,
Do not lament, my friends!

Tomorrow we will see
A realm of true happiness
Of kosen-rufu.

Death awaits
All of us one day;
Thus, be fearless,
Leaving unchallenged
Not a single enemy of the Buddha.

Now, let us set out on a journey
Our hearts emboldened
To spread the Mystic Law
Even to the farthest reaches
Of India.

Shin'ichi wrote each word with his entire life, praying that every member would stand up in faith and realize great development.

NIGHT DEEPENED on Amami Oshima. Midnight came and went, but Shin'ichi did not stop writing.

On the morning of June 23, Shin'ichi departed from Naze Harbor, sent off by members singing Soka Gakkai songs. The ferry took him back to Tokunoshima, where he boarded a plane for Kagoshima. He arrived at Kagoshima Airport at 5:30 P.M. There he transferred to a flight headed for neighboring Miyazaki Prefecture where he was scheduled to attend the Miyazaki General Chapter Leaders Meeting at the prefecture public hall that evening.

At the public hall, Shin'ichi's exhaustion had reached its peak. Even so, he gave his all to encouraging the members, declaring that the growth of the Soka Gakkai was in exact accord with the Lotus Sutra's description of the emergence of the Bodhisattvas of the Earth. He then went to the nearby prefecture education hall to speak with members who were waiting there for him as well.

Shin'ichi's high spirits made it impossible for the members to know just how tired he was and how much he was exerting himself. He lived by the passage in the "Twenty-six Admonitions of Nikko": "Until kosen-rufu is achieved, propagate the Law to the full extent of your ability without begrudging your life" (GZ, 1618). In other words, kosen-rufu will only be possible through the selfless efforts of individuals dedicated to spreading the Daishonin's teachings.

Shin'ichi's mentor, Josei Toda, demonstrated this principle with his very life. He left the world only after achieving the unprecedented membership goal of seven hundred and fifty thousand households. Shin'ichi made a profound vow to embody and communicate his mentor's spirit of total devotion to realizing world peace and happiness for all humankind.

Spiritual succession does not take place in the conceptual realm. It happens only through action and behavior. That is why Shin'ichi poured everything he had into each moment. He consistently gave his all, knowing that one's actions now, in this instant, reveal one's spirit.

The formation of many new headquarters and general chapters was steadily securing the Soka Gakkai's organizational foundation, but Shin'ichi felt deeply that securing the spiritual foundation would breathe real life into the organization. He was determined that the seventh memorial (sixth anniversary) of Mr. Toda's death would be a true gathering of lions who had inherited Mr. Toda's spirit and those who could say with confidence that their mentor was alive in their hearts.

As the leader in the race for kosen-rufu, Shin'ichi ran ahead alone at full speed. He believed that scores of runners, true friends in faith, would definitely follow in succession.

NOTES

1 One of the six treatises that comprise twenty-sixth high priest Nichikan's Six-volume Writings.

2 In those days, the headquarters was the largest local organizational unit in the Soka Gakkai. Organizational units were broken down into headquarters, general chapters, chapters, districts and finally blocks, the smallest organizational unit.

3 Shimousa — Area covering present-day Chiba and part of Ibaraki prefectures, located in the south central part of Honshu, Japan's main island.

4 Shiga — Prefecture neighboring Kyoto in the east.

5 In Japan, public baths were common since hot baths were not available to many households; they are now becoming rare. Public baths often became gathering places for local neighborhoods and communities.

6 Kanto region — In the Soka Gakkai's organizational structure, the area consisting of Ibaraki, Tochigi, Gumma, Saitama and Chiba prefectures in central Honshu, Japan's main island.

7 Kyushu — Southernmost island of Japan's four main islands, comprised of Fukuoka, Nagasaki, Oita, Kumamoto, Miyazaki,

Saga and Kagoshima prefectures. The Amami Islands are part of Kagoshima Prefecture.

8 Amami Oshima — Main island in the Amami group of islands between Kyushu and the Okinawa Islands; part of Kagoshima Prefecture.

9 Ryukyu Kingdom— Beginning in the late 12th century, its domain was the Ryukyu archipelago until Okinawa Prefecture was established in 1879.

10 Shimazu Iehisa (1578–1638) — Japanese feudal lord under the Tokugawa Shogunate (1603–1867) in a southern region of Kyushu known as the Satsuma domain. He conquered the Ryukyu Kingdom in 1609.

11 Satsuma domain — All of present-day Kagoshima Prefecture and part of Miyazaki Prefecture.

12 Kagoshima— Capital of Kagoshima Prefecture in southern Kyushu, the southernmost island of Japan's four main islands. It is a departure point for ships and planes leaving for outlying islands.

13 In Japan, it was traditionally believed that salt had purifying qualities. It was thrown as a form of protection against impurity.

Jeweled Sword

T HE CREATION of a new age rests in the hands of youth. In the summer of 1963, Shin'ichi Yamamoto put his whole life into developing the youth of the Soka Gakkai. He resolutely looked forward to the emergence of tens or hundreds of thousands of young people who were his equals in terms of spirit and capability.

On July 1, he attended a young men's division leaders meeting at the Taito Ward Gymnasium in Tokyo. He announced that the seventh memorial (sixth anniversary) of Josei Toda's death on April 2, 1964, would be the start of the essential phase of the Soka Gakkai's development. His declaration resounded like a lion's roar.

Essential here is a reference to the latter fourteen chapters of the Lotus Sutra. In contrast, the first fourteen chapters are called the theoretical teaching. *Theoretical* in this case indicates a shadow or reflection of the truth,[1] while *essential* means the actual substance of the truth. The core of the Lotus Sutra is revealed not in the first half of the sutra, but in "The Life Span of the Thus Come One" chapter in the essential teaching.

By "essential phase," Shin'ichi meant the time when the actual work of kosen-rufu would begin. This astonished the participants. It was as if an electric current was passing through them. All were consistently amazed at the new developments in the movement to spread Nichiren Daishonin's teachings and at the Soka Gakkai's tremendous growth since Shin'ichi became president. So to hear Shin'ichi declare that a new, essential phase would begin with Mr. Toda's seventh memorial meant that until then they had only been in the theoretical phase. They could not imagine what sort of time the essential phase would be.

Realizing, however, that it would far exceed anything they could conceive of, they were very excited and determined. Their eyes were clear and bright, reflecting the brilliant future image of kosen-rufu. As leaders of the generation who would rebuild society, all of them felt great pride and joy in living with the Gakkai while polishing and developing themselves.

Youth excel where there is hope. Wherever there is progress in the Soka movement, there is also a beautiful atmosphere of hope.

Three days later, on July 5, Shin'ichi attended a young women's division leaders meeting, also at Tokyo's Taito Ward Gymnasium. A new song for the young women's division titled "The Song of Joy" was sung for the first time.

Youth!
Let us sing!
Friends around the world—
We will change history
And let culture flourish.
The Seven Bells shall resound
Heralding the victory
Of freedom and peace.

It was a bright and cheerful song, expressing the young women's fresh determination and awareness of a new beginning.

AT THE YOUNG WOMEN'S leaders meeting, Shin'ichi suggested that the young women's and young men's divisions each aim for a new membership goal of one million. The young women's division at the time had 430,000 members and the young men's division, 640,000. Should they reach their goal of one million, each would be a youth organization of a scale unprecedented in Japan.

It is necessary to have a goal in order to make progress. Once a goal is set and it becomes clear what effort must be made over the days and months to achieve it, momentum increases in that direction. Shin'ichi suggested the goal of one million members for each division because he wanted to give the youth fresh hope.

He also spoke about the way the media provoked criticism of the Soka Gakkai by reporting on the actions of certain members as if they were problems caused by the Soka Gakkai itself. "There are cases in which people suffering from mental illness join the Soka Gakkai and then cause some unfortunate incident," he said. "In other cases, people with criminal records, who are shunned by society, became members and then are involved in another crime.

"Each time something like this happens, the newspapers and weekly tabloids print stories implying that the Soka Gakkai was in some way responsible, intensifying the attacks against us.

"It is the responsibility of politicians and government to look after such people, ensuring that they can live with dignity without endangering others. But this is not happening. Instead, society has abandoned these people and no one is doing anything to help. In fact, many politicians and high-ranking officials simply look the other way when it comes to the unfortunate. Japan's leaders are self-centered and irresponsible.

"We Soka Gakkai members, on the other hand, are working to rid this world of unhappiness. When we meet those who are suffering, we explain to them that all people have the right to be happy and teach them about the Daishonin's Buddhism.

"The Soka Gakkai does not discriminate. Wishing to see all people become truly happy, we devote ourselves wholeheartedly to serving others. People concerned only with their social image and their own needs cannot do this.

"We embrace many people with various backgrounds and problems, and there is a chance that some may get into trouble. But which is right — what we are doing now or turning our backs on such people just because we are afraid of what might happen?"

SHIN'ICHI YAMAMOTO continued his speech with conviction:"The Soka Gakkai is the most noble organization in our society, for it is sincerely embracing even those society has rejected, and is showing them the way to happiness. Any conscientious leader should see this and praise the Soka Gakkai for it.

"If we impose restrictions on our membership, accepting, for example, only those with high social standing, financial means, good health and other qualifications, we would never have been called an organization of the poor and the sick, and many problems could have been avoided.

"But that would mean that we abandon the true spirit of religion, and of Buddhism in particular, which is to save those who are suffering."

Whenever members saw or heard a media report that a Soka Gakkai member was involved in some incident, they did not know what to say to their friends and neighbors, and this frustrated them. By addressing this, Shin'ichi shed light on the essence of the issue. He always tried to keep himself abreast of the problems troubling the members. Once he discovered these issues, he immediately confronted them head-on and clearly refuted them. In a war of words, such quick action is of utmost importance.

Shin'ichi went on: "I hope that all of you, the members of the young women's division, will do your best to personally meet with and encourage each member."

He was concerned that the activities of the young men's and young women's divisions were becoming too focused on organizing meetings and events, and that one-on-one encouragement was falling by the wayside.

The foundation of Soka Gakkai activities are practice for oneself, which consists of doing gongyo and chanting daimoku, and practice for others, which means sharing the Daishonin's Buddhism and encouraging and guiding fellow members in faith. In one sense, introducing another person to Buddhism does not stop with that person joining the Soka Gakkai. Truly enabling others to practice means consistently guiding and encouraging them until they surpass oneself in ability.

Meetings are of course important, but in reality not everyone can attend them. There are usually at least twice as many members in a local organization as the number who regularly participate in any given discussion meeting. Only by personally visiting and encouraging each member in our area can we solidify our organization. This will lead to the Soka Gakkai's growth and development, and in turn, to the advancement of kosen-rufu. Soka Gakkai activities without personal guidance are like a masterpiece without the finishing touches.

OFFERING PERSONAL guidance is of course easier said than done. The Soka Gakkai is made up of all kinds of people. Some may refuse to meet or speak with other members, while others perhaps joined as children along with their parents but do not consider themselves believers. We may even come across members highly critical of the Soka Gakkai. Others may be suffering so deeply from financial difficulties or illness that they are bereft of any hope for the future.

It is no easy task to visit the homes of such members, to try and make conversation, forge bonds of friendship, talk about the importance of faith, and teach them about gongyo and Buddhist principles. Doing so is far more challenging than talking with members we see at meetings or organizing various activities.

But it is these very efforts that enable us to polish ourselves. In striving to help others grow, we grow too. Furthermore, struggling in this way constitutes true Buddhist practice. Promoting activities together with those who regularly attend meetings is simple, but this in itself will not enable the Daishonin's Buddhism to spread. To concern ourselves only with such members would be comparable to the captain of a ship bound for a distant shore contenting himself with sailing around the harbor. Leaders must realize that the main stage of Soka Gakkai activities is not meetings themselves, but the hard work that takes place beyond the meetings.

The network of life-to-life bonds that is the Soka Gakkai was built through the efforts of individuals to visit and personally encourage their fellow members. Just as a broad interwoven nexus of roots that sink deep into the earth supports a mighty tree, it is the consistent and painstaking actions of members to offer personal guidance at the grassroots level that hold up the Soka Gakkai.

A person who does nothing but grandstand, who is

cowardly and lazy, cannot carry out this difficult work, which requires tremendous courage and perseverance. On the other hand, those who personally talk to and encourage their friends and the people they meet are true emissaries and children of the Buddha; they are the real champions of faith.

Shin'ichi was certain that if the leaders of the youth division actively engaged in giving personal encouragement, the Soka Gakkai's future would be firmly and eternally established. He knew that just as a river grows fuller and wider as it flows to the sea, the Soka Gakkai would expand and produce an ever-growing number of talented individuals as the years passed. If the youth division leaders neglected this one crucial area, however, they would be severing with their own hands the roots of the mighty tree of the Soka Gakkai.

That was why Shin'ichi emphasized the importance of offering personal guidance when he spoke at the young women's division leaders meeting.

SHIN'ICHI YAMAMOTO then encouraged the participants to return home from activities at a sensible hour. "The journey to spread Nichiren Daishonin's philosophy throughout the world is a long one," he said. "It will not do any good if you get into a vicious cycle of coming home late every night and pushing yourself to the point of exhaustion.

"It is important to exercise common sense and behave in a way that is socially acceptable. I would not know what to say to your parents if you had an accident because you were out late doing Soka Gakkai activities. I therefore suggest that the young women's division members return home from activities by 10:00 P.M. at the latest. And I want the leaders to see that the members do so, and strictly advise them if they do not."

Time passes quickly when we are earnestly engaged in Soka Gakkai activities. But when we set a limit on our time, we come up with innovative ways to be more efficient and avoid doing things out of habit. We can also prevent accidents. This is how we create value.

At the young women's division leaders meeting, Shin'ichi gave the members a goal for the future, refuted unfounded criticisms of the Soka Gakkai, emphasized the importance of personal encouragement, and even went so far as to offer concrete guidance on the time members should return to their homes.

Youth are the jeweled sword in the endeavor to build a peaceful world based on the Daishonin's teachings, and Shin'ichi spared no effort in polishing that jeweled sword.

On July 6, the day after the meeting, training sessions began for the Suiko-kai and the Kayo-kai, the respective training groups of the young men's and young women's divisions, in Amagi on the Izu Peninsula. Shin'ichi energetically joined in these activities. Some of the participants already graduated from the youth division, but the majority were active members taking central responsibility for both divisions. Shin'ichi devoted every ounce of his energy to the education of youth, so for him these gatherings were highly significant.

The members of the Suiko-kai left Tokyo at 6:00 A.M.

and arrived at Amagi after playing team sports on the beach at Kisami in Shimoda, Izu. Shin'ichi left Tokyo on a train bound for Shimoda just after noon, traveling with General Director Koichi Harayama and others. When he arrived at his lodgings in Amagi that evening, Youth Division Leader Eisuke Akizuki came with other leaders to greet him. Shin'ichi spoke to them with great conviction: "Is everyone raring to go? Let's make this a training session for raising great leaders of the essential phase!"

THE WORDS FLOWED from Shin'ichi's mouth. The training had already begun. "The important thing for a Suiko-kai member is to live out your life upholding the Soka Gakkai spirit. Right now our movement to spread the Daishonin's teachings is advancing in a smooth fashion. But this will not always be the case. The Daishonin writes that one should not 'expect good times, but take the bad times for granted' (WND, 998).

"The Soka Gakkai spirit means resolutely standing up when our organization is faced with great difficulty and under heavy fire. The Daishonin also says: 'Although I and my disciples may encounter various difficulties, if we do not harbor doubts in our hearts, we will as a matter of course attain Buddhahood. Do not have doubts simply because heaven does not lend you protection. Do not be discouraged because you do not enjoy an easy and secure existence in this life' (WND, 283).

"This is the lofty spirit of advancing the spread of the Mystic Law exactly as the Daishonin's Buddhism teaches, regardless of how powerfully the storms of adversity may blow. No matter how severe the obstacles we face or how long they endure, we must not doubt the protection of the heavenly deities. Genuine Buddhist practice is to carry out faith undauntedly to the very end.

"Those who complain, criticize and bemoan the fact that the path to achieving our great goal is rough and difficult are not practitioners of the Daishonin's philosophy. They are not real believers.

"The Daishonin further states: 'This is what I have taught my disciples morning and evening, and yet they begin to harbor doubts and abandon their faith. Foolish men are likely to forget the promises they have made when the crucial moment comes' (WND, 283). Even if believers are told consistently that persecutions will definitely come, many will still end up abandoning the supreme Law of Buddhism. It is the nature of foolish people to forget their vows at the crucial moment. Of utmost importance is what we do—how we decide to live—at that instant, that time when the Soka Gakkai is being persecuted. Such situations reveal a person's true character."

Akizuki and the others sensed extraordinary determination in Shin'ichi's guidance, which poured from him like an ever-flowing fountain. They also felt that Shin'ichi's words expressed his tremendous hopes and expectations for the Suiko-kai and for the youth division.

Shin'ichi continued: "Mr. Toda told me that after his release from prison at the end of the war, he asked his wife in great detail about the attitude and behavior of the members during his incarceration. Later, when his business reached a desperate impasse, he paid close attention to the reactions of his disciples and watched to see what they would do. He was observing their true nature. What we do, how we act, at the crucial moment is what determines ultimate victory or defeat."

"WHEN MR. TODA'S business fell into crisis, I was suffering from tuberculosis. I had a persistent fever and sometimes coughed up blood. Our salaries were still suspended, and my coworkers were leaving one after another. Though they were indebted to him in many ways, some criticized Mr. Toda harshly behind his back.

"But I kept working. I had inwardly determined to give my life to Mr. Toda, to fight alongside him, and to die spreading Nichiren Daishonin's teachings while he was still alive. I believed this was the only way to be an example and show what it means to be a true disciple of Mr. Toda and the Daishonin in the present day.

"Mr. Toda understood everything. He knew me completely, inside and out. He said to me: 'You're trying to kill yourself, aren't you? You've decided to give me your life. But I will not have it! You must live—live out your life to the fullest. I will give you *my* life so that you may do so.' It was a mentor's passionate cry of concern for his disciple and for the future of our movement. With those words, I strongly resolved to live out my life dedicated to the advancement of kosen-rufu.

"To give one's life to kosen-rufu and to live one's life for kosen-rufu are two sides of the same coin. One is not different from the other. Both include the spirit to devote one's life to propagating the Mystic Law.

"Why am I telling you, the Suiko-kai members, these

things? It is because you represent the youth who have been entrusted with the mission of accomplishing the worldwide spread of Buddhism."

This guidance carried profound significance for the youthful leaders. Eisuke Akizuki and the others acutely sensed that Shin'ichi was pouring all his energy into the Suiko-kai.

That evening, the youth gathered for a guidance session in a hall of the inn where they stayed. This gave Shin'ichi an opportunity to hear their opinions, reports and questions. He knew that dialogue that promotes life-to-life exchange was extremely important, for it embodies the principle of oneness of mentor and disciple.

Kenshiro Ishikawa, head of the young men's division, acted as moderator. No sooner did he invite those with questions to raise their hands than did the hands of everyone in the room rise up. All were eager for the opportunity to ask a question or share their thoughts with President Yamamoto.

Shin'ichi felt that all the guidance and encouragement he had been giving to youth was steadily bearing fruit.

SHIN'ICHI had consistently appealed to his precious successors in the youth division: "Above all, I want you to decide that the responsibility for our movement's progress lies with you. I hope you will always deeply consider the many social problems that are sure to arise as we proceed with our great task and think of the wisest possible solutions."

He also said to them: "Whether you are a politician, a company president or in charge of an organization, you cannot fulfill the heavy responsibilities that come with the job if you are passive or inactive. The Daishonin writes: 'The generals in a tumultuous age develop strategy behind drawn curtains, and victory is decided thousands of miles away from the field of battle' (GZ, 183). When generals gather, they bring to the table information they possess and the various issues that need addressing. They examine in minute detail every conceivable approach and consider every solution, creatively working out a plan that will lead to victory.

"I am constantly thinking about how to spread the Daishonin's teachings, and I am devising different ways to reach our goal. Based on your ideas and reports, I draw up plans of action. But without any input, I have nothing to work with. Zero multiplied by any number will always be zero.

"I therefore ask that whenever you come to see me, you bring with you any questions, thoughts, opinions or reports you may have."

These youth, who were in the prime of their development, had put Shin'ichi's guidance into practice. Their questions and ideas ranged widely, from doctrinal issues to the relationship between social reform and human revolution. Many expressed the opinion that if the Komei-kai was really aiming to change Japanese government for the better, it would have to send representatives not only to the Upper House of the Diet but to the Lower House as well.

Opinions were exchanged openly, and various issues were raised. Shin'ichi addressed them all, sometimes going into great detail, and sometimes saying only, "I'll leave it up to you!"

When people are given real responsibility, they become aware of their mission and demonstrate surprising ability. It may be difficult for those with experience to delegate responsibility to the younger generation. There is certainly the risk of mistakes. Nevertheless, it is only by learning from our mistakes and gaining experience over time that we acquire substantial strength.

Youth must be given a stage upon which they can act freely, while being watched over from a distance. It is up to those who are older and have more experience to have the generosity of heart to take full responsibility if they fail.

A YOUNG MAN named Genji Samejima asked Shin'ichi Yamamoto, "What does it mean to have resolute faith?"

Before joining the Soka Gakkai, Samejima belonged to the Hokkeko, another lay organization of Nichiren Shoshu. He became a member of the Soka Gakkai after Shin'ichi became its president. After graduating from Tokyo University, he worked for a certain company, but later was hired by the Soka Gakkai Headquarters and assigned as staff of the *Seikyo Shimbun*, the Soka Gakkai's daily newspaper.

Opinions about Samejima were divided among the other staff. Some described him as a serious and talented young man of good character, while others were convinced that he was overly ambitious and had left the

Hokkeko for the rapidly growing Soka Gakkai because he saw more personal opportunity there.

Shin'ichi was aware of this duality in Samejima's personality. He also knew that Samejima would frequently criticize senior leaders behind their backs and act as though he was the only one who really cared about the organization's future. Everyone, to some extent, has two sides. Buddhism teaches that good and evil exist inseparably in the human heart—that our minds contain both the state of life of the Buddha, Shakyamuni, and of Devadatta, who sought to destroy the Buddha. Shin'ichi wanted to help this young person, who had come to the Soka Gakkai to change his life, realize his full potential at any cost.

In answer to Samejima's question, he said: "People of resolute faith are those who stick with the Soka Gakkai throughout their lives and support their seniors who are devoted to spreading Nichiren Daishonin's teachings. Those who stay with the organization through thick and thin, no matter how others may criticize, attack or try to make them leave, are people of resolute faith. That's all there is to it!"

As he said this, Shin'ichi looked Samejima directly in the eye. He was determined to watch over this young man for the next thirty years. Shin'ichi knew that time reveals who is genuine. If Samejima could continue his faith in earnest for thirty years, then he would gain mastery over himself and show wonderful proof of achieving human revolution. But if he was overtaken instead by ambition and tried to use the Soka Gakkai for his own objectives, in time he would leave the organization.

Shin'ichi put a lot of energy into teaching and train- ing Samejima, and even gave him important responsibil- ities within the organization. Somewhere along the way, however, Samejima became consumed by the desire to control the Soka Gakkai himself. Though he became a vice president, he later turned against the Soka Gakkai and in the end took the tragic road of one who has aban- doned faith.

THE MEMBERS continued asking questions, shar- ing opinions and giving reports. One young man asked Shin'ichi: "There are only a handful of young men's division members in the area for whom I am responsi- ble, and the situation is very tough. What can I do to turn things around?"

Shin'ichi immediately replied, "You need to rise to action!" Tension swept the room, and everyone fell silent. "Youth have to stand alone! By doing so, everything will change. This is what I have done. After President Toda died, the media and others predicted that the Soka Gakkai would fall apart. Some older leaders changed their atti- tude after Mr. Toda's death, and took advantage by becoming willful and selfish. Others plotted to exploit the organization. I realized that if nothing was done, the Soka Gakkai might fall apart. That is why I took a stand. As general administrator of the organization, I worked behind the scenes, taking full responsibility for every- thing. I was thirty years old at the time.

"My spirit all along was to stand up alone amid the harshest of circumstances. This was the case when, as a staff member of Kamata Chapter, I took the lead in introducing people to the Daishonin's Buddhism. At the time, the number of households joining the largest chapters in any given month hovered around one hundred. I knew at this rate we would never reach Mr. Toda's goal of 750,000 member households. Who was going to do it? It was up to his disciples. So I waged a battle, and in one month Kamata Chapter achieved a new membership record of 201 households.

"I was twenty-four years old. There were, of course, men's and women's division members in the chapter. In fact, almost all of the leaders were older than I. But in the end, they all fought alongside me. Why? Because I was so determined. I was more determined than anyone. They all thought: 'We cannot do this on our own, but if we do what this person tells us, we can break through our current deadlock.' And I produced results.

"Wherever I went, the circumstances were the worst they could be, but I won against all obstacles and met Mr. Toda's expectations. That is the way of a disciple. The Soka Gakkai does not need young people who pretend to work hard but are in reality lax and self-indulgent.

"I want *you* to stand up! You have to rise to action! I'll be watching!"

THE DIALOGUE between Shin'ichi Yamamoto and the Suiko-kai members was a true life-to-life exchange. At the end of the session, Shin'ichi added: "Those of you who have not received a message in calligraphy from me, please leave your names with the young men's division leader. I want to present this to each of you as encouragement to commemorate the fresh start we are making here together. I am depending on you. Let's work in unison to spread the Daishonin's teachings around the world!"

Night fell on Amagi as Shin'ichi continued giving inspiration to the Suiko-kai members.

The young women's division Kayo-kai training session was held on July 7, the following day. Once again, Shin'ichi answered the members' questions, pouring all his energy into encouraging them. He sensed that an age in which women would play a central role was near at hand, and that the very future of kosen-rufu hinged upon how many capable and wise women leaders the Soka Gakkai could nurture. These training sessions for the Suiko-kai and the Kayo-kai were perfect opportunities to strengthen further the faith of the young men's and young women's division members, his youthful successors.

Shin'ichi's mind was constantly occupied with the thought of how to educate and cultivate young people. Many leaders in society begin to raise successors only after having achieved success and recognition themselves. In the endeavor to create lasting peace through broadly spreading the Daishonin's teachings, however, that would be too late. That is because it is a task requiring count-less capable individuals whose stage of activities is varied and widespread. Aware of the possibility that he might die young, Shin'ichi felt an urgent need to foster a great many successors who could carry on with his vision and resolve, boldly assuming leadership in his stead.

He began to draw up new guidelines to commem-orate the twelfth anniversary of the young men's divi-sion on July 11, in preparation for the beginning of the essential phase of the Soka Gakkai's development. It was titled "Youth, Become World Leaders!"

Shin'ichi's pen raced: "The Soka Gakkai youth division will be the leaders of the new century. Mr. Toda's essay 'Youth, Be Patriotic!' was a call to the youth to become leaders of not only Japan, but of the world. Mr. Toda clearly outlined his guidelines for the youth division in his two essays 'Precepts for Youth' and 'Youth, Be Patriotic!' These should therefore be the principles of action practiced by the youth division.

"The youth division of the new age must possess an even greater international outlook and be active on all fronts. They must develop into talented, first-rate leaders in their chosen fields of endeavor."

In his guidelines, Shin'ichi also established for the youth division the goals of contributing to the welfare of all humanity and achieving world peace.

SHIN'ICHI went on to identify the source of the impasse facing humankind as a lack of vision on the part of world leaders. New leaders with new guiding principles were needed, he insisted. "Now is the time," he wrote, "for us to embrace as youthful reformers the highest ideals of leadership and show the way to realizing world peace."

He then offered the youth three practical guidelines: first, "establish a strong foundation of faith, practice, and study of the Buddhism of Nichiren Daishonin, the original Buddha"; second, "have lofty ideals while being grounded in reality, always advancing steadily, one step at a time"; and third, "forge unity among members."

Expressing great hopes for his youthful successors, Shin'ichi elaborated on the second point: "Those who aspire to become world leaders should first consistently be winners at their places of work and in other areas of daily life. We build the foundation of our lives during our youth. That foundation must be deep and solid. I hope that you all become dignified, generous and courteous young people."

Concerning the third point, he emphasized that they "should never forget that unity among our youth division members constitutes an eternal bond and a lifeline in the movement to lead people to happiness."

Shin'ichi's pen continued to move swiftly across the page: "The growth of the youth division is the progress of the Soka Gakkai. The progress of the Soka Gakkai is the progress of Japan. We should be confident that our development is directly related to the creation of lasting peace."

In conclusion he wrote: "The Daishonin states in 'The Actions of the Votary of the Lotus Sutra': 'Now, at the beginning of the Latter Day of the Law, I, Nichiren, am the first to embark on propagating, throughout Jambudvipa, the five characters of Myoho-renge-kyo, which are the heart of the Lotus Sutra and the eye of all Buddhas.... My disciples, form your ranks and follow me, and surpass even Mahakashyapa or Ananda, T'ien-t'ai or Dengyo!' (WND, 764–65). Jambudvipa is another name for the entire world. Let us advance courageously under a banner of global citizenship that allows no sacrifice or destruction, committed to achieving the worldwide spread of Buddhism for the sake of the happiness and peace of all people."

His passion for the growth of the youth surging within, Shin'ichi completed his article in one sitting. It would be published as an editorial in the August issue of *The Daibyakurenge,* the Soka Gakkai's study journal, and would serve as a spiritual appeal to the youth to open their eyes wide to the world, and to inspire in them an awareness and sense of responsibility as its future leaders.

IN 1963, Japan was preparing to host the Olympics in October the following year. This sparked a growing interest among the Japanese in internationalization and the world at large. Also in 1963, the English version of the Japanese pop song "I Look Up When I Walk" became a hit in the United States under the title "Sukiyaki." In June that year, it was No. 1 on the U.S. pop music charts.

These events gave the Japanese people a sense of self-confidence and brought the outside world closer to home. However, even though people were becoming more aware of the bigger picture, no one in Japan was offering a way to create peace or thinking about what youth should be doing to contribute on the world stage.

Against this backdrop, Shin'ichi Yamamoto's editorial in the Soka Gakkai study journal *The Daibyakurenge,* "Youth, Become World Leaders," set down concrete guidelines for the youth of the Soka Gakkai. His call was not limited to a select group; he urged all the youth division members to become world leaders, and clearly showed them how to achieve that goal. These guidelines revealed Shin'ichi's philosophy and conviction as a Buddhist.

Japanese society at the time was becoming more and more fixated on academic achievement and credentials, and people were beginning to think that one could not be a leader of society without graduating from a prestigious university. Shin'ichi, however, was not caught up in such an illusion. Of course, knowledge and intellectual ability are important, but academic history is not the same thing. Nor does it equate to one's competence as a human being.

Leaders need knowledge and intellect, but they must also have the wisdom to make the best use of these capacities. They also need courage, conviction, passion and initiative. More than anything, a true leader must possess character and humanity; he or she should be self-disciplined and genuinely concerned about others. These qualities are inseparable from the beliefs and philosophy such a leader upholds. As Nichiren Daishonin writes, "If the Law that one embraces is supreme, then the person who embraces it must accordingly be foremost among all others" (WND, 61).

Shin'ichi was confident that the youth of the Soka Gakkai had the potential to become great world leaders. This confidence struck the hearts of the youth who read his editorial, galvanizing them, and they determined to develop into world leaders to meet Shin'ichi's expectations. The seed of a firm resolve, the source of remarkable growth, was planted in the fertile soil of their young lives.

SHATTERING THE DARKNESS,
The powerful tolling
Of the bell of revolution
Heralds a new dawn.
Wherever its voice may reach

There shall we build
A society humanity has longed for.

As they sang their new "Song of Revolution," the student's voices reverberated throughout the Taito Ward Gymnasium in Tokyo. The Sixth Student Division General Meeting was held on July 14. The participants' faces were bright with excitement, and their fighting spirit energized the venue.

That was only to be expected. They had just reached their membership goal of twenty thousand, which was set at the fifth general meeting the previous year. They had gathered from all over Japan to celebrate their great victory. Those who work toward a clear goal in the endeavor to create peace based on the Daishonin's teachings, who strive to achieve it, and persevere until they win, shine with vitality and life-force.

The student division members present took the lead in the struggle for kosen-rufu in the essential phase of the Soka Gakkai's development. At the meeting, standing secretaries were appointed for the Kansai, Tohoku, Chubu, Chugoku and Kyushu regions, securing the organization's foundation across the nation.

The members were spirited, ready and eager. Goro Watari, the head of the student division, addressed them enthusiastically: "We have surpassed our goal of twenty thousand members set at our meeting last year, and as of today there are twenty thousand three hundred and sixteen student division members. Let us rejoice together at this victorious gathering!

"I propose that toward next year's general meeting we

aim for the goal of forty thousand members! What do you think?" Thunderous applause rocked the gymnasium. The goal meant doubling the membership, and would be next to impossible to achieve in one year without tremendous dedication and effort. Yet the members met this suggestion with an ovation of agreement.

Smiling brightly at this vigorous response, Watari continued: "All right then. Let us work together toward our new goal of forty thousand members.

"Now, regarding our activities on campus. For students, your community is the university. I think, therefore, that it is important that we conduct our activities with our respective universities as home bases. I propose that we form volunteer-led organizations on each campus through which we can actively promote our ideas. Do you agree?"

THE PROPOSAL of Goro Watari for the formation of student division groups at each university was met with a vigorous round of applause. Prior to this meeting, Watari sought guidance from Shin'ichi Yamamoto regarding the direction of student division activities. Shin'ichi was determined to do all he could to support anything the student division felt necessary for the advancement of kosen-rufu. He wanted to respect the group's autonomy and independence.

Following speeches from some vice general directors and the general director, President Yamamoto took the podium. Offering his warm congratulations on the occasion of the Sixth Student Division General Meeting, he said: "A vast sky of boundless hope awaits you. I sincerely pray that you will all live meaningful lives free of regret, and shine with integrity and vibrant life force, always basing yourselves on faith.

"For the past year, I lectured to representative members of the student division on the 'Record of the Orally Transmitted Teachings.' Recently, I began studying Nichiren Daishonin's treatise 'The Object of Devotion for Observing the Mind' with members of the Tokyo University Lotus Sutra Study Group. Also, a group centering around members at Kyoto University in Kansai will study Buddhism's great life philosophy through the Daishonin's work 'One Hundred and Six Comparisons.'"

Shin'ichi regarded these lecture series with Tokyo and Kyoto University students as a model for forming the university organizations that Watari spoke of, and a way in which he could support them. He envisioned that one day the student division groups on each campus would study the Daishonin's writings.

"I am absolutely determined," he said, "that from among the members with whom I am working so closely I will find and raise successors who will be responsible for the Soka Gakkai in the future and become leaders of Japan and the world. I hope you will all strive diligently toward that goal and work hard to forge and develop yourselves!"

Hearing President Yamamoto's high expectations of them moved the members deeply. Shin'ichi staked the Soka Gakkai's future entirely upon the growth of the student and youth divisions. There is an old saying: "When a tiger dies, it leaves its hide behind; when a man dies, he leaves his reputation." Shin'ichi, however, was not concerned in the least with leaving a legacy of personal fame or honor; his only wish was to leave behind talented successors.

SHIN'ICHI continued: "Japanese intellectuals today tend to believe that religion is not compatible with science, or that it is altogether unnecessary. But this is a mistake. The great scientist Albert Einstein himself emphasized the necessity of religion, and Russian writer Leo Tolstoy wrote: 'One of the worst prejudices known is held by a majority of the so-called scholars of our time, who claim that a person can live without faith.'[2] The nineteenth century American writer William Adams called faith the extension of reason.

"When we take a calm and objective look at life and social phenomena, seriously pondering how to alleviate human suffering, what life is, and the primal force of the universe, we naturally arrive at religion. If thinkers and scientists who seek such answers knew of the supreme life philosophy of the Daishonin's Buddhism, I believe they would be deeply impressed, bow their heads in respect, and shed tears of gratitude.

"Let us, who uphold this great religion, strive to create tremendous change in every area of human life, including culture, society, government and business, through our activities to realize religious and human revolution. I want us to continue advancing with our sights set twenty years hence."

Shin'ichi shared his feelings openly: "But whatever I propose, if it stops with me, nothing will be accomplished. If all of you become outstanding leaders in both name and reality, taking a stand as pioneers of the age and as true practitioners of the Daishonin's Buddhism, I can die happily at any moment.

"When we look at government today, we find that our leaders are all incredibly egocentric and selfish. They are arrogant and fixed in their ways. They do not listen to the ideas of youth. If we are to build a new Japan and a new peaceful world, youth must rise to action. I declare that it is you students, the leaders of youth, who must make your stand.

"That is my prayer and my hope. I am blazing the trail with all my strength and being with the belief that you are my true successors. Can I count on you?"

Without a moment's pause, every member shouted, "Yes!" Shin'ichi looked out at the room, at the face of each participant. Gazing back at him, their eyes gleamed with a burning vow.

SHIN'ICHI YAMAMOTO continued, speaking calmly: "It is difficult to maintain faith throughout life. From here on there are liable to be those who betray their fellow members and give up their faith. But Buddhism is about winning. I want each of you to carefully observe the lives of those who are upholding Nichiren Daishonin's teachings and those who left the Soka Gakkai, ten, twenty or thirty years down the line — I want you to witness and experience this contrast first-hand." He closed by calling on the participants to strengthen their foundation and advance with hope toward the future.

Three days later, on July 17, Shin'ichi attended a

district leaders meeting of the Chubu No. 1 Headquarters in Nagoya. The next day, July 18, he participated in the ground-breaking ceremony for the new Chubu Headquarters Building in Minami Ward, Nagoya. Then he left for Kansai, where on the nineteenth he addressed a meeting of student division members studying at Kyoto University, held in the Kyoto Annex. This meeting inaugurated the series of lectures on "One Hundred and Six Comparisons" that Shin'ichi gave to Kyoto University students.

More than twenty Kyoto University students assembled in the room. Three or four student division leaders from other schools in the Kansai area, such as Osaka University and Doshisha University, were also there. Shin'ichi entered the room and said with a smile, "Good evening!"

"Good evening!" replied the students, but there was a bit of apprehension in their greeting. This was not due so much to nervousness as it was to their being overwhelmed by the prospect of the upcoming lectures on "One Hundred and Six Comparisons." When Shin'ichi visited Kansai in June two years earlier, he talked with several Kyoto University students for the first time. "Above all, you need to study the Daishonin's writings in earnest," he said to them. "But understanding Buddhist principles alone will not make you happy. Faith is essential. It is important that you deepen your faith and grow into a person who, ten or twenty years down the road, will truly be able to contribute to the realization of peace and to humanity based on the ideals of Buddhism. This takes time, so there is no need to be hasty.

"I hope you will join me in working throughout our lives for the people's well-being." As he talked with the students, Shin'ichi recalled how Mr. Toda once gave lectures on the Lotus Sutra to the Lotus Sutra Study Group at Tokyo University, and raised many talented people as a result. Shin'ichi determined that he would give lectures on the Daishonin's writings to Kyoto University students in the future and thus create a strong core for the Kansai student division.

THE LECTURE SERIES on "One Hundred and Six Comparisons" was settled upon two months earlier in May, when Shin'ichi visited Kansai. Learning from Yoshihiko Ohya, who was in charge of the Kansai student division, that the number of members studying at Kyoto University increased, Shin'ichi met with Student Division Leader Goro Watari, and they decided to hold lectures for the students on this treatise.

Shin'ichi selected "One Hundred and Six Comparisons" because it was one of the Daishonin's most important writings, explaining his most essential and profound teaching concerning the superiority of the Buddhism of sowing to the Buddhism of harvest.[3] "One Hundred and Six Comparisons" is one of two documents the Daishonin directly entrusted to Nikko Shonin in January 1280, when the Daishonin was fifty-nine, the other being "On the True Cause." Together they are known as documents that transmit the ultimate heritage of the Law, or the lifeblood of faith.

"One Hundred and Six Comparisons" consists of one hundred and six articles in which the Daishonin elucidates in great detail the superiority of his own Buddhism of sowing, which clarifies the profound underlying meaning of the Lotus Sutra, over the Buddhism of harvest as taught by Shakyamuni and T'ien-t'ai, which is based on the literal meaning of the sutra. For this reason alone, it is a challenging piece of writing.

Difficult as it was, however, Shin'ichi thought it appropriate for student division members, as it would give them an opportunity to encounter the core teachings of the Daishonin's Buddhism. In addition, though the students may have been familiar with Western methods of reasoning taught in Japan's post-war educational system, they were not accustomed to traditional Oriental methods of reasoning, and the Daishonin's writings could not be fully apprehended by Western methods alone. "One Hundred and Six Comparisons," which was transmitted directly from mentor to disciple and which transcends formal Western logic, was the best among the Daishonin's writings to help students understand the Buddhist way of thought.

However, the participants assembled there that day had tried to study the document on their own in preparation for the lecture series. The truth, however, was that they had found it incomprehensible.

"Before we start studying 'One Hundred and Six Comparisons,' I want to get to know you all a little," Shin'ichi told the students. "Would you mind introducing yourselves?" He wanted to begin by gaining a deep impression of each person.

The introductions commenced. Two leaders within Kyoto University were the brothers Itaru and Isamu

Nomura. Itaru was the elder and a second-year student in the Agriculture Department. His younger brother, Isamu, was a third-year student in the Economics Department. Though a three-year gap existed between them, Itaru spent a few years away from school studying for the university entrance exam and repeating classes, so his younger brother was a year ahead of him in school.

SHIN'ICHI YAMAMOTO later learned that the Nomura brothers, two leaders within Kyoto University, had lost their father in a traffic accident eight years earlier. He had operated a pharmacy near Dotombori in downtown Osaka, and although they were not wealthy, the family enjoyed comfort and stability until his death.

Mr. Nomura was an atheist. He took good care of his health and was careful in everything he did. Even so, he died in an accident. After his death, the family's situation took a downward turn. They were left with a debt of millions of yen. For the first time, the Nomura brothers felt the force of destiny upon them.

Their mother was also not well. Looking for relief from her suffering and for spiritual support, she began a religious quest. She learned about Nichiren Daishonin's Buddhism from a Soka Gakkai member who came to the shop on business, and though she had doubts, she joined in December 1955. At the start, she did not practice her new faith very energetically. Yet suddenly a growth she had on her back became infected and she chanted daimoku in earnest for it to heal. When it did, she became strongly convinced of the efficacy of Buddhism and she urged her sons to join the Soka Gakkai.

The Nomura brothers witnessed their mother's recovery, and in 1957, partly out of a sense of duty to her, they decided to join. Their interest in the activities of the Soka Gakkai actually piqued the previous year when its participation in campaigns toward the Upper House elections were the focus of much attention. To these two young men, these efforts of the organization to promote social reform revealed its energy as a religious group rooted in the lives of the people.

In 1961, both brothers were accepted into Kyoto University. Through speaking with them, Shin'ichi's impression was that Itaru, the elder, was a good-natured, easy-going person. He did not seem overly concerned with details. These are fine qualities, but without the ability to sharply discern between good and evil and a strong spirit to fight wrongdoing, such a person may end up being used by the ill-intentioned. It is therefore of utmost importance to cast off the shell of one's limitations and thoroughly develop the courage to refute falsehood and reveal the truth, the heart of the Daishonin's Buddhism.

The younger brother, Isamu, was small in physical stature, but he was a passionate idealist who strove to be the best in whatever he did. Passionate idealists, however, may at times neglect to make steady efforts.

As Shin'ichi listened to the introductions of the students at Kyoto University, he thought about how to help each person reveal his or her potential. Moreover, he thought about how to raise each of them to become capable leaders of the movement to spread the Daishonin's great life philosophy around the world.

KOICHI TAGAWA, a slender, bespectacled young man, sat in the front row. Having graduated from Kyoto University's Faculty of Medicine, he was now an intern in the department of microbiology conducting research in immunology. He joined the Soka Gakkai a little over two years earlier. Prior to becoming a member, he suffered from chronic nephritis and at one point returned to his home in Kagawa, Shikoku,[4] for hospitalization. As he struggled with his illness, he began to ponder questions about life and the human spirit. He devoured books on psychology, tried Zen meditation, and read *Passages Deploring Deviations of Faith*[5] and the Lotus Sutra. No matter how much he read, however, he could not find the answers for which he was looking.

Due to his condition, Tagawa often needed to lie down

and rest. The older couple that ran the boarding house where he stayed became concerned, and they told him about the Daishonin's Buddhism. Tagawa attended a discussion meeting where he heard someone say that the Soka Gakkai was based on the "true Lotus Sutra." He decided to join, more out of a desire to study the sutra, than anything else. But as he became increasingly involved in Soka Gakkai activities, his nephritis improved, and this real demonstration of the power of faith gave him confidence.

Naomi Takaoka, like Tagawa, was a medical student. Her face was lackluster and her eyes vacant. She became a member a year earlier at her mother's behest but had doubts about the organization and felt out of place. She also had a fear of speaking in front of others. She was a reluctant participant in this meeting.

Next to her sat Eriko Nakano, a student of pharmacology. She participated in the "Record of the Orally Transmitted Teachings" lecture series in Tokyo and was now a leader of the Kansai young women's student division.

In the back row was a young man who appeared to be about thirty. His name was Yasuo Takigawa, and he worked for Japan National Railways. He received permission from his employer to attend graduate school while working.

One member sat hunched behind the others, as if he did not want to be seen. Yoshiro Takagi only joined a month before and purchased his first copy of the Gosho just prior to the meeting. Sitting in front of Takagi was Takuya Okutani, who introduced him to the practice.

Most of the participants joined the Soka Gakkai a year

or two earlier, and did not have much experience with organizational activities. This was very different from the lectures on the "Record of the Orally Transmitted Teachings," which selected leaders of the student division, including standing secretaries and corps leaders, had attended.

Shin'ichi addressed a male student who was thin and pale: "Are you all right? Are you getting enough to eat?"

"Umm, actually, I often have to skip meals. I do not have very much money."

SHIN'ICHI REPLIED: "You do not have enough money to eat? That must be very tough. Let me help you out a little."

Embarrassed, the student replied, "No, please, that's all right. I cannot accept that kind of help from you."

Shin'ichi smiled and said: "Don't be silly. I hope you will all think of me as an older brother. In that spirit, I intend to nurture each of you to become a person of great ability dedicated to the realization of peace and human happiness based on Buddhist ideals." This was Shin'ichi's firm conviction and desire.

Tomomasa Yamawaki, a graduate of Kyoto University who was now a judicial apprentice, also attended this first session of the lecture series on "One Hundred and Six Comparisons." He had joined the Soka Gakkai four years earlier. At the time, he was taking a long leave from school to tend to his nephritis, and was introduced to Nichiren Daishonin's teachings while he was recuperating from illness. As he practiced his new faith, he gradually regained his health and eventually returned to the university. He studied for the bar exam and passed in the fall of 1961.

As he introduced himself, Yamawaki proudly announced his current status as a judicial apprentice. In his pride, however, one could sense an arrogance that was covering for a lack of self-confidence. Nevertheless, Shin'ichi was glad that a member of the student division had managed to pass the difficult bar examination. He recalled how, when he was arrested on trumped-up charges during the Osaka Incident,[6] there was not a single attorney he could count on. None had the backbone to take a stand for justice. Even though they knew perfectly well that Shin'ichi was innocent, they all advised him to prepare for a guilty verdict.

Shin'ichi fought alone to clear his name. Because of that experience, he long awaited the emergence of attorneys who would uphold the Buddhist principle of respect for the dignity of life and fight for justice and humanism. Now here was Tomomasa Yamawaki, who passed the bar examination and was about to participate in the lectures on "One Hundred and Six Comparisons."

Shin'ichi said to Yamawaki: "So you've become a judicial apprentice? That's quite an achievement. Please do your best as a pioneer!" To all of the members, he then remarked, "I will protect each of you as long as I live." In fact, he continued for years to guide and encourage the students. He gave them unwavering support in many different ways. When, for example, Yamawaki became a full-fledged attorney, he was looked to as a legal advisor to the Soka Gakkai.

YAMAWAKI, however, came to regard the Soka Gakkai, a realm formed from bonds of trust, as an ideal place to realize his personal ambitions. Faith is a struggle between the potential for Buddhahood and the potential for devilish or destructive tendencies — between the good and the evil — that exist within our own lives. Our Buddhist practice, which enables us to polish and develop ourselves, is essential to defeating this inner destructive nature. But Yamawaki, who neglected to make earnest, genuine efforts to strengthen his faith, was an easy target for the devil king of the sixth heaven.

Later, when he officially became legal advisor to the Soka Gakkai, he curried favor with the high priest of Nichiren Shoshu in a plot to bring the organization under the priesthood's authority and gain control of the Soka Gakkai himself. When his ambitions were frustrated, he exploited his position as legal advisor to commit the preposterous crime of extortion against the Soka Gakkai. Thereby, he revealed his true colors as a person of exceedingly malign nature.

Bent on destroying the Soka Gakkai even after serving time in prison for his crimes, he continued to conspire with the priesthood, shrewdly involving certain political forces and segments of the media.

Shin'ichi could see in Yamawaki's demeanor a considerable degree of dishonesty, arrogance and duplicity, and at times would strictly advise him about these shortcomings. But mostly he would warmly encourage and try to guide Yamawaki. Everyone has weaknesses. It is easy to break ties with people, but if we were to turn our backs on every person we deemed to have faults, we would be unable to help anyone grow or develop. Believing in the inherent goodness of human beings is the secret to fostering people; it is also the spirit of a Buddhist.

The more weaknesses or negative tendencies someone had, the more energy Shin'ichi put into encouraging that person. He tried thinking of ways to help the person realize his or her full potential, and gave the person opportunities to take responsibility within the organization.

Shin'ichi was willing to forgive and embrace not only Yamawaki, but anyone who, despite having been deceitful in the past, awakened to the importance of living with integrity and began working wholeheartedly to contribute to kosen-rufu. But people often took advantage of this good faith. Shin'ichi, however, was not afraid of being hurt, and because he continued to put great effort into fostering people, he raised capable individuals who became active in the various areas of endeavor necessary for the realization of peace.

After the participants finished introducing themselves, Shin'ichi told them: "There will be many temptations along the way to achieving kosen-rufu. There will be obstacles. Unless you strive in all sincerity to deepen your faith, you will succumb to your inner weaknesses. Some among you here today may abandon your faith or betray the Soka Gakkai in the future. But even if there is only one of you left, I will continue to encourage that one person and to work with them to realize our goal.

"Having said that, however, I hope all of you remain to the very end. I hope that we will continue striving together to spread the Daishonin's teachings around the world as long as we live."

NEXT, SHIN'ICHI invited questions. The first person to raise his hand was Eikichi Uehata, a sophomore in literature. He had thick, dark eyebrows and strong features, and there was a pensive air about him. "I'm thinking of studying modern philosophy," he said, "and am wondering if, from the perspective of the Daishonin's Buddhism, there is any value in that." Uehata had been questioning the meaning of learning philosophy at the university level for some time.

Shin'ichi's response was clear: "Philosophy taught at universities today is for the purpose of broadening one's knowledge; it is training for the intellect. To put it plainly, the purpose of studying such subjects these days is to enable you to acquire a degree or title. This is the problem with current university education in general.

"What is the true purpose of studying philosophy? It is to learn how to live, and how to establish a state of unsurpassed joy and fulfillment. Only Nichiren Buddhism offers such a great philosophy. Buddhism is a supreme philosophy of life. It is a teaching firmly rooted in daily life that can bring happiness to all people. So Buddhism is the basis. If you study the Daishonin's Buddhism thoroughly, you will gain penetrating insight into all things.

"However, you will still need to acquire knowledge and intellect to become active leaders in society. Faith is the key to tapping the wisdom that will help you put that knowledge to the best use. If you base yourself on faith, nothing you do will be wasted." Shin'ichi then looked straight at Uehata and said: "In your case, now is the time to put energy into your university studies. Your time at a university is short. If life is like a marathon, then school is like a sprint, don't you think?"

As soon as Shin'ichi had answered Uehata's question, another hand shot up. This time it was Isamu Nomura, who asked: "At the student division general meeting the other day, you encouraged us to be people of "backbone" and life force who always base ourselves on faith. What exactly do you mean by being a person of backbone?

Shin'ichi smiled, nodded, and said: "I mean to live magnanimously, with strong conviction and composure. People are easily affected by their circumstances. For example, if you spend your days working part-time jobs, living on nothing but junk food, narrowly squeezing in time for your studies, you yourself are likely to become a person of narrow vision and capacity."

THE MEMBERS listened intently to Shin'ichi.

"Students today tend to be concerned only with their personal happiness. I am worried about this trend among young people. We must not live without beliefs, without philosophy, ignoring the questions of how to improve society and the world and what it is to live a meaningful life. If young people live this way, in the end they will suffer, as will society at large.

"So how can we become people of backbone, of great caliber? We need to revolutionize the state of our lives. We must do our human revolution. If you chant daimoku earnestly and work for kosen-rufu together with the Soka Gakkai, your life will naturally develop and you will become a person of real substance.

"The Soka Gakkai is the only organization that is nurturing people in this way and taking responsibility for the future of humanity. That's why I urge you to stick with the Gakkai!

"You are young, and you may think that there is still a long, long road ahead of you, but life passes by in a flash. Time really does fly. It has been said that life is a one-way ticket, and that is very true. We may wish to return to our younger years, but we cannot.

"But you have encountered this faith and are striving to create the best life possible. It is my sincerest wish that you will all live wonderful and dignified lives to the very end."

After responding to a few more questions, Shin'ichi continued to express his feelings: "I hope that great scholars, scientists and political leaders will emerge from this group. I will be supporting you wholeheartedly, so please be confident and follow my lead. At times I may be strict about matters concerning faith, but that is because I have your best interests in mind. I am truly praying for the growth and progress of the youth, of all of you. I intend to do everything I can to ensure that in ten, twenty or thirty years you will be playing active roles in all spheres of endeavor the world over.

"You are my treasures. You will build a new century with your own hands. Let's do it together. Let's always stick together. Please keep that spirit, even after you've graduated."

Shin'ichi then shook the members' hands. Praying in his heart for the growth of these young "eagles," he grasped their hands firmly, warmly encouraging each one.

SHIN'ICHI YAMAMOTO'S series of lectures to Kyoto University students on Nichiren Daishonin's "One Hundred and Six Comparisons" finished in August of the following year, 1964. They met a total of seven times, including the opening session. After that, Shin'ichi began a new lecture series on the "Record of the Orally Transmitted Teachings" for leaders of the student division in regions of Japan west of Kansai as well as Kyoto University students.

Shin'ichi recalled his fond memories of studying "One Hundred and Six Comparisons." This was because President Toda had assigned it to him as study material when Shin'ichi was a Study Department professor (around 1955). Every evening after work, he met with Toda for a lesson on the treatise. Toda spent three days on the first comparison alone: "The theoretical three thousand realms in a single moment of life and the threefold contemplation in a single mind—theoretical and essential." He then divided the section into key phrases—"The Buddhas of the three existences"; "Appearing in the world and attaining the way"; "The meaning of the Life Span chapter of the Buddhism of harvest"; "The theoretical three thousand realms." He lectured on each one in great detail, from many different viewpoints.

The lectures were a guide for Shin'ichi into the infinite, boundless realm of Buddhism; at the same time, they constituted a transmission——a direct passing on of the teachings—from mentor to disciple. When the lecture on the first comparison ended, Toda said to Shin'ichi: "Memorize everything I taught you so far and engrave it in your life. If you thoroughly study this first comparison and understand it deeply, you will understand the remaining one hundred and five.

"In addition, if you understand this treatise, you will understand the rest of the Daishonin's writings. It is very important to grasp each and every word correctly and completely. It is unacceptable for a professor or assistant professor in the study department to make mistakes on matters concerning study."

The lessons continued, covering two or three comparisons at a time. Whenever Shin'ichi's attention seemed to wane in the least, Toda would snap the Gosho shut and say: "That's all! I'm not a machine!" Each time that happened, Shin'ichi felt dejected and ashamed, but he continued to pursue his studies, determined to etch every word into his heart. The pages of Shin'ichi's copy of the Gosho were black with the notes he took from Toda's lessons.

In his lectures to the Kyoto University students, Shin'ichi did his best to explain the Daishonin's teachings in the most accessible way possible, since many of the participants did not yet master the fundamentals of Buddhist study. "One Hundred and Six Comparisons" strictly distinguished the Daishonin's Buddhism from that of Shakyamuni, establishing which was theoretical and essential and which was superior or inferior. Shin'ichi therefore began by discussing the difference between the essential teaching and the theoretical teaching from every angle and explaining how that applies to daily life.

What is the foundation of our lives? This question became the focus of his lectures.

THE GREAT TEACHER T'ien-t'ai of China compared the essential teaching to the moon in the sky and the theoretical teaching to a reflection of the moon on the water, thus pointing out that the essential is superior and the theoretical inferior. *Essential* means the actual substance of the truth, reality, while *theoretical* indicates a shadow or reflection of the truth. Just as theory derives from reality, the theoretical teaching derives from the essential teaching.

In one of his lectures, Shin'ichi introduced these concepts in detail, yet in a way that was easy to grasp: "Theory is an example of a measure. It is a model for explaining reality, but not reality itself. For example, a person's life is changing every moment. That ever-changing reality is the actual substance of life. Theory, on the

other hand, is abstracted from this reality and universal-
ized. It is very important to be able to differentiate clearly
between reality and theory, and to remain firmly
grounded in reality.

"The basis of all reality is life itself. It is human beings
who live in the midst of reality. There are countless examples in history of absolute trust being placed in theory
and ideology, which degenerate into dogmatism, and ultimately, oppression. I hope that you intelligent young people will put an end to this tragic legacy of history."

The last of the "One Hundred and Six Comparisons"
says, "One must distinguish essential and theoretical,
superior and inferior, in all things, even the swelling waves
and the blowing wind" (GZ, 869). In reference to this,
Shin'ichi said: "This passage tells us that the essential and
theoretical are to be found in our own lives, and that we
must draw a distinct line between them.

"For example, when we are sleeping, we are in a theoretical phase of our existence, but when we are awake,
we are in the essential phase. For students, whose job it
is to study, indulging in fun and entertainment is the theoretical while studying hard is the essential. In addition,
those who are studying with the sole aim of making
money or gaining status are living only for themselves
and are thus choosing a 'theoretical' way of life that is
caught up in the pursuit of worldly things. As members
of the student division, the essential is to study with a
deep sense of purpose, and develop yourselves so that you
can contribute to kosen-rufu.

"Our real identity is that of Bodhisattvas of the
Earth who have come forth to carry out the widespread

propagation of the humanistic teachings of Buddhism. For us, the essential way of life is to dedicate ourselves to that endeavor. In contrast, no matter what social status or position you may acquire later on, that is all just based on the theoretical. I hope you will never make a mistake about this."

SHIN'ICHI YAMAMOTO'S voice grew stronger as he spoke to the students: "All of you will eventually become active members of society and experience the challenges and obstacles that go along with that. There may be times when you cannot participate in Soka Gakkai activities as much as you would like. Herein also lie the essential and theoretical aspects of life. If you are determined to fulfill your unique mission for kosen-rufu, no matter what your circumstances, you are living the essential. But if you allow yourself to be defeated by your situation, lose faith and forget your mission, your way of living has only been theoretical.

"In one sense, it can be said that the difference between the essential and the theoretical is slight, for both boil down to one's state of mind, one's determination, and are invisible from the outside. However, when seen with the eyes of Buddhism everything is clear, and the difference between the two becomes abundantly evident.

"In terms of our inner determination, the essential is our prime motivation; our commitment to spreading Nichiren Daishonin's teaching. It is the spirit to advance, the spirit of challenge. The theoretical, on the other hand, is inertia, compromise and retreat.

"The way we can distinguish between the essential

and the theoretical in our lives is by asking ourselves: 'Am I living for the sake of kosen-rufu and striving to do my human revolution? Am I thoroughly resolved in my goals?' The person who does this will triumph in life.

"Living the essential is a moment-to-moment struggle. Therefore, the place we are right now is the training ground for our Buddhist practice."

Shin'ichi's lecture on the essential and the theoretical made a deep impression on the participants, and became a very important guide for them in later years. Shin'ichi did not want these lectures to be simply a lesson in Buddhist doctrine. He made a tremendous effort to help each student expand his or her life. With that in mind, he always left time at the end of the session for questions and open discussion, during which he offered guidance and encouragement to anyone who was struggling with a problem.

After a lecture held at the Kansai headquarters in January of the following year, 1964, Eriko Nakano, a pharmaceutical student, announced: "Recently I went to the doctor because I was exhausted and I could not stop coughing. I was then diagnosed with tuberculosis. The doctor told me that I should be hospitalized."

"Tuberculosis?" Shin'ichi asked with great concern. "Do you have any appetite?"

"Not much," Nakano replied.

"Are you sleeping at night?"

"I am, but I have a hard time falling asleep."

Shin'ichi asked Nakano in detail about her symptoms. Having suffered through tuberculosis himself, he knew something about the nature of the illness.

SHIN'ICHI addressed Eriko warmly: "I recovered without hospitalization, but sometimes hospitalization is recommended. I think either way can work.

"You have a mission. If you dedicate yourself whole-heartedly to faith, you will definitely change your karma. In 'The Object of Devotion for Observing the Mind,' the Daishonin quotes these words of Chang-an: "*Great Concentration and Insight* reveals the teaching that T'ien-t'ai Chih-che himself practiced in the depths of his being' (WND, 355). In *Great Concentration and Insight*, T'ien-t'ai expounded the principle of a single life-moment pos-sessing three thousand realms—the idea that all aspects of existence are present in the mind of each person. Chang-an is saying that T'ien-t'ai experienced this prin-ciple, himself, in his own life.

"In other words, the entire universe exists within a single human life. The causes and effects of all phenom-ena are present within your own mind, and they are all a reflection of your life. This is the teaching of Buddhism. That is why you will heal yourself through faith."

Nakano nodded, but she still looked uncertain.

"Getting sick," Shin'ichi continued, "is difficult and painful. But depending on the way you look at it, it may also provide you with a chance to discover the true mean-ing of faith and of life. The Daishonin said, 'Illness gives rise to the resolve to attain the way' (WND, 937). This is your opportunity to summon forth the power of faith.

"In that sense, your illness is a good thing, isn't it? Please take your time and rest well. We will be waiting for you."

Nakano felt the warmth and sincerity in Shin'ichi's words.

She obtained a leave of absence from school and entered the hospital. At first she thought that all she needed to recover was a little rest, and she was even slightly relieved to have a chance to take a break, even if it was in the hospital. She was so busy as a student division leader alongside her studies. Tired of her hectic schedule, she privately wished for some time just to relax and read some good books.

Unexpectedly, her wish came true. But she could only rest and enjoy her reading for a few days before she began to worry. The shadow across her lungs was not going away. She wondered why, even though she was young and strong and now receiving medical attention, she was not getting better. If she had to be hospitalized for several years, what would happen to her life? She became more anxious each day.

She began to appreciate how happy she was spending her days busily engaged in study and Soka Gakkai activities.

ERIKO NAKANO set up her Gohonzon at her hospital bedside and began to chant daimoku in earnest. As she did, she recalled the guidance President Shin'ichi Yamamoto gave her when he explained the Gosho passage: "*Great Concentration and Insight* reveals the teaching that T'ien-t'ai Chih-che himself practiced in the depths of his being" (WND, 355).

"Sensei was telling me that all karma, including illness, is a reflection of one's inner determination, of one's life," she thought. "I wonder then what was my inner determination?" For the first time, she began to think seriously about her life.

As she looked carefully at herself and her actions, it suddenly struck her: "Though I thought I was devoting myself to kosen-rufu and helping others do the same, I was also wishing somewhere in the back of my mind that I could have a break from my Soka Gakkai activities and just rest a little....

"Now my wish has come true. As long as I continue thinking this way, I will never get better. It may be my karma to suffer this illness, but the fundamental cause for it lies within my own mind. I have to change my attitude!"

From this time on, Nakano chanted with increased intensity. Finally, after eight months in the hospital, she decided to leave. Her tuberculosis was not completely cured, but she wanted the freedom that being at home afforded her to chant daimoku to her heart's content and to begin participating, even if only a little, in Soka Gakkai activities once again. Understanding that she had been unaware of her own noble mission, she apologized deeply and prayed to the Gohonzon to become well enough to work for kosen-rufu again.

Her daimoku was so powerful and focused that it seemed to shake the altar. Three months after she left the hospital, the tuberculosis completely disappeared. She returned to the university and reclaimed her strong and healthy self again. She overcame the theoretical in her life and established the essential.

Meanwhile, Yasuo Takigawa, a thirty-three-year-old graduate student, was extremely worried about his wife, Suzuyo. She was diagnosed with uterine cancer, and the doctor told them that even with surgery her chances for recovery were only about fifty percent. Joining the Soka

Gakkai a little more than a year earlier, Suzuyo decided to see her illness a test of her faith and began to chant fervent daimoku. As she chanted, her desire to receive direct guidance from President Yamamoto grew, and she told this to her husband.

Yasuo decided to ask Shin'ichi for guidance on his wife's behalf after one of the lectures on "One Hundred and Six Comparisons." The day of the lecture, Suzuyo accompanied her husband to the Kansai Headquarters and was waiting in another room. Yasuo's shyness, however, made it hard for him to bring up his wife's situation.

SHIN'ICHI looked around at the faces of the students attending that day and asked: "Many of you here today are faced with personal issues, aren't you? I'm here to listen to whatever you have to say, so please speak freely."

With this invitation, Yasuo at last asked about his wife's situation. "My wife was diagnosed with uterine cancer," he began. "She is chanting daimoku and is determined to beat her illness through faith."

Shin'ichi immediately replied: "To uphold the Gohonzon is to uphold the body of the Buddha. Your wife has a mission to fulfill as a Bodhisattva of the Earth, so everything is going to be fine.

"But even if a person who practices this Buddhism should die young, his or her life will not have been in vain. That person's life and death will have profound meaning and will serve to teach something very important to those who remain. No matter what happens, do not give in to fear or panic, but instead keep arousing stronger faith.

Let's all chant daimoku. I will pray for her, too. I would also like to present her with some prayer beads."

When Suzuyo heard this guidance from her husband, she thought: "I have a mission. I know I can beat this cancer, and I will!"

As surgery approached, she continued chanting abundant daimoku. In the end, she triumphed over her illness. Her experience also gave her husband tremendous confidence in the power of faith and became the fuel for his further development.

One lecture participant Shin'ichi was particularly concerned about was Naomi Takaoka, a medical student. She always wore a gloomy expression and Shin'ichi imagined that she was struggling each day. Lost in a maze of abstract theory and unable to find her own path in life, she became withdrawn. It also seemed that she grew skeptical about life itself, and loath to do Soka Gakkai activities.

Shin'ichi wanted to teach her about the importance of one's state of life. One day he said to her: "When we break through our outer shell and develop our lives, we begin to see and feel things differently, even though our circumstances remain unchanged. For Einstein, the stars in the night sky no doubt sparkled with the light of the theory of relativity, while for Beethoven they were playing a beautiful symphony. For Goethe, they glimmered with the beautiful poetry of the universe. Each perceived things according to their profound state of being.

"Buddhahood, however, is the deepest, broadest realm of life. You must not give up your faith before you reach that state."

"YOU MUST NOT isolate yourself from others. If you do, you will only become deadlocked. The Soka Gakkai is an organization that provides us with inspiration and encouragement, allowing us to open our hearts. You need the courage to engage yourself fully in Soka Gakkai activities and to work for the well-being of others.

"One day you will be a doctor, a profession in which the spirit of dedication to others, the spirit of a bodhisattva, is most important. Without it, no matter how skilled you become, selfishness and egoism will prevent you from making a real contribution to society."

Another time, a student attending one of Shin'ichi's lectures at Kyoto University said: "To be honest, I do not like the Soka Gakkai as an organization. However, through attending your lectures, I developed a desire to grow into a person who can protect you and work together with you for the happiness of others."

Shin'ichi responded immediately: "You say you want to protect me, but protecting the organization is protecting me. Protecting one, ten, a hundred or a thousand Soka Gakkai members is protecting me. This is because I have made the Soka Gakkai the sole purpose of my life.

"Our aim of kosen-rufu can be called a bloodless revolution, but I am prepared to give my life for the sake of our members, for Buddhism and for society. Without such courage and determination, I could not lead our movement. I do not exist apart from the Soka Gakkai or its members. If you have even the slightest desire to protect me, I hope you will take a place at the front lines of this organization and work there to protect all our members."

Throughout these lectures on Nichiren Daishonin's "One Hundred and Six Comparisons," Shin'ichi paid close attention to the life-state of each student and gave guidance accordingly, thinking hard about what he should say and what he wanted to impress upon them. He did this for their lives, for their future. In this way, he was teaching them the essential path that human beings should follow. It is through such diligent, painstaking and wholehearted effort that others grow.

In fact, almost all of the participants in this lecture series showed great development and began to shine as jeweled swords in the endeavor to achieve world peace based on the widespread propagation of the Daishonin's teachings. They later realized great achievements and made important contributions to society in their various capacities as leaders of the Soka Gakkai, doctors, scholars, members of parliament, or as contributors to many other fields as well.

Shin'ichi devoted his life to educating youth. Life is limited. Only so much can be accomplished in one lifetime. That is why the fostering of successors of the next generation who would carry on his work were indispensable to achieving kosen-rufu.

MANY SOKA GAKKAI members who saw the headline on the front page of the July 25 *Seikyo Shimbun*, the Soka Gakkai's daily newspaper, were astonished. There, in big letters, were the words "HIGH PRIEST ADMONISHES ALL PRIESTS AND HOKKEKO[7] MEMBERS." What was the reason for this sudden directive from the high priest, they wondered? Two subheads for the article read "Priests and Laity to Join Forces for Kosen-rufu" and "With the Unity of 'Many in Body, One in Mind.'"

The newspaper's introduction to the directive began: "High Priest Nittatsu issued a directive to all Nichiren Shoshu teachers,[8] general priests and Hokkeko members. The high priest expressed his hopes that at this time of rapid development within Nichiren Shoshu and when the Soka Gakkai initiated a fresh and brilliant advance toward the future, the priests and laity will further unite in purpose in order to spread the teachings of the school throughout Japan and the world."

This introduction provided no clue as to why the high priest issued a directive at this time. Only by reading the document itself could one get a sense, however vague, of what might be behind it.

There were actually two directives, one to all teachers and general priests, and another to Hokkeko members. The actual wording of both was very abstruse and literary, but the one to priests said: "The Great Pure Law of the Daishonin, our founder and the sun of wisdom in the Latter Day of the Law, is flowing ceaselessly out into the world like a rising tide, and our school continues to flourish. For the sake of the Law and Nichiren Shoshu, this is truly wonderful.

"The source of this tremendous development is the magnificent power of the Dai-Gohonzon, to which all people of the Latter Day of the Law should devote themselves and base their lives upon. At the same time, it is also due to the dedication of the Soka Gakkai members who, under the leadership of their president, have united to spread the teachings of the Daishonin and realize his wish of worldwide kosen-rufu as quickly as possible.

"Their wholehearted efforts deserve our recognition. Already, approximately one-tenth of the households in Japan have discarded their faith in erroneous teachings, embraced the True Law, and are basking in the light of the Daishonin's great desire to empower all humanity. In addition, the sincere donations of Soka Gakkai members have built the Grand Lecture Hall of True Buddhism as well as the resplendent Grand Reception Hall, which is now near completion. Furthermore, the number of temples nationwide that were built and donated by the Soka Gakkai has already reached eighty."

The directive highly praised the hard work of Soka Gakkai members to realize the widespread propagation of the Daishonin's teachings.

HIGH PRIEST Nittatsu's directive continued to cite the Soka Gakkai's accomplishments: "The Soka Gakkai has operated on the noblest of ideals and done away with the evils of the past, taking action in exact accord with Nichiren Daishonin's sacred teaching of Buddhist principles for the betterment of society. With great compassion as its foundation, it has initiated a broad range of activities to promote the well-being of all people.

"Basing its endeavors on the correct Buddhist teaching, the Soka Gakkai is speaking out for truth, profoundly influencing not only practitioners and non-practitioners alike, but also moving widely into the realms of academia and culture while advancing steadily toward kosen-rufu.

In all of its efforts, it presses forward unceasingly one step at a time and exhibits tremendous strength.

"Through everything, the Soka Gakkai maintained a solid seeking spirit, never wavering or compromising its ideals. It deserves our deepest respect.

"It is time for the priests of Nichiren Shoshu to devote themselves to their Buddhist practice and to fulfill their duties. It goes without saying that to be a priest means to have firm and unshakable faith, to exert oneself in practice and study and offer sincere gratitude to the Buddha. It is to serve as a model for others through our actions, behavior, study and understanding of Buddhism.

"Instead, there are rumors of those who lack an appreciation of the significance of the incredible circumstances we are now in and who betray the nature and role of the priesthood through their words and actions. This is truly deplorable. If these rumors are indeed true, we face a very grave situation.

"If the disciples of the Buddha who wear the three garments [the robe, the surplice and the prayer beads] and whose purpose it is to dedicate themselves selflessly to Buddhist practice and propagate its teachings are guilty of such lapses, they are like warriors who destroy their own castle from within (see WND, 21). As a matter of course, such priests must be ousted and punished.

"Let us not be reprimanded as priests who 'spend their time in idleness and chatter' (see WND, 760), are 'idle and negligent' (WND, 303), are no better 'than animals dressed in priestly robes' and are 'disciples of non-Buddhist teachings' (see WND, 760). Rather, let us be discreet in our behavior, living by the principle of desiring little yet knowing satisfaction, and with the ferocity of a mighty lion, rise to action and devote ourselves wholeheartedly to our Buddhist practice.

"I hope that all Nichiren Shoshu priests will understand my intent and will implement the instructions of our predecessor to unite with the laity and realize the principle of 'many in body, one in mind,' striving to the fullest extent to accomplish our great desire."

The end of the document read, "The above directive was made by Hosoi Nittatsu, Chief Administrator of Nichiren Shoshu, on July 15, 1963." Such an official reprimand of the priests' behavior was an extraordinary event.

THE HIGH PRIEST'S directive to the Hokkeko members was also very severe. The Hokkeko was an association of parishioners belonging to various local Nichiren Shoshu temples. This directive started out by attributing the present surge of advancement toward worldwide kosen-rufu to the appearance of the Soka Gakkai. It praised the organization as acting in accord with the Daishonin's great vision of widespread propagation and hailed the efforts of its members to unite as Bodhisattvas of the Earth and introduce many others to the practice.

The document further stated: "The selfless dedication of Soka Gakkai members in propagating the Law is an absolutely unprecedented occurrence in the history of our school.

"Under the leadership of the Soka Gakkai president, the Soka Gakkai's more than 3.4 million member households have worked in complete unison and initiated a

variety of indispensable activities aimed at spreading the
Daishonin's teachings across the globe. These efforts are
producing remarkable results.

"The Daishonin is surely applauding their actions,
which should also be shown the utmost respect from
both priests and laity alike. Let it be known that anyone
who, with or without basis, slanders the great and harmonious body of practitioners that contributed to and
protected our school with such unparalleled noble sincerity, is guilty of holding an erroneous view that
obstructs the pure practice of kosen-rufu, and will be
bound for the hell of incessant suffering."

The directive concluded: "Let the genuine seeking
spirit of the Soka Gakkai members be appreciated, looked
to and revered as a true model of Buddhist practice. I
hope that all Hokkeko members will work together with
their counterparts in the Soka Gakkai in our endeavor to
create a Buddha land, and continue to advance side-by-
side with them."

When the members of the Soka Gakkai, who for the
most part had little contact with either priests or Hokkeko
members, read these directives, they realized for the first
time that some within those groups had been slandering
and criticizing the Soka Gakkai, and they could not con-
ceal their astonishment. On the other hand, those who
had contact with priests and Hokkeko members were not
in the least surprised. They frequently heard members of
both groups speak ill of the Soka Gakkai and President
Shin'ichi Yamamoto, and saw with their own eyes corrupt and degenerate behavior among the priests. This concerned them deeply. Reading the directives, however,

brought them comfort as they felt the Nichiren Shoshu administration now understood the real nature of the situation with its priests and was at last taking appropriate measures. They hoped this would awaken the priests and Hokkeko members to the true meaning of faith.

High Priest Nittatsu's directives reassured the Soka Gakkai members that he correctly understood the organization, and inspired them to work even harder.

SOKA GAKKAI members suffered immeasurably before matters reached the point that a directive needed to be issued by the high priest.

Shin'ichi Yamamoto had received various complaints from members about the priests' behavior. In one case, a Soka Gakkai member was bringing a friend whom he introduced to the practice to his local temple to receive a Gohonzon. They ran into some congestion on the road caused by a traffic accident and ended up being just a few minutes late. When they arrived, however, they were refused conferral, even though the priest was just sitting inside watching television.

Some priests complained that because Soka Gakkai members were introducing many new people, they were always busy performing Gohonzon-conferral ceremonies and had no chance to relax. Others did not like the fact that Soka Gakkai members used the temple for their meetings, and a few would not open the doors to the altar enshrining the Gohonzon when Soka Gakkai members used the temple's main room.

How frustrating it was for these Soka Gakkai members, who were working diligently for the happiness of others, to be taken to task by the priests for introducing new people and for holding meetings! Some priests even made outrageous remarks such as: "The Gakkai is always talking about elections and culture, but those things have nothing to do with faith. Instead of conducting all those unrelated activities, Gakkai members should stick to their temples and listen to the guidance of the priests. They're just a bunch of lay people, after all."

These priests did not seem to make any attempt to understand the intent of the Daishonin, who sought to help suffering people, nor did they appear to have the desire to propagate Buddhism widely. As a result, they could not grasp the significance of any of the Soka Gakkai's activities.

The behavior of the priests was also a serious problem. There were numerous accounts of priests who did not perform gongyo, or who spent every night drinking and carousing.

There were also members of the Hokkeko who spoke ill of the Soka Gakkai. The Hokkeko began as groups of lay believers affiliated with respective local Nichiren Shoshu temples. But a year earlier, in July 1962, they were organized into a nationwide organization called the National Hokkeko Federation. Up until then, Hokkeko members received virtually no guidance in faith and were hardly aware of the importance of working for kosen-rufu. Many Nichiren Shoshu followers of old did not even know how to do gongyo, let alone introduce others to the practice. What is more, the activities of each local organization were conducted independently of the others. This left room for people seeking to line their pockets to exploit the members. They did this by moving from temple to temple forming local Hokkeko organizations and placing themselves at the head.

THERE WAS a growing movement within Nichiren Shoshu, stimulated by the Soka Gakkai's tireless efforts to realize kosen-rufu in accord with the Daishonin's wish, to reorganize and strengthen the Hokkeko. This led to the formation of the National Hokkeko Federation. Many members of the Federation looked on Soka Gakkai members as newcomers and strongly felt that as longtime practitioners of the school they deserved special consideration. They were also displeased by the fact that society in general now identified Nichiren Shoshu with the Soka Gakkai.

Some were openly jealous of the Soka Gakkai and slandered it repeatedly. "All you hear," they would say, "is Gakkai this and Gakkai that, but Gakkai members are all new to our faith. We are on a different level, because our families have belonged to Nichiren Shoshu for generations."

Another criticism was that the efforts of Soka Gakkai members to introduce others to the practice brought "low-class" people into Nichiren Shoshu. Soka Gakkai members bore the brunt of such remarks, continuing to single-mindedly fulfill their mission to bring happiness to others and work for kosen-rufu.

Shin'ichi was deeply pained whenever he heard the priests' shameful behavior or the injurious remarks of Hokkeko members. He communicated these incidences to the school's administration, strongly urging that something be done to discipline those priests, but there were no signs of change. This did not surprise him, however, since a number of the unfortunate reports that he heard from Soka Gakkai members were about the escapades of senior priests themselves.

On July 8, Shin'ichi attended the opening ceremony for the Soka Gakkai's Fujinomiya Community Center in Shizuoka Prefecture. This center would be an important base of operations for the Soka Gakkai's three-million-member general pilgrimage to the head temple scheduled to start from April the following year to celebrate the completion of the Grand Reception Hall. When they arrived at the center, Shin'ichi and the leaders traveling with him met with newly appointed Shizuoka Headquarters Leader Ritsu Ohyama and other leaders in the area.

Ohyama was also vice-leader of the pilgrimage department, which meant he had frequent contact with the priests and knew very well what was going on at the head temple. He looked troubled as he spoke: "This is the home base of the head temple, and there are many Hokkeko members whose families have been Nichiren Shoshu followers for generations. They criticize Soka Gakkai members saying that we are too confident for newcomers.

"Yet they do not even do gongyo, and go so far as to say that they will attain Buddhahood simply by living within earshot of the head temple's bell."

SHIN'ICHI YAMAMOTO responded to Ritsu Ohyama: "I am well aware that there are people within the Hokkeko who do not look kindly on the

Soka Gakkai, but I want us to be tolerant and try to reach out to them. It is important at this point in our movement to encourage them to rise up and work together with us to achieve kosen-rufu.

"Most of the Hokkeko's criticism of the Soka Gakkai stems from not fully understanding the spirit of Nichiren Daishonin, nor do they appreciate what the Soka Gakkai is about. I have been talking with the president of the National Hokkeko Federation. I am sure they will eventually see what a wonderful organization the Soka Gakkai is and will come to respect us.

"I know there will be times when you will feel angry, but please be patient a little while longer. Actually, there are some factions within the Hokkeko that oppose the federation's attempt at unification, and the federation itself is having a hard time of it right now."

Ohyama nodded, and then said gravely: "Sensei, I am more concerned about the priests than the Hokkeko members. Around here, the priests at the head temple have a bad reputation. People call them the 'debauched priests.' Soka Gakkai members are really disappointed in them. They see priests frequenting taverns or indulging in the entertainment of geisha. There are rumors of sexual affairs, too. There are some instances where priests who have gone out drinking together have been overheard criticizing Soka Gakkai members, who after all are practicing their faith diligently.

"Although both you and President Toda have done your utmost to serve the school in earnest, most priests do not seem to feel any gratitude. They act as if it were expected. In Osaka there was a temple that refused to confer the Gohonzon on Soka Gakkai members. Here in Shizuoka, they do not refuse, but at some temples the priests make it very obvious that they are not happy about it.

"When they conduct the Gohonzon-conferral ceremony, they take on an unbelievably arrogant air and strictly order the new member to come every month to offer a *toba*[9] tablet for the repose of deceased family members for which temples charged believers. Sensei, we will do whatever is necessary to protect Nichiren Shoshu for the sake of kosen-rufu. No matter how difficult it may be financially, we are still willing to make offerings. In fact, this is exactly what we have done.

"But we do not want to donate one cent to corrupt priests who malign the Soka Gakkai, the organization dedicated to widespread propagation, just so they can spend it on pleasure seeking. This is not just my opinion —all the members feel this way."

AS OHYAMA SPOKE, his anger rose, and gradually his words burned with emotion: "I heard from a Soka Gakkai member who is on good terms with the priests that they think the Soka Gakkai has become too much of a nuisance," he reported. "They are worried if things continue the way they are, the Soka Gakkai will take over everything, and they will be left out in the cold. They are talking about disbanding us after we have built them enough temples.

"If we object, they say they will take away our Gohonzon and bar us from visiting the head temple. That is why they decided to increase the membership of the

Hokkeko and to organize and strengthen it. There are priests who simply want to milk the Soka Gakkai for all they can and then dissolve it. They have no qualms about using the Gohonzon, the very foundation of our faith, as a trumpcard to control practitioners and make them subservient. It's really frightening.

"The reason there are so many in the Hokkeko who see the Soka Gakkai as a threat is because that attitude is instigated by the priests. The priests declare that they are superior to lay believers. They look at Soka Gakkai members as little more than slaves or machines to bring them offerings. I do not think they have ever taken kosen-rufu seriously. All they think about is themselves. They have no faith and no compassion. They are corrupt." Tears filled Ohyama's eyes.

"This really is deplorable," Shin'ichi replied. "I understand how you feel. It is only natural for you to be angry. In fact, just the other day Soka Gakkai General Director Harayama strongly appealed to the school's administration to rectify the situation."

Shin'ichi then turned to Koichi Harayama at his side and asked, "Mr. Harayama, how did they respond?"

"Well, they said they would take care of it, but they have not given us a concrete answer yet. They say the same thing every time. It is a real problem."

When Ohyama heard this, his face flushed with anger, and he said: "Sensei, I cannot put up with this any longer. Not just me, but the entire Shizuoka young men's division will not stand for it. Many members are exasperated and ask why we should remain faithful to priests who make no effort to realize kosen-rufu yet torment Soka

Gakkai members. If you will permit us, we would like to go to the head temple and lodge a serious protest."

SHIN'ICHI addressed Harayama: "Mr. Harayama, the members have reached the limits of their patience. At this rate, we'll never get anywhere. I'm going to put in a call to the Nichiren Shoshu administration. Everyone is fed up. Next spring the Grand Reception Hall will be completed and three million members will make a pilgrimage to the head temple. We are about to begin a new phase in the development of kosen-rufu. Now is the time for priests and laity to unite and make a fresh advance in the spirit of many in body, one in mind.

"Simply constructing a building like the Grand Reception Hall is not what is important—we must create a treasure tower of unity and pure faith aimed at the widespread propagation of the Daishonin's teachings. Isn't it compassionate, therefore, to admonish that which must be admonished and thereby cut out the iniquity that is taking root within the priesthood?

"I am sure that there are people who will react against this and hate me for it, but I am prepared to bear the brunt of everything."

As Shin'ichi headed toward the office, Harayama followed him and said, "Please let me try to talk to them first." With that, Harayama placed a call to a senior priest at the head temple. Listening to Harayama's side of the conversation, it was clear to Shin'ichi that no progress was being made. Shin'ichi then picked up the phone and asked point-blank what practical steps the Nichiren Shoshu administration intended to take to deal with all of the problems they were facing.

Flustered, the priest replied: "We are aware that these are serious problems that need attemtion. I have spoken with the high priest about how regrettable these attacks on the Soka Gakkai are, as well as the behavior of the priests that you are referring to."

It was a half-baked answer that skirted the issues. Irritated, Shin'ichi replied: "I have heard this over and over again. We have been waiting for your response for a long time, but you refuse to take any concrete action. All the while, Soka Gakkai members continue to suffer from these attacks. This is utterly irresponsible!" Shin'ichi's sharp voice echoed throughout the room.

"As we near the completion of the Grand Reception Hall, it is of utmost importance that harmony is forged between the priesthood and the laity, and that the Hokkeko joins us in generating a great flow toward kosen-rufu. Why are you not treating this matter seriously? Why do you let evil go unchecked?

"I WANT YOU to confer with the high priest and come to an immediate decision. We will not be satisfied with excuses or explanations any longer," Shin'ichi said as he hung up the telephone.

After this, he did gongyo with local members at the center and participated in the center's opening ceremony. He then traveled by car to the Fuji Community Center in neighboring Fuji City to attend the inaugural meeting of Shizuoka Headquarters. In the car, Shin'ichi could not help but think about why the priesthood so easily fell prey to corruption and licentiousness.

It was common knowledge that during World War II, Nichiren Shoshu accepted the Shinto talisman out of fear of suppression by the military government. But the truth was that long before that time the priests of the school violated the fundamental doctrine of "strictly admonishing slander of the Buddhist law." There were numerous examples of such corruption, even just counting the major ones from the early twentieth century on. For example, in November 1914, representatives of the Nichiren schools met at Hommonji temple of Nichiren Shu (the Minobu school), in Ikegami, Tokyo, and drew up a basic plan for unification.

Nissho Abe, the fifty-seventh high priest of Nichiren Shoshu, and Houn Abe (later Nichikai, the sixtieth high priest) attended this conference. Nichikai Abe was the father of sixty-seventh high priest Nikken. On that occasion, Nissho Abe signed a document stating his agreement to the unification of all the Nichiren schools, including the Minobu school. The plan for unification later collapsed, but Nissho Abe again cooperated with representatives of the other Nichiren denominations when they requested that the emperor bestow the honorific title Great Teacher Rissho on the Daishonin, which was granted in October 1922.

It was Nissho Honda, chief administrator of the Kempon Hokke school of Nichiren Buddhism, who started the drive to have the emperor confer the title of "Great Teacher" on the Daishonin, just as many centuries earlier the title had been bestowed upon Dengyo and Kobo.[10] Nissho Abe of Nichiren Shoshu signed the petition, and on the day it was granted, he joined other Nichiren school priests in reciting the "Life Span" chapter of the Lotus Sutra and chanting daimoku led by the head of the Minobu school. The actions of these priests to ingratiate themselves with authority were absolutely contrary to the spirit of the Daishonin. In addition, the other Nichiren schools, while using the Daishonin's name, completely went against his spirit, revealing themselves to be like parasites that devour the mighty lion of the Daishonin's Buddhism from within.

Nissho Abe's act of reciting gongyo together with the head of the Minobu school was a clear violation of Nikko Shonin's admonition "You should not sit together with slanderers of the Law [at religious ceremonies] for fear of suffering the same punishment as they" (GZ, 1618). Such slander of the Law by high priests of Nichiren Shoshu continued.

In October 1931, just prior to the six hundred and fiftieth memorial service commemorating the Daishonin's passing, the Minobu school was moving ahead with its plan to have the emperor inscribe on a plaque the Daishonin's new title, Rissho, to be kept at Kuonji, the head temple of the Minobu school.

B Y BEING the recipient of the emperor's hand-written inscription of the Daishonin's new title, the Minobu school hoped to make itself appear the most important of all the Nichiren denominations. Before approving the Minobu school's application, however, the

Japanese Ministry of Education required the agreement of the heads of all other Nichiren schools. The senior priests of Minobu therefore went to the heads of each school asking them to sign a memorandum giving their consent. This included Nichiren Shoshu, whose high priest at the time was Nichikai Abe.

The memorandum stated in effect that since the Daishonin's tomb was located at Kuonji temple[11] on Mount Minobu, the undersigned supported the petition submitted by the temple's chief priest requesting that the plaque bearing the emperor's inscription be kept there. In other words, by signing the agreement, one assented to the claim that the tomb containing the Daishonin's remains — his grave — was located on Minobu. Yet Nichikai Abe signed and officially sealed the document as the chief administrator of Nichiren Shoshu.

The second high priest, Nikko Shonin, left Minobu because Mimbu Niko, the chief instructor of priests at Kuonji temple, permitted the local steward of Minobu, Hakiri Sanenaga, to build a statue of Shakyamuni Buddha and make pilgrimages to Shinto shrines. These were violations of the Daishonin's teachings, and Minobu thus became a place of slander of the Law and a nest of devilish influences. Nikko Shonin could not allow such a place to be the residence of the Daishonin's remains, and so, heartbroken, he took them and left the mountain.

At the time, he wrote, "My pain and chagrin at leaving Minobu valley is beyond description" (*Hennentai Gosho*, 1733). There is no knowing the depths of his sadness. When high priest Nichikai Abe signed, sealed and assented to the memorandum stating that Minobu was the location of the Daishonin's tomb, he completely defied Nikko Shonin. More than that, he trampled on the Daishonin's spirit and the correct teachings.

It was the Soka Gakkai that finally removed this stain from Nichiren Shoshu's history. On March 11, 1955, a debate took place between the Soka Gakkai and the Minobu school in Otaru, Hokkaido.[12] In proving that neither the Dai-Gohonzon nor the Daishonin's remains were located on Minobu and completely refuting the errors of the Minobu school, the Soka Gakkai gained an enormous victory.

The moderator for the Soka Gakkai was Shin'ichi Yamamoto, the youth division chief of staff. From the start, Shin'ichi pointed out the fact that countless followers of the Minobu school were joining the Soka Gakkai, and he sharply illuminated the opponent's erroneous doctrines. This opened the way to the Soka Gakkai's victory, and the correct teachings of Nikko Shonin were protected.

DURING WORLD WAR II, when the military government drew up a plan of uniting all Nichiren schools under its policy of thought control, there were some priests of Nichiren Shoshu who consented. But Tsunesaburo Makiguchi, the Soka Gakkai's first president, emphasized that in order to protect the correct teachings and doctrines of the Daishonin and Nikko Shonin, Nichiren Shoshu should apply to the government for independent status. Finally, in March 1941, through President Makiguchi's tireless efforts, Nichiren Shoshu was granted status as an independent religious body.

In September 1941, two years before the arrest of President Makiguchi and his disciple, Josei Toda, the Nichiren Shoshu administration had fourteen important passages excised from the Gosho, including "I, Nichiren, am the foremost sage in all Jambudvipa..." (WND, 642). They were afraid of being charged with *lese majeste* by the military government which made State Shinto its spiritual foundation.

This act of deleting passages that were, in essence, the Daishonin's great declaration of his true identity, was on a level equal to the actions of the five senior priests at the time of his death. Thinking that the Daishonin's writings in the easily readable kana syllabary were a disgrace to his name, these priests destroyed them, reprocessed the paper on which they were written, or burned them. The Daishonin, however, wrote his letters for the sake of the lay followers he was addressing.

Finally, the head temple enshrined the Shinto talisman and ordered Soka Gakkai members to do the same. But the Soka Gakkai stoutly refused to do so, and as a result presidents Makiguchi and Toda were arrested and imprisoned. The fear of being linked with the two Soka Gakkai leaders prompted the priesthood to expel them and prohibit Soka Gakkai members from visiting the head temple.

Though the priests proclaimed that Nichiren Shoshu preserved "the direct heritage of the Law from one high priest to the next" and that it was as perfect as if the "water of the pure Mystic Law had been transferred from one vessel to another without a drop being spilled," they completely discarded the Soka Gakkai, which was fighting in the genuine spirit of the Daishonin. This astonishing act revealed the school's true nature.

There is deep significance in the priesthood's slanderous acts and cold treatment of the Soka Gakkai. According to the Daishonin's writings, those who devote themselves to spreading the true teaching in this defiled age of the Latter Day of the Law are certain to face persecution. That is why kosen-rufu is a sacred undertaking that can only be achieved by those who are determined to work selflessly. Nikko Shonin therefore says, "Until kosen-rufu is achieved, propagate the Law to the full extent of your ability without begrudging your life" (GZ, 1618). However, many of the priests of Nichiren Shoshu demonstrated not the faintest hint of that spirit. Caring only for themselves, they hid away from persecution and, guided solely by narrow self-interest, sought to live in the lap of luxury.

Those who make self-interest their guiding principle will naturally forget the lofty goal of realizing peace and happiness for all people and instead curry favor with the authorities.

THESE PROFESSIONAL priests, who cared only about protecting themselves, ended up repeatedly distorting and seriously disgracing the Daishonin's teachings. Having grown completely accustomed to keeping up the appearance of authority and passing themselves off as guardians of the correct teaching and doctrine, they showed not the slightest remorse or regret for their slanderous actions. Their lives were based not on the Buddhist Law but on their own interests.

When one abandons the lofty goal of kosen-rufu and seeks only to protect oneself, one loses the foundation of one's life and becomes a slave to desires. The priests' betrayal of Buddhism and their debauched way of life were two sides of the same coin. Each reduced himself to the level of what the Daishonin described as an "animal dressed in priestly robes" (WND, 760).

A closer look at the history of Nichiren Shoshu reveals that, aside from Nichikan and a small number of priests who remained faithful to the Daishonin's teachings, over the centuries the heritage and lifeblood of faith was lost time and again. The Daishonin's spirit had long been missing from within the priesthood.

In sharp contrast, even in prison both presidents Makiguchi and Toda continued to uphold their belief in the Daishonin's teachings, and President Makiguchi gave his very life. The true light of Buddhism, the spirit of the

Daishonin, in this way was protected by the Soka Gakkai, which carried on the heritage of faith. The Soka Gakkai prevented the Daishonin's Buddhism from being extinguished.

When President Makiguchi stood up to take the lead in realizing kosen-rufu, priests who were not inclined to work for that noble endeavor viciously attacked him. What's more, when Soka Gakkai members introduced this Buddhism to suffering people and brought them to a temple to receive the Gohonzon, most temples refused. With their cold, heartless attitude, these priests ridiculed the great compassion with which the Daishonin strove to rescue all people from suffering. At the time, there were only two temples that would confer the Gohonzon on Soka Gakkai members. In contrast, the priests gave special consideration to believers with wealth and high social status.

Though the Daishonin had declared, "This is the correct Law in which every single person from the ruler down to the common people should take faith" (GZ, 1301), most Nichiren Shoshu priests never treated the people with compassion nor did they make any effort to share the Daishonin's teachings with them. Because most ordinary citizens at the time were suffering from sickness and poverty, the priests regarded them as an unprofitable bother.

They also feared the attacks and persecution that attempts to spread the teachings might stir. How much trouble and concern these priests must have caused President Makiguchi! It was in fact the priesthood itself that posed the greatest obstacle to the religious revolution he envisioned.

PRESIDENT MAKIGUCHI once said, "The Tendai school of Buddhism at the time of the Daishonin corresponds most with Nichiren Shoshu than of all the Nichiren Buddhist schools today."

The Tendai school during the Daishonin's day showed signs of corruption and degeneracy. The Great Teacher Dengyo founded the Tendai school of Buddhism based on the Lotus Sutra and the teachings of T'ien-t'ai of China, and endeavored to establish the first Mahayana Ordination Platform in Japan on Mount Hiei.[13]

However, his disciples, who should have inherited and transmitted his teachings faithfully, incorporated erroneous esoteric teachings into Tendai Buddhism and lost Dengyo's original intent and true spirit.

President Makiguchi continued: "We must ask ourselves who among the followers of Nichiren Shoshu through the ages has 'actually encountered the three obstacles and four devils' (WND, 501)? Aren't those who claim to lead others on the correct path without summoning forth such obstacles no more than 'wardens of hell who drive others toward the evil paths' (WND, 501)?"

The "followers of Nichiren Shoshu" in this passage refers not to mere practitioners of the Daishonin's teachings but to the priests whose responsibility it is to lead others. In his writings, the Daishonin clearly states that if the three obstacles and four devils do not arise, it is because the struggle for kosen-rufu has been abandoned. President Makiguchi sharply points out the cowardice and evil of such priests' choice of self-interest over kosen-rufu.

His disciple, President Toda, also continuously fought

against the corruption of the priesthood, stating the following: "A priest who does not propagate the Daishonin's teachings himself and then complains about those who actually do is worthless. A priest who has done nothing to deserve respect but hides behind the Daishonin's greatness and demands respect is cunning. A priest who only cares about donations is a beggar.

"There are priests who say, 'We're not going to hand out the Gohonzon to just anyone.' That's outrageous. If they will not grant us the Gohonzon even though we built them temples, then we did not build temples at all, only dormitories for priests.

"We must protect the Nichiren Shoshu organization at all costs, respecting the good priests, remonstrating with corrupt priests and refuting them, preserving the school from external enemies, and aiming for the unity of priests and laity.

"We must not allow the chief priests of local temples to become arrogant.... They have an unfortunate tendency to treat believers as if they were retainers or servants.

"There are priests who are incapable and irresponsible and who cozy up to powerful followers to try to solidify their position. Practitioners influenced by such priests always end up discarding their faith and come to a regrettable end."

JOSEI TODA was always strict with priests who had fallen off the correct path. He gave no quarter to priests who became spoiled and decadent. Sometimes he actually shouted at them. As a result, whenever he went to the head temple, priests with a guilty conscience would sneak away. But once he left, they would get together again and bad-mouth him over drinks: "He's only a follower, but he's constantly nagging us...."

Unable to put up with the abusive comments of the priests any longer, Soka Gakkai members working at the head temple would go to their leaders in tears and tell them what was going on.

President Toda fought against this evil trend among the priests because he wanted to protect Nichiren Shoshu. That is why he put tremendous effort into reconstructing the struggling head temple which lost many of its agricultural holdings in the post-war land reform of 1946. In addition, he led donation campaigns to secure a financial base for the temple, enabling it to repair its five-storied pagoda and to construct many new buildings, including the Hoanden and the Grand Lecture Hall. He also spearheaded efforts to build Nichiren Shoshu temples all over Japan.

He did this because he wanted the priesthood, as guardian of the Dai-Gohonzon and inheritor of the noble spirit of Nichiren Daishonin and Nikko Shonin, to awaken to their original mission. He hoped that they would strive to create harmonious relations with the Soka Gakkai in order to carry out the sacred task of kosen-rufu. Toda's main objective in working for the revival of the priesthood was to revive its faith. That is why he so firmly and strictly rebuked "this one evil," (WND, 15) that is, corruption among priests who were only too ready to defame the Buddhist Law for their personal interests. He acted in complete accord with the Gosho passage "If one befriends another person but lacks the mercy to correct him, one is in fact his enemy" (WND, 286).

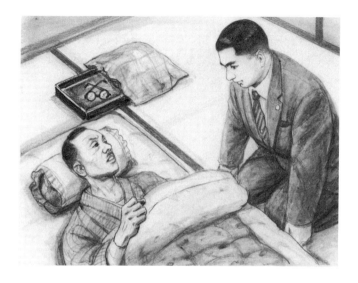

This way of religious reformation will lead to the worldwide spread of the Daishonin's teachings. It is for this reason that on his deathbed President Toda said to his disciple Shin'ichi Yamamoto: "Fight adamantly against any corruption that takes root within the priesthood. Do you hear me, Shin'ichi? You must never retreat a single step. Never slacken in your resolve against such evil!" It was one of his final instructions.

Imprisoned for his beliefs, and fully aware of the school's history, President Toda knew that these priests who draped themselves in the robes of authority but lacked any desire to develop themselves would become in a sense "possessed by demons" and cause the destruction of the kosen-rufu movement. However, he was firmly determined not to let this happen; he was utterly devoted to protecting the Daishonin's teachings.

IN THE CAR on his way to the Fuji Community Center, Shin'ichi decided that if he were going to act in accord with the spirit of his mentor, he absolutely could not ignore the corruption of the priests and their abuse of the Soka Gakkai. But he also knew that if he pursued the issue relentlessly, he would be inviting a hostile reaction from many of the priests. Still, it was clear that if he overlooked the present situation, the corruption in the priesthood would continue and the problem would only be aggravated.

Shin'ichi was profoundly aware that he was the only one who could remonstrate with Nichiren Shoshu. He also believed that sensible priests would listen to his sincere protest and understand his intent. "I must fight," he thought, "for kosen-rufu, for the members, and to protect the priesthood." He was firmly resolved. From the car window he could see Mount Fuji rising majestically above the clouds in the sky.

When Shin'ichi arrived at the Fuji Community Center, he received a phone call from the priesthood official with whom he had spoken earlier. The official said that the priests whose behavior was in question would be individually censured, and he hoped things could be settled amicably.

Shin'ichi said: "I want to know what you think about the situation! We've heard you say this time and again, but the same problem keeps arising! The priests and the

Hokkeko have been attacking the Soka Gakkai, which is practicing Buddhism just as the Daishonin instructed and working hard to spread his teachings. They have discriminated against Soka Gakkai members and bullied them. We in the Soka Gakkai have done nothing to deserve this treatment.

"I want Nichiren Shoshu to understand this and take a clear stand. I want you to stop trying to evade the problem. That will only be the cause for more trouble later. I am not satisfied with your response thus far." Before long, the priest replied: "I understand. We'll discuss it," and hung up the phone.

Shortly after 3:00 that afternoon, Shin'ichi attended the inauguration ceremony for Shizuoka Headquarters. Not long after the ceremony was over, the priest Shin'ichi had been talking to arrived at the Fuji Community Center. Shin'ichi reiterated his complaint, citing concrete examples of unacceptable behavior on the part of priests, of abuse hurled at the Soka Gakkai and problems with the Hokkeko. He explained clearly and in no uncertain terms just how Soka Gakkai members suffered and were abused.

The priest, however, acted as though it did not concern him, simply repeating, "That's really unfortunate." Finally he said, "Mr. Yamamoto, please do not be so hard on me." He showed no sign of regret.

KEEPING HIS ANGER in check, Shin'ichi strongly argued that unless Nichiren Shoshu fought against the corruption within, it would eventually be destroyed by it. "Next spring the Grand Reception Hall will at last be completed and three million members will visit the head temple in celebration," he said. "Soka Gakkai members are exerting themselves wholeheartedly in the spirit that the time has come for priests and laity to work together in harmony toward the realization of kosen-rufu.

"There is evidence, however, that some priests are harshly criticizing the Soka Gakkai and inciting Hokkeko members to do the same. In addition, there are priests who continue to act licentiously, becoming the objects of ridicule. Their shameful and decadent behavior deceives pure-hearted believers. It is also a betrayal of Nikko Shonin's injunction, 'My disciples should conduct themselves as holy priests.'

"If Nichiren Shoshu has anything it wants to say about the Soka Gakkai—whether it be opinions, wishes or complaints—I would like you to tell me directly. The fact is, however, there are priests who vilify the Soka Gakkai in secret and harass our members, without conveying a word to me. This is simply intolerable.

"Soka Gakkai members are verbally abused and even ostracized by society at large, yet they continue to do their best introducing others to the Daishonin's teachings and working hard for the prosperity of Nichiren Shoshu. The Daishonin would embrace these members, these noble children of the Buddha, for their sincere efforts. But the words and actions of certain priests who call themselves disciples of the Buddha are like a slap in the face.

"This is unacceptable. If the school administration says it can do nothing about this, you can be certain that I will!"

The priest hurriedly replied: "No—we will definitely

take action. I will confer with the high priest and we will make sure such things never happen again."

"Can I really believe you this time?" Shin'ichi asked, looking intently at the priest.

"Yes."

"All right. I'll leave the details up to you. But I really expect the administration to take responsibility this time and not try to gloss over the problem."

Shin'ichi escorted the priest to the entrance of the community center and then said to himself, "The members do not deserve this kind of treatment...."

The high priest issued the directives to Nichiren Shoshu priests and Hokkeko members a week later on July 15.

AFTER the high priest's directive appeared in the July 25 issue of the *Seikyo Shimbun*, the head of the Nichiren Shoshu General Affairs Office published his comments in the *Seikyo Shimbun* as well. He said: "As the directive states, it is due to the great power of the Gohonzon and the enthusiastic efforts of sincere Soka Gakkai members to share the Daishonin's teachings with others that Nichiren Shoshu has become an international religion.

"In accord with the high priest's wishes, the school administration is determined to proceed in unity with the laity. As the completion of the Grand Reception Hall approaches, we vow to uphold the high priest's directive, as well as the instructions of the former high priest, and to work together with the Soka Gakkai."

The president of the National Hokkeko Federation

also published his remarks in the *Seikyo Shimbun,* stating: "Every member of the Hokkeko, without exception, accepts and is prepared to carry out the high priest's directive. We are determined to respond to the high priest's deep consideration by overcoming any obstacle that stands in the way of kosen-rufu, and to dedicate ourselves to practice for oneself and others following the Soka Gakkai's lead."

He concluded by expressing his hope that under the compassionate leadership of President Yamamoto, whom he referred to as a senior lay Hokkeko representative and a great and unparalleled leader, each member of the Hokkeko would advance with strong faith toward victory in the struggle to achieve kosen-rufu and create a Buddha land.

With the announcement of the directives, Rengeji temple in Osaka and Daijoji temple in Kochi, which had consistently harassed Soka Gakkai members, eventually seceded from Nichiren Shoshu. Criticism of the Soka Gakkai by some priests and Hokkeko members abated for a time, and there were fewer incidents of Taisekiji priests seen drinking and partying in Fujinomiya. But essentially nothing had changed. Behind closed doors, verbal attacks on the Soka Gakkai continued, and the priests' profligate behavior just took place in less conspicuous locations. In later years Nikken Abe proved himself to be the epitome of self-interest and hunger for power when he assumed the school's top ranking position of high priest and chief administrator. Nichiren Shoshu and the Daishonin's teachings were then completely reduced to a den of iniquity and degradation.

Shin'ichi was relieved that at least the high priest published these directives, but at the same time he knew that the corruption taken root in the hearts of the priests was not severed. A look at history reveals that devilish functions entered the priesthood at the very core of kosenrufu in order to halt the advance of that movement. To prevent the priesthood from becoming the "one evil" (WND, 15) that destroys Buddhism, Shin'ichi picked up the jeweled sword of faith and began to battle the demonic nature of authority that had clothed itself in priestly robes.

NOTES

1 Theoretical here is a translation of the Japanese term *shaku,* which literally means *shadow.* It suggests a conceptual outline or image of the ultimate reality or truth.

2 Leo Tolstoy, *A Calendar of Wisdom,* trans. Peter Sekirin (New York: Scribner, 1997), p. 14.

3 The Buddhism of sowing means Nichiren Daishonin's Buddhism, which reveals the Law of Nam-myoho-renge-kyo, while the Buddhism of harvest indicates the essential teaching revealed in the latter half of the Lotus Sutra.

4 Shikoku — The smallest of Japan's four main islands.

5 (Jap. *Tannisho*) A record of the words of Shinran (1173–1262) of the Jodo Shin school of Buddhism, believed to have been compiled by his disciple, Yuien.

6 In the Osaka Incident, President Ikeda, then Soka Gakkai youth division chief of staff, was arrested and wrongfully charged with election law violations in an Upper House by-election in Osaka in 1957. At the end of the court case that

dragged on for almost five years, he was fully exonerated of all charges in January 1962.

7 Hokkeko — Lay organizations affiliated with Nichiren Shoshu temples.

8 A priest with a particular rank.

9 *Toba* — Traditional memorial tablets for the deceased for which temples charged believers. Priests would inscribe them with passages from the sutras, the deceased's posthumous name, etc.

10 Kobo (774-835) — The posthumous name of Kukai, the founder of the Shingon school of Buddhism in Japan.

11 Kuonji temple — Located on Mount Minobu, it was the center of the Daishonin's activities toward the end of his life. After his death, however, it gradually deviated from the Daishonin's teachings. His successor, Nikko Shonin, thus moved the center to the foot of Mount Fuji.

12 Hokkaido — The northernmost island of Japan's four main islands.

13 Until that time, even Mahayana priests in Japan were ordained only in the Hinayana precepts. Dengyo struggled against opposition by the established Buddhist schools to gain the necessary approval from the emperor to establish a Mahayana ordination center. This goal was finally realized soon after his death.

Pure Stream

WRITING and speech are the mark of humanity. They are forces capable of resisting violence and building true and lasting peace. Kosen-rufu is a fresh, humanistic movement to enable the human spirit to triumph, creating happiness and peace for all people through the written and spoken word.

On July 28, 1963, Shin'ichi Yamamoto attended the first all-Japan Soka Gakkai Writers Department general meeting at the Kyoritsu Auditorium in Kanda, Tokyo. The Writers Department was founded two years earlier, on May 3, 1961, when the Culture Bureau was established. At that time, Youth Leader Eisuke Akizuki had been appointed as its head.

The Writers Department at first consisted of two groups: The first, Group 1, included young men's and young women's leaders, and the second, Group 2, was for professional writers. Later, at the request of the women's division, a third group was established primarily for women's division members. Its aim was to be a forum for women to voice their ideas toward building a new society. Group 2 subsequently became a men's division section of the Writers Department. Professional writers joined whichever of the three groups was appropriate to their circumstances.

The Writers Department established branches not only throughout the Tokyo metropolitan area but gradually across the country, and they became very active. In November 1962, the first issue of *Opinions*, the Writers Department monthly journal, was published. It provided a place where department members could express their ideas, and included articles on current issues and pointed rebuttals to criticisms of the Soka Gakkai in the mass media.

Shin'ichi contributed a short essay to the first issue where he declared that initiating a war of words dedicated to truth and justice could change the direction of the Cold War and the numerous armed conflicts around the world. It would be based on the conviction that "the pen is mightier than the sword." He also emphasized that Nichiren Daishonin's many letters and treatises, written out of a great desire to lead all people to happiness, were testimony to the "war of words" he waged in accord with the fundamentals of democracy.

"The time has come for us to speak out courageously for truth and justice and advance for the sake of kosen-rufu and the well-being of the people." It is the people who are responsible for ensuring that there is sound speech and writing. In Japan, however, the people gave up thinking for themselves and ceased to speak out for the protection of their own rights and dignity. Shin'ichi regarded giving the power of words back to the people as the mission of the Writers Department.

WORDS have tremendous power. They can change people's awareness and change the times. That is why those in power wishing to control the people have always tried to manipulate words and eliminate the influence of reformers in society. Such people misuse the mass media to spread lies, branding reformers as evil, deviant and insane, and trying to stir up hatred and fear.

The Soka Gakkai, an organization striving to open a celebrated age of the people, has been consistently subjected to such critcism. Unless such wrongdoing is challenged and justice revealed, the truth will continue to be distorted and trampled upon. Moreover, the people will never win.

For this reason, Shin'ichi put his energy into developing the Writers Department. Whenever he considered the power of words, he recalled the struggle for American independence.

In January 1776, a pamphlet titled *Common Sense* was published in Philadelphia. It appeared nine months after the battles of Lexington and Concord, where the first shots of the American Revolution were fired.

This small, forty-seven-page pamphlet had tremendous influence, and stirred people's desire for independence. At the time, any public call for independence invited strict surveillance from British colonial authorities. In addition, public opinion was divided on the issue. Only about one-third of the American people supported independence. Another third were loyalists who wanted to remain a colony of England, and the remaining third were neutral. Many who were satisfied with having gained a degree of self-rule were skeptical about full independence, and stood by silently to see what would happen.

Against this backdrop, a thin pamphlet cried out that

independence from England was a natural conclusion of common sense. It stated: "There is something very absurd in supposing a continent to be perpetually governed by an island."[1] "O ye that love mankind! Ye that dare oppose, not only tyranny, but the tyrant, stand forth!"[2] "Nothing can settle our affairs so expeditiously as an open and determined declaration for independence."[3]

These were not complicated words. They were clear, simple and understandable to all, words that advocated the need for independence with passion and conviction.

The author signed the pamphlet, "Written by an Englishman."

IT EVENTUALLY became known that the author of the pamphlet *Common Sense* was a thirty-nine-year-old editor named Thomas Paine. He arrived in America from England only two years earlier and was a complete unknown. Yet his small pamphlet garnered a stunning response, selling one hundred and twenty thousand copies in just three months, at a time when the population of the colonies was only about 2.5 million. While this was an astonishing figure in itself, in the end the pamphlet is said to have sold more than five hundred thousand copies.

Those who read *Common Sense* were struck deeply by its message and came to believe that independence was America's future. The old common sense they once believed in collapsed and was replaced by a new one. An English newspaper described the effectiveness of the pamphlet, saying, "As many as read [*Common Sense*], so many became converted."[4] George Washington, later to become the first president of the United States, commented on the pamphlet's "sound doctrine and unanswerable reasoning," remarking, that it "will not leave numbers at a loss to decide upon the propriety of separation [from England]."[5]

Farmers and poor city dwellers rushed to buy copies of *Common Sense* and soon joined the ranks of those who supported independence. One reader noted that "the public sentiment which a few weeks before [the publication of *Common Sense*] shuddered at the tremendous obstacles, with which independence was environed, overleaped every barrier."[6]

The pamphlet gave people in the colonies confidence that independence could be won, and roused in them the courage to stand up and act. The power of a people determined to do something is tremendous. Nothing can stop them.

Soon after, on July 4, 1776, the Declaration of Independence was signed. Though the mood of the times called for independence, there can be no denying that this little pamphlet, written by an ordinary citizen, was instrumental in its realization.

Paine wrote, "Who the Author of this Production is, is wholly unnecessary to the Public, as the Object for Attention is the *Doctrine itself,* not the *Man*."[7] The power of his words changed history. It is the people who speak out for justice against the tyranny of authority and the inequities of society that are the foundation of democracy.

In any case, when we break through the falsehood of evil with truth, we can open the way to a bright future.

TO SAY BOLDLY what must be said, to declare right what is right and wrong what is wrong—this is the true way of Buddhists. The early Buddhist teaching of the Eightfold Path, which outlines the way to enlightenment, exemplifies this with its inclusion of "right speech." Right speech is defined as refraining from lying, bad language, slander and frivolous speech. In this way, Shakyamuni taught that we should only speak the truth.

When Shakyamuni began to preach in Rajagriha,[8] people of excellent caliber flocked to him one after another and became his disciples. Envious and fearful of this rapid development, others in the city attacked Shakyamuni with a storm of abuse. This worried his disciples, but Shakyamuni remained unfazed. He taught them to respond to such attacks by saying, "The Buddha is inviting people by means of the true dharma. Who would be jealous of this?"

These words gave his disciples the courage to rise to action. From then on, whenever they heard people criticizing the Buddha, they would resolutely speak out. They talked until they convinced their opponents of Shakyamuni's true intent. This is what it means to refute people's erroneous views and lead them to the correct teaching. Eventually, the slanderous remarks ceased completely.

When Devadatta revealed his real nature by trying to seize control of the Buddhist order, Shakyamuni immediately told Shariputra and his other disciples to go to Rajagriha and expose Devadatta for the scoundrel that he was. It was thus that Shakyamuni staunchly challenged all wrongdoing. He clearly distinguished right from wrong, his words piercing injustice like bullets.

The Daishonin's life was also a constant fierce struggle to communicate the truth. Establishing his teachings at the age of thirty-two, he stood alone and pointed out the errors of all the Buddhist schools of Japan at the time. He was not a person of rank or status, but he had no fear of the powerful military government. He knew that enemies would attack him from all over Japan, and he was prepared for intense persecution.

His words were a lion's roar to relieve the people of suffering, bring them happiness, and build a peaceful and prosperous society. That is why his life was a series of endless persecutions.

NICHIREN DAISHONIN remonstrated with Hojo Tokiyori, the de facto ruler of Japan in his day, and harshly rebuked the slanderous behavior of Ryokan[9] of Gokuraku-ji temple, a powerful religious figure. The Daishonin's struggle was one of swift words and actions. He always responded immediately to attacks from his enemies, as well as to reports from his disciples. In particular, the Daishonin's response when his disciples were in trouble or some incident occurred was astonishingly rapid, on the mark, and detailed.

In June 1277, Shijo Kingo fell into disfavor with his lord and was pressed to sign a vow to give up his faith in the Lotus Sutra. The source of the problem was a trumped-up report that Shijo Kingo along with others had disrupted the preaching of a priest named Ryuzo of the Tendai school.

Upon reading the document Kingo urgently sent to him explaining the incident, the Daishonin immediately discerned the reality of the situation and took up his brush to write a letter to Kingo's lord on his behalf called "The Letter of Petition from Yorimoto."[10] In the letter, the Daishonin came boldly to Kingo's defense, declaring, "This is a groundless falsehood" (WND, 803).

Silence allows the darkness of falsehood to spread. Communicating the truth is the light that breaks through that darkness. To stand by and watch as people suffer shows an utter lack of compassion. Failing to speak out for truth and justice when clouds of iniquity threaten to obscure the skies of truth is cowardice.

During the Atsuhara Persecution in October 1279, the Daishonin wrote letter after letter, including "On Persecutions Befalling the Sage," "Reply to Reverend Hoki[11] and Others," "Petition of Ryusen-ji" and "Reply to Sages." Some are encouragement to disciples who were farmers and were persecuted. One is a petition the Daishonin wrote to the authorities on behalf of his disciples declaring their innocence. In another, he gave detailed instructions to Nikko Shonin and other priests regarding a court appeal in the Atsuhara case. In this way, the Daishonin took control of the situation and responded swiftly to the rapidly changing circumstances.

It is crucial always to obtain correct information and respond to it quickly. In a battle with one's enemies, speed can make the difference between life and death. Furthermore, for words to be truly powerful and effective, they must expose the very nature and essence of injustice.

The Daishonin identified Ryokan, who had the support

of the military government and was looked up to by
many as a "living Buddha," as the third of the three powerful enemies described in the Lotus Sutra. He
denounced Ryokan for pretending to be a sage but in
reality caring only for fame and profit, and for deceiving
the people. Ryokan hated the Daishonin for this, and so
made false statements about him to the authorities and
plotted his demise.

IN MARCH 1275, a fire broke out at Ryokan's
Gokuraku-ji temple and the complex burned to the
ground. There was also a fire at a palace of the military
government, which was strongly supportive of Ryokan.
In light of the sutras, it was clear that the fundamental
cause of the fires was Ryokan's slander of the correct
teaching. When the Daishonin learned of these incidents,
in a phonetic play on words, he referred to Ryokan as
"Ryoka-bo" meaning "Priest Two Fires." He strongly
rebuked him, saying that Gokuraku-ji [Paradise Temple]
had been reduced to Jigoku-ji [Hell Temple] (see WND,
488). He also warned that the fires not only "ravaged the
country in this existence," but foretold that the "teacher
and his disciples throughout Japan will in their next life
fall into the hell of incessant suffering, where they will
burn in the Avichi flames" (WND, 488). By calling Ryokan
"Priest Two Fires," the Daishonin was exposing him flat-
out as a false sage.

These words were not intended as mere insults. They
were a relentless bombardment of truths based on Buddhist scriptures and clear reasoning. If wrongdoing is not
stopped, good will be lost forever. If the truth is not

declared, lies will spread unchecked. If the correct teaching perishes and erroneous teachings reign, it is the people who will suffer.

The Daishonin's fierce and tireless volley of words came from his deep commitment to the correct teaching (see WND, 302). Achieving victory for the people through the power of words is no easy feat. There will be all sorts of difficulties and obstacles along the path of kosen-rufu, just as there were during the Daishonin's lifetime.

However, like the Daishonin who said, "But still, I am not discouraged" (WND, 748), what is important is to continue speaking out for justice. Such an invincible cry of the spirit moves the hearts of others. A true warrior of words is a person with indomitable conviction. Shin'ichi Yamamoto hoped that the Writers Department would comprise such people.

The Kyoritsu Auditorium, where the first all-Japan Writers Department general meeting was being held, teemed with the excitement of such "warriors" from across the nation. At the meeting, Vice General Director Kazumasa Morikawa announced that a fourth group of the Writers' Department was being established specifically for members of the young women's division, who had been in Group 1 with the young men. With this change, each of the four divisions now had a group in the Writers Department.

This announcement was followed by activity reports and two speeches denouncing corruption in the mass media titled "Critique of Modern Journalism" and "The Distorted Mass Media."

FOLLOWING words from several leaders, President Yamamoto took the podium. Praising what the Writers Department accomplished over the last two years, he spoke on the importance of the written word in achieving kosen-rufu: "Using the power of words to change society is fundamental to democracy. Writing about the truth is a weapon to protect the people, creating a world in which the people come first and are triumphant. This is the movement of kosen-rufu."

While he emphasized that freedom of expression must never be compromised, he pointed out the abuse that can occur in the name of free speech. This was evident, he said, in the proliferation of irresponsible and arbitrary journalism, as well as that which distorts the truth and deceives the people.

Freedom of speech does not give license to the spread of lies and rumors. "What will happen," asked Shin'ichi, "if Japan falls under the control of a small group of ill-intentioned journalists or leaders who agitate and influence the people?

"The mission of the Writers Department is to challenge such malicious reporting, to expose lies, and to forge a fresh climate of public opinion in which true peace and happiness can develop. I declare that the age when freedom of speech can be exploited by a handful of critics or the privileged few is over. Freedom of speech must never be the exclusive right of such people. Let us raise the curtain on a new age through a passionate war of words waged by an alliance of good!"

True freedom of speech will only be realized when the people boldly speak out for truth and justice. Every abusive and unfounded statement must be met with ten declarations of the truth. It is precisely such effort that gives life to the Daishonin's teaching "The voice does the Buddha's work."

In closing, Shin'ichi called on the members of the Writers Department to always be allies of the people and courageous champions in the great struggle of words. People, in other words. who move people's hearts with their passion, ideals and penetrating logic.

Many intellectuals in Japan believed that the strength of the Soka Gakkai lay in its ability to gather and organize ordinary people. However, it wasn't being organized in and of itself that gave the Soka Gakkai its strength. As members of the organization, ordinary people fostered a spirit of independence as well as proudly voiced their opinions. As a result, they were also able to contribute to society. This is what gave rise to a solid alliance of the people's power, a force that would not bow to authority.

ON JULY 30, Shin'ichi visited Nagano City to attend the Chubu No. 2 Headquarters leaders meeting at the Nagano Civic Hall. At the time, the headquarters included chapters from the Koshin[12] and Hokuriku[13] regions. When the meeting was first announced, the members of Chubu No. 2 Headquarters began a serious effort to introduce many people to the Daishonin's Buddhism in order to welcome President Yamamoto amid the joy of triumph.

Tremendous progress was made in July. In particular, Koshin General Chapter, which encompassed the area where the meeting was to be held, achieved the highest results, surpassing general chapters in Tokyo and Osaka previously known for their strength in propagation.

Located in a basin, Nagano is very hot in the summer. On the morning of the meeting the temperature continued to rise, until it reached ninety-nine degrees inside the auditorium by the time the meeting began at 2:30 in the afternoon. Many members from Kanazawa and Toyama in central Honshu had left home by bus the previous evening, arriving in Nagano at 6:00 A.M. Shin'ichi was worried that everyone would be exhausted, but the participants were all in high spirits.

Shin'ichi sensed in their hearty applause the joy that came from dedicating their lives to kosen-rufu. People who work for kosen-rufu experience great joy and benefit. At the meeting, Shin'ichi said: "Nothing makes me happier than seeing all of you so full of energy. Since you are so vigorous, may I assume that each of you is receiving great benefit?"

The members applauded in response. Shin'ichi asked another question: "How many of you have experienced benefit since becoming a member? Please raise your hand."

"I have!" came the thunderous reply as they all raised their hands.

"That's wonderful," Shin'ichi said. "Since that's the case, I can end my speech here." Laughter filled the auditorium. "The purpose of faith, after all, is to obtain benefit."

Indeed, the purpose of faith is to receive benefit. That is also the purpose of Buddhist practice and Soka Gakkai activities. The Soka Gakkai organization and its leadership exist to ensure that each member receives benefit. If we lose sight of this, our organization will lose its vigor, stagnate and become idle.

SHIN'ICHI then announced the construction of the Chubu No. 2 Headquarters Building. The members expressed their joy with enthusiastic applause. Shin'ichi went on to say that the secret to happiness was winning over oneself, and in addition, practicing to the Gohonzon with doubt-free faith that flows like a pure stream no matter what happens.

"The validity of the Daishonin's Buddhism is confirmed," he said, "by documentary, theoretical, and actual proof. But some people begin to have doubts as soon as their business suffers a little downturn. Or some say the Gohonzon has failed to protect them if, for instance, their child gets injured. Moreover, there are those who, when certain sectors of the mass media criticize the Soka Gakkai, begin to doubt the guidance of their seniors, lose faith in the Gohonzon and stop doing gongyo altogether.

"These are people who tend not to reflect on themselves or their faith. Instead, whenever the slightest problem or setback occurs they start doubting the Gohonzon or the Soka Gakkai. However, this only erases the great benefit they would have otherwise accumulated.

"Babies thrive because they unconditionally drink their mother's milk. If they stop drinking it too soon, however, their growth can be stunted and they can become weak and susceptible to illness. In the same way, if we continue to have faith in the Gohonzon and chant daimoku throughout our lives, we will absolutely tap into the life force of the Buddha. The way we live, likewise, will reflect a condition of absolute happiness.

"Please do not doubt the Gohonzon, but continue to chant daimoku and work together in the Soka Gakkai, the organization dedicated to kosen-rufu. This is the way to enjoy a truly meaningful and happy life." Shin'ichi's guidance expressed his earnest wish that each of his fellow members would enjoy a life of great fulfillment, abundant benefit and good fortune.

The Chubu No. 2 Headquarters leaders meeting closed with Shin'ichi leading the members in the "Song of the New Century." Afterwards, Shin'ichi went to offer encouragement to the overflow of members waiting outside. He then attended a chapter leaders guidance meeting, presenting each participant with a separately handwritten copy of a poem that had been composed by his mentor, Josei Toda. It had taken him until late the previous night to copy down each of these poems in his own handwriting.

After the chapter leaders guidance meeting, he visited the construction site of the new Chubu No. 2 Headquarters Building. He then attended a district leaders meeting being held at a local Nichiren Shoshu temple, where he spent nearly half an hour pouring his heart into offering guidance and encouragement to members.

IN THE EVENING, Shin'ichi had a meeting with leaders of the local general chapters. By the time all of his engagements were over, his neck and shoulders were stiff and his back was sore. He asked the inn where he was staying to send a masseur, and soon a blind man in his late middle ages came to his room. As he massaged Shin'ichi's shoulders, the masseur said, "I'm surprised how stiff you are for someone so young. I have massaged many people, but I have never encountered anyone so stiff before."

"Really?" said Shin'ichi. "You are very skillful. It feels good. And you have so much energy."

"I joined the Soka Gakkai about six months ago, that's why I'm so energetic. I was born blind, but since becoming a member I am convinced that I will be able to see in my next life." Then he asked Shin'ichi, "Do you know about the Soka Gakkai?"

"Yes, of course," Shin'ichi replied. "If you practice your faith even harder, you will be able to see clearly with your mind's eye, even if you don't regain your sight." Realizing it would now be awkward to tell the man he was president of the Soka Gakkai, Shin'ichi did not mention it.

"I think I can already see with my mind's eye," said the masseur. "Every day is just so wonderful."

"Is that so?" asked Shin'ichi. "Then I hope you'll keep up your practice and receive even more benefits."

"You sound just like my district leader," said the masseur. "He is a very good man."

The masseur began to go on about the Soka Gakkai, but after a while Shin'ichi interrupted him. "I understand how happy you are to have found faith," he said, "but I am sure many of your clients want to rest quietly while you're massaging them. Maybe you should not talk about your faith and the Soka Gakkai while you're working."

"Yes, you are right," admitted the masseur. "My chapter leader says the same thing. You really sound like him, too."

After about twenty minutes of silence, Shin'ichi

expressed his appreciation to the masseur: "Though you are older than I, you have worked hard to give me a fine massage. I am very grateful. You must be tired. Let's take a little break and drink some juice."

"This is my job," added the masseur, "so I always do my very best."

Shin'ichi went to the refrigerator, took out some juice, and offered it to the masseur, who gulped it down with gusto.

THE MASSEUR resumed massaging Shin'ichi. He said: "Actually, Soka Gakkai President Yamamoto attended a meeting here in Nagano today. Recently, one of the directors of the Soka Gakkai came to Nagano. He told us that President Yamamoto is a great leader whose vision and actions are indispensable to both Japan and the world. I really wanted to go to today's activity and meet him.

"I kept praying that I would be able to, but then all of these jobs came in today that I could not refuse, and I could not go. I am so disappointed."

Hearing this, Shin'ichi began to feel awkward, and the tension seemed to return to his shoulders. "That is too bad," he said. "But haven't you been told that if you really chant in earnest, your prayers will be answered? Please do not worry. If that was your wish, I am sure it will come true."

Smiling, the masseur replied: "Thank you so much for your encouraging words. You are very considerate for someone so young. I almost feel as if I were meeting with the president of the Soka Gakkai right now."

After about thirty or forty minutes, Shin'ichi finally felt relaxed. He politely thanked the masseur.

"You are very thoughtful," commented the masseur. "That must be why your shoulders are hard as rocks!"

"I guess that is it," said Shin'ichi. "But it is not good to have such rock-solid shoulders. On the other hand, having solid faith is a good thing!" Their cheerful laughter rang through the room.

When the masseur later found out that he had been massaging President Yamamoto, he deepened his appreciation of the remarkable power of prayer.

In July, the Soka Gakkai membership had reached an astonishing 3.6 million households. Shin'ichi was happy to see Bodhisattvas of the Earth springing up across the country. These people of noble mission were practicing Buddhism joyfully and gaining great benefit. Kosen-rufu is an effort to bring hope and happiness to blossom in people's hearts.

Shin'ichi returned to Tokyo on July 31, and that evening the August young men's division leaders meeting was held at Taito Ward Gymnasium. The new "Song of Worldwide Kosen-rufu" debuted at the meeting.

Look! Grand and heroic
The Himalayan peaks sparkle with snow
The Yellow River flows
Like the stream of human history
We set out
Our hearts ablaze with new ideals
Resolved to achieve worldwide kosen-rufu!

THE LYRICS to "Song of Worldwide Kosen-rufu" greatly inspired the audience. The music rose with each phrase, symbolizing a future of unfolding possibilities.

Kenshiro Ishikawa had been appointed head of the young men's division at a general meeting of that division in December the previous year. Since then, there had been a growing demand for the creation of a new song. Beginning in January, members across Japan had been encouraged to submit ideas, but none of the submissions were quite what the leadership had in mind.

One entitled "Song of Worldwide Kosen-rufu," however, caught their attention. Though some revisions would be necessary, the grand scale it expressed was what they had sought. It sang of the Pacific Ocean, the Rocky Mountains and the Gobi Desert, and closed with the line, "Ah! The bell of worldwide kosen-rufu rings." A group of young men active in the chapter that included Ota City in Gumma Prefecture and Ashikaga City in Tochigi Prefecture[14] had composed the lyrics. They would often gather at their chapter activity center after meetings and discuss ideas for the song.

Though preoccupied with the immediate demands of life, they were also aware of President Yamamoto's determination to accomplish worldwide kosen-rufu. For this reason, they agreed to break through the shell of their limitations and write a song that would inspire members to work actively on the world stage for peace alongside President Yamamoto.

After several late nights, they finally came up with some lyrics. These were then edited by a staff of leaders of the young men's division, who refined and polished them over the next several months.

When the lyrics were ready, they were given to Takeshi Arimura, head of the brass band, who composed the music. The final product was new and original, unlike any Gakkai song before that time. The song was ready, but the time to introduce it was still undecided.

To commemorate the twelfth anniversary of the founding of the young men's division on July 11, President Yamamoto contributed an essay to *The Daibyakurenge* entitled "Youth, Become World Leaders!" This offered an excellent opportunity to introduce the new song. The young men's leaders decided to revise the song further to express their vow to respond to President Yamamoto's call, and they finally introduced it at the August young men's division leaders meeting held on July 31.

Heroes of the Gakkai

Our voices resound across the seven seas
Young Bodhisattvas of the Earth soar skyward
Celebrating together the creation of peace
Ah! The bell of worldwide kosen-rufu rings.

As pioneers of the essential phase of the Soka Gakkai's development, the young men pledged to achieve global kosen-rufu and began their journey afresh with this song on their lips.

AUGUST, known in the Soka Gakkai as "the month of training," began with the second nationwide meeting of the Education Department at the Taito Gymnasium in Tokyo on August 1. At this meeting, Hisao

Seki, a vice general director and culture bureau leader, was appointed the new department head, replacing Katsu Kiyohara.

The annual summer training course began on August 3 at the head temple. This year it was expected that twenty thousand members from all divisions throughout Japan would participate, which was to be conducted in four sessions over nine days. In addition to his responsibilities in overseeing the course, President Shin'ichi Yamamoto led question-and-answer sessions, wholeheartedly encouraging the members in each group.

On the evening of August 11, the last day of the training course, Vice General Director Seiichiro Haruki and Director and South America General Chapter Leader Hiroshi Yamagiwa departed from Tokyo's Haneda Airport for Argentina.

They were the first of the leaders who embarked on overseas guidance trips that summer. After a layover in Vancouver, British Columbia, they flew on to Argentina, after which they visited Paraguay, Brazil, Peru and Bolivia. In all these countries, they met with members to offer guidance and encouragement. They were scheduled to return to Japan on August 29.

Hisao Seki and others left for North America on August 15 and returned on the 27. Vice General Director and Southeast Asia General Chapter Leader Kazumasa Morikawa and others then departed on August 17 and returned on the 25. The regional summer guidance tours that were conducted around Japan since the early years of the Soka Gakkai were now taking place on a global scale.

Before departing for South America, Haruki and Yamagiwa, who were in charge of some of the sessions during the summer training course, went to see Shin'ichi. After confirming that they were going to pass through Mexico, Shin'ichi said: "I will never forget that just before Josei Toda died, he told me happily that he dreamt he had visited Mexico. He said that everyone there was waiting, that they were seeking the Buddhism of Nichiren Daishonin. He said he wanted to go there, to go everywhere for kosen-rufu.

"I want you two to go to South America with the strong awareness that you are going in President Toda's stead. Wherever I go, I always act with that in mind. I ask myself, 'What would President Toda do in my place? How would he approach this challenge?' I also always ask myself if President Toda would be pleased with what I am doing. That has allowed me to give my best and to have courage. That, to me, is how to live the way of mentor and disciple."

SHIN'ICHI continued: "If I could, I would like to go to Mexico, Argentina and Peru myself. I would like to visit every country in the world and encourage everyone I meet with all my might. But I just do not have the time right now. So you are going in my place, too. Since you are making this trip, you must pour your all into encouraging and guiding the members. It would be a disservice to them to do anything less." After this, Haruki and Yamagiwa left for South America with renewed determination.

During the summer training course, Shin'ichi met a

number of times with the leaders who were being sent abroad to discuss in detail the development of Soka Gakkai organizations around the world. He wanted to firmly establish the organization in each country and prepare the way for future growth and development. These plans were officially announced after they had been discussed with the leaders in those countries during the summer guidance tours.

The most important new development was the creation of the first headquarters organization outside Japan, the Europe and All-America Headquarters, with Nagayasu Masaki as its head. In the United States, the America General Chapter was divided into two, forming the America West and America East general chapters. The new Europe and All-America Headquarters thus consisted of four general chapters: one in South America and Europe, and two in the United States.

In the United States, chapters were established in San Diego, Colorado and Kentucky. A group was also formed in Canada.

In South America, Paraguay Chapter was created and Brazil Chapter was split into three, the two new chapters being São Paulo West and São Paulo North. Including the already existing Brazil, Peru and Bolivia chapters, South America now had six chapters. In addition, a district was formed in Argentina and a group in Mexico.

In Southeast Asia, Jakarta Chapter was established in Indonesia and Manila Chapter in the Philippines, and districts were set up in Singapore and in Phnom Penh, Cambodia. The foundation of kosen-rufu was being steadily built around the world.

On August 14, after the summer training course, Shin'ichi visited Hokuriku to attend the funeral of Toyama Chapter Leader Toshiharu Takamatsu, which had been organized by Toyama Chapter. He had died on July 31 while returning home by overnight train from the Chubu No. 2 Headquarters leaders meeting in Nagano, which Shin'ichi had attended.

A̲T THE CHUBU NO. 2 Headquarters leaders meeting, Toshiharu Takamatsu joined other chapter leaders in joyfully leading the singing of Soka Gakkai songs. His movements were especially vigorous that night. When the meeting finished, Takamatsu caught up with Shin'ichi as he entered a reception room, and said with a smile, "Sensei, it's been a long time since we have met!"

"Yes! How good to see you! When are you returning to Toyama?"

"I am going back on the train tonight with the others," Takamatsu replied.

"I see. Well, please have a safe journey back. By the way, in commemoration of today's meeting, I would like to present you with one of President Toda's poems that I have copied out by hand." Shin'ichi handed the calligraphy to Takamatsu.

Believe in the Buddha,
The treasure of the universe,
And as a Buddha's child,
Enjoy protection
Without fail.

Takamatsu's eyes brightened as he read the poem. "Thank you!" he exclaimed. "I am deeply encouraged!"

Takamatsu had joined the Soka Gakkai in 1955. He was a good-natured and simple man. At one point he managed a welding shop, but his trusting nature often led him to be taken advantage of, which did not fare well for business. Eventually he fell so deeply into debt that his house was confiscated. He and his wife and their six children moved into a small shack, and from there into one cramped row house after another. But all the while, he remained earnest in his faith.

The family was destitute and Takamatsu's wife, Shizuko, was forced to make frequent visits to the local pawnshop just to make ends meet. Still, they both kept their spirits up and continued to work hard for kosen-rufu.

In September 1960, when Toyama Chapter was established, Takamatsu was appointed chapter leader and Shizuko, chapter women's division leader. Eventually their financial situation took a turn for the better. Then, in the spring of 1963, urged by his friends and neighbors, Takamatsu ran for the local city council and won.

On the train back from the leaders meeting, Takamatsu walked through the cars encouraging his fellow members. He continued giving personal guidance late into the night, and then he fell asleep in his seat.

As the morning dawned, he seemed to be sleeping soundly. But when the person in the seat in front tried to wake him, saying, "We will be in Toyama soon," Takamatsu did not answer.

SHIZUKO also tried to wake him but in vain. He had stopped breathing. It was a peaceful death. He seemed to be smiling.

When Shin'ichi learned of Takamatsu's death, he immediately telephoned the family. Shizuko answered, and from her description of Takamatsu's appearance, Shin'ichi knew that Takamatsu had attained Buddhahood. Shizuko said with a steady voice: "I am fine. Please do not worry. I am more concerned about the other members...."

She had lost her loving husband and she must have been wracked with grief, yet she was concerned about her fellow members. Her strength and dignity moved Shin'ichi. He promised he would visit Toyama soon. On August 14, he went to attend Mr. Takamatsu's funeral ceremony, which had been organized by Toyama Chapter.

Takamatsu was only fifty-three when he died, young compared to the average life expectancy in Japan. No one can avoid death, however, and by the same token, life is eternal. It is good to live a long life, but even more important is what one has done in life, whether one has carried out one's mission. That is why Nichiren Daishonin wrote: "Life is limited; we must not begrudge it. What we should ultimately aspire to is the Buddha land" (WND, 214).

Takamatsu had made kosen-rufu his personal goal and taught numerous others the way to genuine happiness. At the same time, he had helped raise many capable people. He had fulfilled his mission as a Bodhisattva of the Earth in this life and departed for Eagle Peak. The many others he had nurtured would now inherit and carry on his dream.

Those who devote their lives to working for kosen-rufu will attain Buddhahood without fail, just as the Daishonin's writings promise. Shin'ichi believed that Takamatsu would be reborn immediately and that by the arrival of the twenty-first century, he would be a courageous, youthful leader in the Soka Gakkai.

At the funeral, Shin'ichi warmly encouraged all of the family members. He knew that for them, living happy lives from this point on would be proof of Takamatsu's attainment of Buddhahood.

When the services were over, Shin'ichi attended the Hokuriku General Chapter leaders meeting held in the Toyama Civic Hall. The Hokuriku General Chapter had just been established in May of that year, and this was the first leaders meeting of the new general chapter to be attended by Shin'ichi. The meeting began with Shin'ichi's arrival shortly before 2:00 in the afternoon.

SHIN'ICHI YAMAMOTO was concerned with how the members of Toyama Chapter would react to the death of their chapter leader, Toshiharu Takamatsu. But when he saw the faces of the members who filled the hall, he was relieved. They had overcome their sadness and appeared firmly resolved to carry on Takamatsu's spirit of dedication to kosen-rufu.

In his speech, Shin'ichi encouraged the members to uphold the Mystic Law throughout their lives and become true winners. He could see that they fully grasped his message. Even in death, Takamatsu's strong determination continued to influence the members of his chapter, and was beginning to have an impact on the entire region.

On August 24, the sixteenth anniversary of his joining the Soka Gakkai, Shin'ichi visited Hokkaido, where his mentor, Josei Toda, spent his youth. He attended a leaders meeting at the Hokkaido headquarters building that day, and on the next day he went to the Fifth Soka Gakkai Hokkaido Sports Festival, held in Sapporo.

This "festival of youth" was the first of the year. Similar events would follow across the country, culminating in a national gathering on September 22. In fostering youth, it is important to provide a stage on which they can exercise their talents. The sports festivals offered just such an arena as they presented these young people with an excellent opportunity to give full play to their strengths and abilities.

Shin'ichi carefully observed how the youth in each area were preparing for these events, watching what they were planning and how they were growing as a result. He wanted to see if they would concentrate simply on putting on a show, or if they would give the occasion special meaning and come up with something original and unique that would launch them toward further progress. Depending on their effort and attitude, the sports festivals would have very different meaning and value.

Soka Gakkai activities are all aimed at helping members deepen their faith and at advancing the cause of kosen-rufu. If this basic purpose is forgotten by just trying to put on a good show, then such activities lose their meaning and purpose.

The Hokkaido sports festival overflowed with youthful energy and passion. Individual events were unique and well thought-out. When the word "trailblazing" was spelled out with hand-held cards on the field, a rousing cheer rose from the audience. In preparation for this day, the members had worked very hard to introduce their friends to the practice. They wanted to celebrate this occasion through a groundswell of propagation, blazing a great trail of Nichiren Daishonin's Buddhism throughout Hokkaido.

Shin'ichi was overjoyed to see the growth of the youth in Hokkaido, where just six years earlier, during the Yubari Coal Miners Union Incident of 1957.[15]

ON SEPTEMBER 1, under a bright sun and beautiful blue skies, a grand chorus of joyful voices rang through the Nihon University Auditorium in Ryogoku, Tokyo. The Twenty-Sixth Headquarters Leaders Meeting was being held to commemorate the completion that day of the long-awaited new Soka Gakkai Headquarters building in Shinanomachi. This facility was to be an energy source from which an important new movement in the essential phase of kosen-rufu would be launched.

The meeting started just past 9:30 A.M. Beneath the clear autumn sky, members who had gathered from all over Japan rejoiced at the building's completion and cheerfully exchanged vows to make a new start in their activities.

In his speech at the meeting, Shin'ichi related that High Priest Nittatsu had told him excitedly: "President Yamamoto, kosen-rufu is here! The time has arrived at last!" Shin'ichi also announced that the Soka Gakkai had realized President Toda's goals of three-million-member households and of opening the way for the spread of the Daishonin's teachings throughout Asia.

In fact, the Soka Gakkai now had more than 3.6 million households. Seven chapters had already been established in other parts of Asia where President Toda desired so much to shine the light of happiness. The foundation for worldwide kosen-rufu was steadily being built.

Shin'ichi declared that, based on the Daishonin's Buddhism, the Soka Gakkai would without a doubt lead all the people of Japan to happiness. He closed by saying: "My sincerest wish is that all of you will put faith first and enjoy wonderful benefit in your lives. I hope our leaders will do their utmost to serve the members toward that end. We must never grow arrogant or negligent because of the Soka Gakkai's tremendous growth.

"Let us be humble about our victories and continue to advance in high spirits one step at a time as allies of the people."

After this joyous leaders meeting, the completion ceremony for the new headquarters building was held in

Shinanomachi at 1:30 P.M. The pristine white structure sparkled against the cloudless sky. The site measured 14,639 square feet, and the building itself covered 10,226 square feet. With four stories and a basement, it boasted a total floor space of 41,355 square feet. Its surface was plain concrete inlaid with pieces of marble. The solid diagonal pillars gave the building a feeling of simple fortitude and grandeur.

The members' eyes glistened and their faces beamed as they took in the splendid edifice. They were excited to think of the fresh surge of progress that would arise from this place.

NOTHING could have made Shin'ichi happier than to witness his fellow members' joy at the completion of the new Soka Gakkai Headquarters building in Shinanomachi. Thinking back, he recalled that for the first eight years after President Toda had been released from prison on July 3, 1945, the Soka Gakkai had no place of its own. During that time, President Toda was busy rebuilding the organization, and the second floor of his business offices in Nishi Kanda, Tokyo, served as the Soka Gakkai Headquarters. It was here that he held lectures on the Lotus Sutra and established the young men's and young women's divisions.

This was also where the Soka Gakkai's Joju Gohonzon bearing the inscription "For the Fulfillment of the Great Desire for Kosen-rufu Through the Compassionate Propagation of the Great Law" was enshrined. From here, the organization had launched its colossal effort to introduce seven hundred and fifty thousand households to the Daishonin's Buddhism.

During those eight years, whenever a senior leader would propose constructing a headquarters, President Toda would flatly reply: "We don't need a building. That's just an outward form. Wherever I am is the headquarters!"

In fact, however, no one felt the need for an independent headquarters building more than President Toda. At his offices in Nishi Kanda, only two rooms were available for Soka Gakkai use and both were quite small. People who came to attend meetings or to receive guidance would often overflow from the building into the street. President Toda felt terrible about those members who could not enter, and it pained him to no end to see them standing in the cold and rain.

Since he could not afford to build a headquarters on his own, doing so would require asking the members for donations. At that time, however, most Soka Gakkai members were so poor that they could barely make ends meet. Not wanting to increase their burden, President Toda decided to hold off on the construction of a headquarters building until a later date.

When he was alone with Shin'ichi, President Toda often shared his true feelings. "Shin'ichi," he would say, "let's build a magnificent headquarters building someday. I'd like the Soka Gakkai to have other great structures, too."

Plans for a Headquarters building finally took shape in the summer of 1952. Things were going smoothly when the Soka Gakkai purchased a lot measuring 15,096 square feet at Twenty-five Shinanomachi, Shinjuku Ward, near the Nishi Kanda Headquarters, but soon they hit a snag. The five-story pagoda at the head temple had sustained weather damage, and repairs were urgently needed. President Toda gave first priority to maintenance of the head temple and set about repairing the pagoda.

REPAIRING the five-story pagoda depleted the Soka Gakkai's funds for building a headquarters. As a result, in 1953, they sold the land they had bought a year earlier and purchased instead an old Western-style building with an area of 7,353 square feet at Thirty-two Shinanomachi and refurbished it. In November that year, the Soka Gakkai Headquarters moved to this building in Shinanomachi.

For the next nine years, this was the base camp for kosen-rufu activities. Many members received guidance and encouragement from President Toda there. It was a training center for the nurturing of new energy. The ceremony officially recommending Shin'ichi as the third president of the Soka Gakkai after President Toda's death also took place in this building.

Plans for tearing down the old building and putting up a new one on the same site had been under consideration even while President Toda was alive. After Shin'ichi became president, however, the Soka Gakkai's movement experienced such great progress as well as a dramatic increase in membership that the need for a new headquarters building became urgent. The project was therefore undertaken at last.

Stones from forty-two nations around the world, from locations such as Egypt and the Ganges River in India, were encased in the concrete base of the altar where the Joju Gohonzon was to be enshrined. Shin'ichi had collected these stones on his overseas travels, and he had them placed there to symbolize the prayer for world peace.

The basement of the new headquarters contained a utility and electric facilities, a cafeteria and storage space. The first floor had a lobby, offices and reception rooms. On the second floor were more offices, meeting rooms, reception rooms, and rooms for each Soka Gakkai division. On the third floor were a large main Gohonzon room and the president's office, and on the fourth was a large conference hall.

The completion ceremony took place in the Gohonzon room on the third floor. Amid the joyous voices of members reciting the sutra and chanting daimoku, Shin'ichi vowed that from this new headquarters he would continue giving his all in leading worldwide kosen-rufu.

Addressing the participants, Shin'ichi said: "For the first time in the thirty-five years since President Makiguchi took faith in the Daishonin's Buddhism and began to spread its teachings far and wide, the Soka Gakkai has built a real headquarters. This headquarters is a castle of the Law dedicated to kosen-rufu. It is a castle of champions who work for the people's happiness. Though there is a room for each Soka Gakkai division here, I hope you will make the most of all the facilities in your respective activities.

"I hope all of you will take full responsibility for our movement, becoming allies to those who are suffering and courageously taking the lead in spreading this Buddhism throughout Japan and the world." The sunlight streaming in through the large windows of the new building illuminated the faces of all present.

MANY GUESTS attended the reception that was held after the completion ceremony. Shin'ichi Yamamoto walked around the room greeting everyone and thanking them for coming. Some commented to him on the new headquarters: "It combines grandeur and simplicity." "It exudes the strength of a great ship!"

Among the guests were people from the neighborhood. "Thank you for taking the time to join us today," Shin'ichi said to them. "I'm Soka Gakkai President Yamamoto. There will be a lot of traffic passing through this building, but we will do our best not to be too much of a nuisance. I sincerely hope we will enjoy your continued support.

"We want to do whatever we can for the community, so please let us know if there is anything you need from us," he said, bowing politely. The neighbors at the reception seemed surprised and grateful for Shin'ichi's remarks. The reception ended in high spirits.

To gain understanding and support for Soka Gakkai activities and spread the teachings of Buddhism in the community, it is crucial to be considerate of those living near Soka Gakkai facilities. The organization will only develop as a movement firmly rooted in society if the communities where its centers are located thrive, and the people living there feel secure and undisturbed by their presence. The reception ended amid high spirits.

The Soka Gakkai initiated a fresh wave of activities with the new headquarters as its focal point. The members advanced toward the essential phase that would commence the following year on the seventh memorial (sixth anniversary) of second Soka Gakkai president Josei Toda's death on April 2. The essential phase referred to a time when every area of human endeavor, including education, art, government and finance, would be brought to full bloom upon the current foundation of kosen-rufu. It was a move from theory to action; a time when the humanity of Buddhist philosophy and ideals of respect and compassion for life would be actively applied in society. Moreover, they would contribute substantially to social prosperity and peace.

It was also the age in which Shin'ichi, having fulfilled

the vow he made to his mentor to achieve a membership of three million households, would create his own
vision of kosen-rufu as the disciple, spreading his wings
and taking flight toward its realization.

Around this time, a wave of excitement was sweeping
the young women's division. Shin'ichi had published
guidelines for them in the editorial of the September
issue of *The Daibyakurenge,* the Soka Gakkai monthly
study journal. This was the first time they had received
concrete guidelines from Shin'ichi, and young women
around the country were overjoyed.

THE EDITORIAL BEGAN, "My mentor often
said that the young women's division members
should be as bright and beautiful as the sun." President
Toda had continuously prayed for the happiness of the
Soka Gakkai young women. After sharing his words,
Shin'ichi discussed how in the course of history women
have wept over their destiny while enduring the shack-
les of social oppression. He then explained the Lotus
Sutra's teaching of the enlightenment of women, stating,
"In other words, by firmly maintaining a correct view of
life, of daily living and of society, you can create value
toward realizing happiness in your families, your work-
place and society."

He encouraged them not to allow their circumstances
to control or sway them and thereby succumb to misery
as had happened so often in the past. Emphasizing the
importance of carrying out their mission in this life, he
further urged them to act boldly in all fields of endeavor.

Shin'ichi asked that they not be subservient or

ingratiating, but that they hold their heads high as truly modern women of wit, culture and passion taking the lead in building a new age. Their mission, he said, was to work for social prosperity and world peace while striving to become happy themselves. He suggested four practical guidelines for them to apply in their daily lives toward that end:

1) Devote yourself wholeheartedly in faith and practice, and study the teachings of Buddhism in earnest.
2) Ensure that Soka Gakkai meetings attended by young women's division members are always warm and brimming with joy and compassion.
3) Enjoy each day by establishing a positive rhythm in daily activities at work and at home.
4) When choosing a marriage partner, seek the advice and counsel not only of your parents, but also of fellow members and seniors, and look to the graduates of the young women's division as models for how to build a happy life.

Shin'ichi then cited a few passages from Nichiren Daishonin's writings, including "There should be no discrimination among those who propagate the five characters of Myoho-renge-kyo in the Latter Day of the Law, be they men or women" (WND, 385).

"As young women who uphold and protect the Mystic Law," he declared, "you are all children and emissaries of the Great King of the Law." He ended his article, saying: "At this time of the creation of a 'third civilization,' it is my great hope that the members of the young women's division will surpass even Joan of Arc, who saved her homeland of France."

No leader of Japanese society at the time had ever charged young women with a lofty mission or encouraged them to change society and the nation. It was in this climate that Shin'ichi entrusted the Soka Gakkai young women with the responsibility of building a peaceful society based upon the humanistic ideals of Buddhism.

JAPAN had entered a period of rapid economic growth and was becoming wealthier by the year. People had begun to spend more money and leisure activities were on the rise. At the same time, young women were becoming more self-centered. Interested only in superficial glamour, they were starting to lose touch with their spiritual core. This concerned Shin'ichi.

No real joy is to be found in a life that seeks only personal happiness and self-interest. Furthermore, preoccupation with glamour or image and spiritual emptiness are two sides of the same coin.

The key to living a truly wonderful life is to build a strong spiritual center during one's youth. To do so, we need a sound philosophy. Shin'ichi dedicated his editorial in the *Daibyakurenge* to young women because he wanted them to exercise their full potential in benefiting others and society as a whole, to create real value and genuine happiness in their lives.

Shin'ichi's article gave these young women a clear direction in which to proceed. They were overjoyed and rose excitedly to the challenge of changing the course of the history of women. With their motto "Be a Joan of Arc of the Mystic Law," they brightened their discussion meetings and places of work with fresh smiles that sparkled like a pure stream.

Shin'ichi spent the month of September devoting himself to the growth and development of young people. He attended a series of Soka Gakkai youth division sports events, including the Tohoku Sports Festival (September 8), the East-West Swimming Competition in Osaka (September 14), the Kansai Sports Festival (September 15), the Tokyo Sports Festival (September 21), the All-Japan Sports Festival (September 22), and the All-Japan Judo and Kendo Meet (September 30).

He also attended the first meeting of the editorial

committee of the student division journal, where he and committee members considered names for the new publication. They finally decided on *Gakusei Journal* (Student Journal). This later became *Gakuen Journal* (School Journal), and then *Daigaku Shimpo* (University News). Years later the student division journal was dissolved to make way for the present journal of the youth division, *Soka Shimpo* (Soka News).

Helping youth develop means meeting them face-to-face, talking and working with them, and giving them inspiration. Shin'ichi gave himself wholeheartedly each day to raising the next generation, while at the same time leading the kosen-rufu movement.

IN OCTOBER, district leaders meetings for each local headquarters in the Tokyo and Kanto regions were held in succession at the Soka Gakkai Headquarters in Shinanomachi. The new building was for use by all members. Shin'ichi was eager to make a fresh start from the headquarters with these men's and women's division district leaders, who were the main support and center of chapter activities.

He attended all of the district leaders meetings, conducting question-and-answer sessions and pouring his life into encouraging the participants. Until now, he had met with men's and women's division chapter leaders on numerous occasions to offer guidance and encouragement, but he hadn't had many opportunities to meet with district-level leaders. Shin'ichi felt the time had come to spark a new surge of progress by focusing on district leaders.

During this time, while traveling to Kushiro and

Muroran in Hokkaido, the Tohoku and Chugoku regions, and other parts of Japan to encourage the members and offer guidance, Shin'ichi was also steadily building a base for the Soka Gakkai's cultural movement.

On September 15, the opening ceremony for the Asian Culture Research Center in Kansai was held, and on October 18, a concert to celebrate the establishment of the Min-On Concert Association took place at Bunkyo Civic Hall in Tokyo.

Shin'ichi conceived the idea of the Min-On Concert Association during his first visit to India and Southeast Asia in February 1961 as he was traveling back from India through Burma (now Myanmar) toward Thailand and Cambodia. Shin'ichi's elder brother died in Burma during World War II, and throughout that trip he thought about what was needed for humanity to break away from the tragedy of war and build lasting peace. He realized that some means of promoting mutual understanding among the peoples of the world was indispensable to this end, and that cultural exchange through music and the other arts was essential. Shin'ichi decided to found an organization with the Soka Gakkai as the parent body for the purpose of promoting exchange in music and the arts.

The Soka Gakkai leadership carefully considered the matter, and at the second national convention of the Education Department on August 1 that year, Shin'ichi announced plans for forming a cultural association. A preparatory committee was set up and final steps taken toward the association's establishment. This included selecting its name, defining its guiding principles and goals, choosing its president and directors, and proposing a concrete program of events.

On October 18, a concert celebrating the association's establishment was held. It began at 6:30 P.M. with a rousing performance of the march "Anchors Aweigh" by selected members of the Soka Gakkai Brass Band. The logo of the Min-On Concert Association, a stylized design of musical notes, hung at the back of the stage.

THE EVENT celebrating the founding of the Min-On Concert Association featured a chorus, a musical ensemble and performances by a leading violinist and cellist. The president of a local music college gave a brief congratulatory speech on behalf of the other guests, followed by words from Eisuke Akizuki, who had been appointed Min-On's executive vice president.

Akizuki began by stating that the full name of the organization was Minshu Ongaku Kyokai, or "The People's Concert Association," and that its goal was to promote music widely for all to enjoy. He explained that at first there was talk of calling it "The Public Concert Association," but Soka Gakkai President Shin'ichi Yamamoto had suggested changing it to "people's" to express that it is the people who are the true sovereign of society and the nation, and they play the leading role in fostering music and the arts.

Akizuki continued: "I would next like to introduce the five principles of the Min-On Concert Association. They are: 1) to promote a vibrant and thriving musical movement widely among the people; 2) to create and develop a new music for the people; 3) to promote music education

for youth, and raise the general level of music appreciation, toward the realization of a rich cultural life for the
people; 4) to deepen international cultural exchanges
through music and establish friendly ties linking people
around the world; and 5) to foster musicians and present
their finest works and performances at home and abroad.

"In order to develop a new musical movement of the
people in accord with these five principles, the association will sponsor regular performances, which will
include the metropolitan areas. Our goal is to create a
new current in music culture that will return music to
the people."

After Akizuki finished speaking, Hiroshi Izumida, a
Soka Gakkai vice general director and now executive
president of Min-On, asked the audience for its continued support of the association and its activities. Next, the
Fuji Wind Ensemble played the *Light Cavalry Overture*
and other pieces, and for the finale, the famous Japanese
composer and conductor Hidemaro Konoe conducted
the march, "Old Comrades."

When the performance was finished, the hall erupted
in enthusiastic applause. This was the Min-On Concert
Association's maiden voyage into society as the flagship
of a new musical and cultural movement of the people.
There were many guests in attendance that day, and they
all expressed support for Min-On's guiding principles
and goals. Such a flourishing of music born from the
people was long-awaited.

AT THE TIME, the average person in Japan listened
mostly to popular music, but wasn't so familiar with

classical music or opera. Tickets to such concerts were very expensive, most likely because promoters were looking to make a profit, which made them inaccessible to a large part of the population. Shin'ichi believed that the first priority of the Min-On Concert Association was to provide people with an opportunity to enjoy all types of music, including classical, opera and that of the traditional Japanese variety.

Music is for everyone. It is not the exclusive possession of the privileged or wealthy.

The Workers' Music Councils (Ro-On) was another major organization promoting musical appreciation at the time, but most people thought it was too political and ideological. In 1963, the same year of Min-On's founding, the Japan Federation of Employers' Associations established the Musical Culture Association (On-Kyo), but its scope was still rather small.

Shin'ichi was pleased with the prospect that both of these organizations might also offer fine music to a broad spectrum of people. His hope was that Min-On's birth would spark the creation of fresh culture by giving ordinary people more opportunities to experience music of the highest caliber.

During the concert celebrating the founding of Min-On, Shin'ichi was at Soka Gakkai Headquarters chanting for the success of the event and the association's growth and development. After the concert was over, Hiroshi Izumida and Eisuke Akizuki returned to the headquarters. It was just after 10:00 P.M.

"It was a great success," Izumida told Shin'ichi. "The

guests were very receptive to the founding principles of Min-On, and they expressed great hopes for its future."

"That's wonderful. Congratulations!" said Shin'ichi.

Akizuki elaborated: "Actually, until tonight's concert, many people in the music world seem to have been of the opinion that the Soka Gakkai founded Min-On in order to use music and art to expand its influence.

"Also, one guest asked whether Min-On would avoid sponsoring performances of music related to any other religion, such as that celebrating Christmas. Since the Soka Gakkai does not compromise in matters of religion, this person thought that Min-On, as an affiliated organization, would reject any art or music that had religious overtones."

Izumida then added: "Mr. Akizuki, there are some Soka Gakkai members who think the same thing."

THE SOKA GAKKAI has always distinguished clearly between superior and inferior, deep and shallow, and correct and erroneous when it comes to religious teachings. This is because whether we are genuinely happy or not is determined by the beliefs we uphold. Consequently, there were many members who felt uncomfortable about performing or listening to music that was related to other religious traditions.

Religion and art are certainly intertwined. Religion cultivates the earth of our being, our life itself, while art brings the flowers and fruits of culture to bloom in that earth. Appreciating the art that is born from a particular religious tradition, however, is not the same as believing in that religion. Though religious feeling may be the wellspring of artistic creation, once the art is created, it transcends religion.

A beautiful flower delights and refreshes the hearts of all people equally, no matter what soil it grows in. That is the power of beauty. The same is true of great art. It is this spirit that the German poet Heinrich Heine sang of when he wrote that once the peapod bursts open, the sugar peas inside are for everyone to enjoy.[16]

To categorize art by its religious or ideological content and reject it on that basis is to reject humanity itself. Furthermore, Buddhism teaches respect for the dignity of life, of freedom and equality. It is a philosophy of compassion that enables us to bring our humanity to full bloom. Since the Soka Gakkai's musical movement is based on Buddhism, it is completely mistaken to categorize and reject any music that is an expression of our shared humanity. This was Shin'ichi's feeling and also his firmest conviction.

Shin'ichi addressed Izumida and Akizuki: "I am concerned about Soka Gakkai members falling into a narrow and dogmatic way of thinking. Our strictness is aimed at religious teachings themselves. We must make it understood by both our membership and society that we are entirely open-minded when it comes to art and culture.

"Art is not a slave to ideology or politics, nor is it a slave to religion. It has a value all its own, and so it is only natural to recognize and treasure it. Furthermore, I have not the slightest intent to use the activities of the Min-On Concert Association to propagate Nichiren Daishonin's

Buddhism or bring music lovers into the Soka Gakkai. That must also be made very clear. My purpose in founding Min-On is to return music to the people. It is to create a humanistic culture, join the hearts of people around the world through music, and contribute to world peace."

SHIN'ICHI spoke with determination: "Many religions have used art and culture and even the cause of peace as a means to expand their influence. Rather than seeking to develop and contribute to the arts, they have exploited them temporarily for their own interests. Such pretension, however, cannot endure. Eventually, the true intentions of such religions are exposed and those who were once supporters begin to leave. Deceit is always uncovered in the end.

"But our movement for culture and peace is different. Our goal is to contribute to the arts. We are serious about this. We are advancing a great movement for the people, for humanity.

"At first, many people will probably be skeptical about our motives, but eventually they will see that they are wrong. Thirty or forty years down the road, they will appreciate the profound significance Min-On has come to have in society. At the same time, it is up to us to make that happen. I want Min-On to become a global music association. I want people to say that it revived the musical world, that it gave rise to wonderful music, and that it linked the hearts of people and united the planet."

Izumida and Akizuki nodded deeply in agreement.

The Min-On Concert Association soon expanded

nationwide, and in January 1965 it was incorporated as a foundation. It went on to make great contributions to music and art, growing into a major Japanese musical and cultural organization with 1.3 million members.

Its activities were varied, and it sponsored concerts of a vast range of musical genres, including classical, popular and traditional Japanese. It also promoted free town concerts, as well as school concerts to contribute to the musical education of children and young people. In addition, it started the Tokyo International Music Competition to discover and foster new musical talent.

As part of its international exchange activities, in 1965 Min-On brought an Israeli pianist to Japan, and in the following year the Soviet National Academy Novosibirsk Ballet. Later it sponsored in Japan tours of world-renowned companies such as the Vienna State Opera and the Scala Theater of Milan. It also sent many Japanese musicians and dance troupes overseas. Its international exchange activities have extended to seventy-seven countries and regions to date.

The establishment of the Min-On Concert Association under the auspices of the Soka Gakkai breathed fresh life into the world of music and art in Japan.

AROUND THIS TIME, a serious problem arose in a certain region of Japan involving a region leader and money.

The situation came to light through the courageous actions of a young women's leader named Yukiko Kishizaka. She had a good head on her shoulders and a strong sense of right and wrong. When she went to visit and encourage the young women in her area, she also got along well with their mothers. She was trusted by the women's division, too.

The incident took place in the spring of 1963. Kishizaka was at her job as a bank teller when a women's division member she was acquainted with came to her window. The woman, who ran her own business, addressed Kishizaka in a low voice: "I'd like to talk to you about my financial situation. Would you mind coming by my house when you get off work today?"

Kishizaka supposed that the woman wanted to talk about her fixed deposit account or some similar matter, and so that evening she headed toward the woman's house lightheartedly. When she got there, however, she was told a rather upsetting story.

"The truth is, I lent Koji Numayama 100,000 yen, but it's been quite a long time, and he hasn't repaid me. I don't know what to do," explained the woman.

Koji Numayama was a central figure in the region. Kishizaka was speechless. From the time of second Soka Gakkai president Josei Toda, borrowing and lending money among Soka Gakkai members was strictly forbidden. There was no way Numayama could not have known this.

"Have you asked him to repay you?" asked Kishizaka.

"No," replied the woman.

"It has always been a rule that Soka Gakkai members don't lend or borrow money among one another," said Kishizaka. "It is especially wrong for a leader to borrow money from the members. It may be hard for you to speak up to him because he is a leader, but I think you should be brave, come right out and ask him to repay the loan.

"I'll also discuss this with the appropriate people," she promised.

Kishizaka almost could not believe what she had heard, but subsequently two other women came to her with the same story: that Numayama had borrowed money from them and had not repaid it. They, too, asked for her advice because they were at their wit's end. At the same time, they did not want to cause any trouble.

This was a very serious problem, and Kishizaka was at a loss for what to do. She realized that she should report the incidents immediately to the top men's and women's leaders in the region, but she did not want to seem like she was being a snitch.

She spent several days mulling over the situation.

KISHIZAKA knew Numayama because they had participated in Soka Gakkai activities together. After pondering the matter for several days, she decided to go directly to him and ask him about the stories she had heard. Then, if need be, she would issue him a warning.

Kishizaka paid a visit to Numayama's home in late September. Her heart was heavy. When Numayama appeared in the entranceway, she got right to the point: "I have something I want to talk to you about. You know, Mr. Numayama, that lending and borrowing money among Soka Gakkai members is strictly prohibited, don't you?"

He nodded without expression.

Kishizaka related each of the incidents that she had heard about to Numayama, who stood there in silence growing clearly annoyed.

"Are these stories true?" Kishizaka asked. "If they are, I hope that you will find a way to return the money. Please. I think it is outrageous for a Soka Gakkai leader to behave in this fashion."

At this, Numayama became incensed, and his manner suddenly transformed. "What right is it of yours to tell me what to do?!" he yelled.

He looked ready to strike Kishizaka. Just then, his wife Mieko, who was a women's leader, rushed to where they were. She had been listening to their conversation.

"Ms. Kishizaka," she said, "It's not his fault. I made him do it. I'm the one to blame, so please forgive my husband!"

She pleaded with Kishizaka, tears in her eyes. Returning to his senses, Numayama began muttering excuses. The company he was co-managing was facing difficulties, and he was desperately trying to raise funds but to no avail. An earlier business of his had also failed, and he borrowed money to pay back those debts, too.

"In any case," Kishizaka said sharply, "you know that it is wrong to borrow money from Soka Gakkai members, don't you?"

"You're absolutely right," replied Mieko. "I know what we've done is inexcusable. But don't worry, we will pay everyone back right away."

Believing the problem now solved, Kishizaka felt as if a great weight had been lifted from her shoulders. But when she saw one of the women who had lent money to Numayama again some time later, she learned that he still had not repaid the loan.

KISHIZAKA began to suspect that the problem of Numayama borrowing money from members ran much deeper than she had originally thought. Several days later, she met with a men's region leader and reported what she had heard. The leader could not hide his astonishment: "Is that what he's been doing? How many members has he borrowed from?"

"I don't know the full extent of it, but I have heard of several incidents," Kishizaka replied.

Realizing the gravity of the situation, the leader immediately contacted Soka Gakkai Headquarters for instructions. Without delay, a vice general director and other senior leaders in charge of the region began an investigation into the matter.

Their inquiry revealed that Numayama had borrowed money from more members than anyone had imagined, and that he had accumulated an enormous debt.

Furthermore, in each case, he had done it by cleverly exploiting the members' faith. One of his victims, a men's district leader named Shotaro Okajima, had been tricked into loaning Numayama some 1.8 million yen. Okajima ran his own company, and business was going smoothly. Numayama would frequently visit his home and ask about the business. Okajima was grateful for Numayama's interest, feeling it was a sign that he was a leader who really cared about the members.

One day Numayama said to Okajima with a serious look, "To tell you the truth, I'm in a bit of a bind...." He went on to explain that the payments from a certain area for the *Seikyo Shimbun* had not yet arrived. The area was rather remote and lacked good transportation, which meant that it often took three or four days for money and goods sent from there to be delivered. At that time, the system for selling and distributing newspapers was in the process of being established across Japan, and there were still some regions that collected *Seikyo Shimbun* payments through the local Soka Gakkai organization. Today, with a daily circulation of 5.5 million nationwide, the *Seikyo Shimbun* is operated through a system independent of the Soka Gakkai organization.[17]

"Remittance of the payment can't be late," Numayama said, "so I was wondering if you could cover the outstanding amount temporarily. I'll return it to you as soon as the money arrives."

This sounded like an emergency to Okajima. It just so happened that it was payday for his fifteen employees, and he had five hundred thousand yen on hand, which he lent on the spot to Numayama. Okajima trusted Numayama as a Soka Gakkai leader, so he did not even ask for an IOU. Okajima believed wholeheartedly that the newspaper payment would arrive soon and that Numayama would then repay him. Numayama's story, however, was a complete fabrication.

ONE MONTH passed, then another. Numayama didn't repay the loan or say another word about it. Then, three months later, Numayama appeared at Okajima's home unannounced. Okajima naturally thought he had come to repay him, but instead Numayama had a surprising announcement: "We're in another jam. The members' payments for the visit to the head temple have not arrived."

Okajima cut him off before he could say anything further: "Mr. Numayama, you haven't returned the money you borrowed for the newspaper payment yet."

"I know," Numayama replied. "We still haven't received it, and now the money for the pilgrimage hasn't arrived either, which only makes matters worse. It comes to about one million yen, and if it isn't paid, the members won't be able to go."

Seeing Numayama's troubled expression, the good-hearted Okajima thought: "A million yen is a lot of money, but it will be terrible if the members can't visit the head temple. I'll take care of it somehow. It's for the sake of my fellow members, after all." He went to the bank, withdrew the money and gave it to Numayama.

Some time later, Numayama showed up at Okajima's home again. Without the slightest hesitancy, he asked for another loan: "Leaders are coming from Tokyo and I have to take them to dinner and entertain them, but I don't have any cash on hand. Can you help me out, Mr. Okajima?" Once again, he entreated Okajima in earnest.

The entertainment of leaders was prohibited in the Soka Gakkai. Unaware of this, Okajima lent Numayama the money, thinking that if it was indeed necessary for him to entertain visiting leaders from the headquarters, it was sure to be expensive.

By now Okajima had lent Numayama more than 1.8 million yen, but Numayama showed no sign of returning any of it. When Okajima asked him if the newspaper or pilgrimage payments had arrived yet, Numayama, clearly annoyed, replied, "Not yet."

Eventually, Okajima came to suspect that something was not right. Numayama may have noticed that Okajima was starting to get suspicious, because one day, as if trying to curry favor, he visited Okajima carrying an incense container that he said he received from the high priest at the head temple. "This is very valuable," he said. "I'd like to give it to you."

"I don't want it," Okajima retorted. Then he asked for his money back.

"I don't have any money," Numayama said. He defiantly added, "It hasn't arrived yet. There's nothing I can do about it!"

Realizing he had been duped, Okajima shook with anger.

KOJI NUMAYAMA had deceived several other Soka Gakkai members by the same method of borrowing money from them under false pretenses. A group leader had ended up lending him 1.65 million yen after Numayama told him that payments for the pilgrimage to the head temple and donations from members living in remote areas had not arrived. As the investigation proceeded, it became clear that his wife, Mieko, had also acted in an inappropriate manner. Exploiting her role as a central leader in the women's division, she would make frequent trips to the chapter office presenting a variety of excuses in order to be reimbursed for such expenses as her personal taxi fares.

Mieko was extravagant and liked to show off. She

always wore the most expensive clothes and would call a taxi for even minor shopping trips. Spendthrift that she was, she admitted to Yukiko Kishizaka that she had indeed pushed her husband to borrow money.

The Numayamas had joined the Soka Gakkai about a decade earlier. At the beginning, both of them participated eagerly in Soka Gakkai activities. They were soon appointed district leaders of their respective divisions. Their marital relationship was rocky, however, and they were always fighting. Mieko had a reputation as a flirt, and there were constant rumors about her involvement with other men. But Koji was clumsy with words, and he had no chance of holding his own in an argument with Mieko, who could talk her way out of anything.

Members of their district were frequent witnesses to their arguments, and they were fed up with it. Even though they felt it best not to interfere in the marital problems of another couple, the consensus was that Mieko was to blame, and that Koji did not deserve the treatment he got.

One day, Mieko received guidance from second Soka Gakkai president Josei Toda. After she laid out her husband's many faults, President Toda addressed her sternly: "You are the worst wife in the world. Don't you see that you are completely undermining your husband? Stop complaining about him and take a look at yourself!" President Toda saw right through her.

After that, it seemed to those around Mieko that she was seriously reflecting on her behavior. She and Koji later became chapter leaders, but then Mieko disappeared. She had run away with another man. Although she returned after a brief interval, it was decided that she should be relieved of her post as chapter women's leader.

SOME YEARS later, Mieko was reinstated as chapter women's leader. Her appointment was met with considerable resistance, but because she showed remorse for her misdeeds and was now getting along well with her husband, it was decided to provide her with another opportunity. Another large reason was that there was not anyone else qualified to fill the position.

As an organization based on faith in Nichiren Daishonin's Buddhism, the Soka Gakkai first and foremost trusts and believes in people, and goodwill toward others is essential to its activities. Mieko was therefore given a second chance. If this had occurred in any other type of organization, where people are not so ready to give others the benefit of the doubt, she would never have been reinstated. But the Soka Gakkai was accepting and forgiving to the point of vulnerability. Negative influences therefore took advantage.

Mieko had a talent for getting people to like her. She was also good at taking care of others. She used these skills to surround herself with a group of admirers, and gradually created a warped relationship of boss and underlings in the local organization. She played favorites in all leadership appointments, building a faithful following and eventually an atmosphere in which no one dared oppose her.

Mieko was merciless against anyone who did not agree with her. She would engage in an insidious campaign of harassment, attacking the person fiercely in front of everyone on the one hand, and completely ignoring anything the person had to say on the other. She came to be known as "the dragon lady," and everyone feared her. Among her cohorts, there were some who, even if she called in the middle of the night saying, "I'm in the mood for some sushi," would drive around town looking for a sushi shop that was open and then deliver it to her.

The local organization was still producing results, however, so the senior leaders in Tokyo had no way of knowing what was actually going on. Still, Shin'ichi Yamamoto was very strict with Mieko. Whenever he met her at leaders gatherings, he would caution her, saying: "The role of leaders is to serve the members. You must never exploit the members for your own purposes."

On one occasion, General Director Koichi Harayama and the leader in charge of Mieko's region proposed to Shin'ichi that she be promoted. "Are you sure that's wise?" Shin'ichi asked.

"IN MY OPINION, yes," the leader in charge replied. "Mieko has a lot of energy and tremendous power."

"It's her character I'm worried about," Shin'ichi said. "The question is how deeply committed she is to faith."

"She's a different person since she was relieved of her post and then reinstated as chapter women's leader," the leader continued. "She's making a real effort. Besides, there isn't anyone else qualified to fill the spot, and she and her husband have worked hard in the area since the early days. I think the members will agree with her appointment."

"Mr. Harayama, as general director, what do you think?" Shin'ichi asked.

"I agree," Harayama said.

Shin'ichi fixed his gaze on both men. "If this matter has been considered carefully by everyone and this is your conclusion, I won't object," he said. "But an error in the appointment of a leader could produce disastrous results. Please look after Mrs. Numayama and regularly offer her guidance."

In fostering top leaders, it is necessary to entrust them with a variety of responsibilities, including personnel matters. There were, however, many cases in which Shin'ichi felt that the Soka Gakkai leaders' decisions were sure to result in problems. Yet if he made every decision, they would not grow into capable leaders. This was Shin'ichi's dilemma.

Fujiko Kakutani, a woman who worked at the local chapter office and had frequent contact with Mieko, was beginning to wonder about Mieko's casual attitude toward money and the fact that she seemed unable to distinguish between her personal expenditures and official Soka Gakkai business. Perhaps Mieko had sensed this, because one day she drew Kakutani aside and said: "As you know, I was dismissed from my post as chapter women's leader. That's why the members still don't completely trust me. But after my dismissal, I began my practice anew as a general member. I knew I had brought it all on myself, but it was still very difficult.

"Once I was relieved of my duties, the people who were close to me changed overnight. They began treating me so coldly. I desperately wanted to receive guidance, but when I showed up at a district leaders' meeting, they turned me away saying I didn't belong there. I felt so sad and lonely. It was awful.

"I went home, sat down in front of the Gohonzon and chanted daimoku in tears. It was all I could do."

LOOKING SORROWFULLY off into the distance, Mieko continued telling her story: "President Yamamoto never said a kind word to me, either—not even after I became chapter women's leader again. But I know he was watching me to see what I would do.

"Then, two years ago, I drove for hours to a town where President Yamamoto was going to give guidance, and I waited for a chance to speak to him. When I finally was able to, for the first time he praised my efforts. I was so happy. 'He understands all of my struggles. That's all that matters,' I thought. I decided then that whatever happened, I wouldn't let myself be defeated and I would follow President Yamamoto as a true disciple."

Tears glistened in Mieko's eyes. She looked at Kakutani again and said: "Ms. Kakutani, there are many complicated issues one must deal with as a leader, things that can't be talked about with others. Taking care of the members requires money. A lot of that ends up coming out of one's own pocket.

"I know there are people trying to get rid of me. But whatever anyone says, I want to devote my life to working for kosen-rufu alongside President Yamamoto. That's my determination."

It was a very moving speech, but it was nothing more than Mieko's attempt to dispel Kakutani's doubts by putting on an act of purity and devotion to President Yamamoto. At the same time, carried away by her own words, Mieko may have been unconsciously justifying her own misdeeds to herself. This is the working of devilish functions in one's mind.

Kakutani did not believe Mieko's story. Why would someone who had "devoted her life to working for kosen-rufu with President Yamamoto" behave in such an irresponsible way? The way in which Mieko described it, right and wrong subtly traded places, and she presented herself as a tragic heroine.

The vice general director and other senior leaders carrying out the investigation met with each of the members who had lent money to Koji Numayama and asked them about the amounts of the loans and the methods that Numayama had used to obtain them. Mieko Numayama was then confronted, and the facts were confirmed. He admitted to every incident without exception. As the full story unfolded, it turned out that he had borrowed a total of more than twenty million yen from members.

AS THE INVESTIGATION of the Numayama affair proceeded and the severity of the situation came to light, the Soka Gakkai Headquarters decided that serious measures needed to be taken to encourage and offer guidance to the members. General Director Koichi Harayama and Vice General Directors Kiyoshi Jujo, Hiroshi Izumida, Hisao Seki, Katsu Kiyohara, Eisuke Akizuki and Seiichiro Haruki were therefore dispatched to the region.

The members who lent money to Koji Numayama knew the Soka Gakkai's strict policy against the lending and borrowing of money among members. But when a leader, Numayama, told them that he was in a fix because payments for the *Seikyo Shimbun*, pilgrimages to the head temple, or donations from the members were late, they lent him the money against their better judgment thinking it was for the sake of kosen-rufu.

If they had followed Soka Gakkai policy, however, the problem would never have occurred. In fact, there were many who avoided being victimized because they did just that. The reason that second Soka Gakkai president, Josei Toda, strictly prohibited borrowing and lending among members was to prevent them from being exploited for financial gain. In addition, the disputes that sometimes arise from such dealings were bound to have an impact on the organization as a whole and rouse sentiments of anger and resentment among members.

Some members felt that it was the individual's right to loan money if he or she saw fit, but to this President Toda said: "I have prohibited the borrowing and lending of money among members, because in the end it will harm members' faith and destroy the Soka Gakkai, an organization that stands for truth and justice. A leader who has borrowed from members will no longer be able to offer them proper guidance, nor will they be objective. Leadership appointments can also be influenced.

"On the other hand, if a member makes a loan to a leader or a fellow member and that person doesn't repay it, the member will begin to doubt his or her faith or the Soka Gakkai, will become resentful, and eventually discard faith altogether. Whenever this has happened in the past, the outcome has been the same. I have prohibited these transactions in order to protect the members. If in spite of this you still want to lend money to another member, go right ahead, but don't expect the Soka Gakkai to have anything to do with it. If you don't get your money back, don't complain. If you simply must lend money, do it as if you were giving it away."

President Toda was so strict about this issue because he wanted to protect the purity of the realm of faith.

Those who had lent money to Mr. Numayama each took different steps to resolve the problem, some even turning to the law. But because it was a leader who had acted so dishonestly, the organization itself was strongly affected.

After returning from the area, General Director Hara-yama and the others discussed the matter and then rec-ommended that both Koji and Mieko Numayama be dismissed from their positions. They asked President Shin'ichi Yamamoto to make the final decision.

SHIN'ICHI agreed to the consensus that the Numa-yamas must be dismissed from their leadership posi-tions. "Of course this is unavoidable," he said. "President Toda said that the Soka Gakkai was more important to him than his own life. It is completely unacceptable for anyone to use the organization for their personal gain and trick members into loaning them money. It is a grave offense that requires a strong response."

Everyone nodded in agreement.

Shin'ichi then said something that took everyone by surprise: "Still, I want to help the Numayamas out somehow."

Clearly baffled, one of the leaders said: "Sensei, these people have caused the Soka Gakkai a great deal of trouble!"

"I know," Shin'ichi replied, "but Mr. Numayama's business is crumbling, and he is going to have a very difficult time repaying all his loans. He's in a desperate situation. When I think of this, I can't help feeling sorry for him.

"If he truly regrets what he has done, I want to personally help him and do something to get him back on his feet."

The leaders were shocked by Shin'ichi's words. Some could not believe how good-hearted he was. Others were moved by his deep concern for the members and how far he would go to help even those who had caused trouble for the Soka Gakkai. In the end, the unscrupulous Numayamas were dismissed from their posts and replaced by Kiyoshi Ohara and his wife, Hisako, who had been active as leaders in another area.

A vice general director remained in the region to follow up on the problems caused by the Numayamas. One day, when the leader was at the member's home that served as the meeting place for the local chapter, Koji Numayama came storming in, in a terrible rage.

"I've worked hard for the Soka Gakkai!" he roared. "How dare you fire me!"

He glared threateningly at the leader.

The vice general director tried to calm him down: "You agreed to your dismissal...."

But Numayama was not in the mood to listen. "You bastard!" he shouted. Then, grabbing the vice general director by the lapels, he struck him.

"You're only going to bring further hardship upon yourself," the vice general director said.

"Shut up!" Numayama spat as he fled the room.

The vice general director dropped his head. It was not that he was surprised or angry at having been hit. He was profoundly disappointed in Numayama, who was not sorry in the least for his actions and knew nothing of Shin'ichi's concern for him.

THE QUESTION of how to deal with the Numa-yamas was taken under further consideration, and in the end it was decided that they would both be expelled from the Soka Gakkai. Shin'ichi viewed this incident as a matter of grave import.

The Numayamas had been pioneers in the local Soka Gakkai movement. For that reason, the other leaders in the area respected them and held them in high regard. For a time they both had participated sincerely in organizational activities. That was why they were made leaders in the first place.

The desire for fame and fortune, personal gain and self-profit exists within everyone. However, when we practice Nichiren Daishonin's Buddhism in earnest and fully dedicate ourselves to working for kosen-rufu, those negative aspects remain dormant. But as soon as we grow negligent and start acting out of force of habit, our negative tendencies emerge to pollute our heart and mind. That is why the Daishonin said, "Strengthen your faith day by day and month after month. Should you slacken in your resolve even a bit, devils will take advantage" (WND, 997).

Faith is a struggle between the devilish functions and the Buddha nature in one's life. There is a fine line between walking the path of attaining Buddhahood in this life as a leader dedicated to kosen-rufu and discarding one's faith and turning against the Soka Gakkai. This change can happen in a single life-moment. Koji and Mieko Numayama were defeated by the negative forces in their lives. They came to see the Soka Gakkai and their fellow members as nothing more than means to their own greedy ends.

How can this problem be prevented? If we see a fellow member deviate even slightly from the guidance of the Soka Gakkai, it is important that we have the courage to point it out and advise against his or her actions immediately, no matter who they may be. By doing so, we will protect both the Soka Gakkai and that person.

The bottom line was that each member needed to develop wisdom. For this to happen, Shin'ichi realized that he must continually encourage the members to be able to spot evil and injustice, and dauntlessly fight against them.

After their expulsion from the Soka Gakkai, the Numayamas' true colors began showing more than ever. They started to attack the Soka Gakkai as if they were the victims. The local members were absolutely astonished. They knew that devilish functions were certain to arise in the effort to spread the Daishonin's teachings, and many had in fact experienced opposition and been criticized for their faith. But this was the first time they had encountered a situation in which leaders who had once guided them in faith had caused serious problems within the organization and then went on to attack it.

MANY MEMBERS were shaken by the Numa-yama incident. When leaders were sent to the area from the Soka Gakkai Headquarters to offer guidance and encouragement to the members, they were frequently asked: "If the Numayamas were appointed leaders because of their strong faith and integrity, why did they behave this way? Who can we trust to guide us in faith?" Their questions were not unreasonable. But in light of the Daishonin's writings, there was nothing extraordinary about what had occurred.

The Daishonin teaches that this world is the realm of the devil king of the sixth heaven, and that as kosen-rufu advances, the devil king begins to fear that he will lose his kingdom to the forces of the Buddha. He therefore uses every conceivable method to persecute the votaries of the Lotus Sutra. The problem caused by the Numayamas was one example of this.

In "Letter to Misawa," the Daishonin describes how the devil king orders his followers to harass the votaries of the Lotus Sutra, saying: "Each of you now go and harass that votary, according to your respective skills.... Enter into the minds of his disciples, lay supporters, and the people of his land and thus try to persuade or threaten him" (WND, 894).

In other words, he instructs them to enter into the minds of believers and, by causing confusion among the Buddha's children, stop the advance of kosen-rufu. That is one highly effective way that negative forces are manifested in order to take people by surprise and cause them to have doubt. Because the movement for kosen-rufu is a never-ending struggle between devilish functions and the champions of the Buddha, those functions will never let up in their effort to provoke corruption among leaders, make them abandon their faith and become enemies of the Soka Gakkai.

This, however, is nothing to be feared. Once we recognize such devilish functions for what they are, we can defeat them. The important thing is not to be led astray by the mere surface of events, but to open wide the eyes of faith and always base our actions on the Daishonin's teachings. Even the most seemingly complex problems become clear when viewed through the eyes of faith.

The leaders that went to the area from the Soka Gakkai Headquarters poured their whole lives into explaining to the members that the aim of devilish functions was to cause people to lose their faith. Kiyoshi and Hisako Ohara, who had been sent to replace the Numayamas, also made an earnest effort to encourage members. They realized that in order to eliminate the doubts that were causing the members to suffer, they themselves had to set an example of what it was to be a true Soka Gakkai leader, thereby conveying the pure stream of faith. This would require a selfless commitment to serving the members and honestly, sincerely speaking with each and every one of them.

KIYOSHI and Hisako Ohara set out on a campaign of earnest, steady efforts to encourage the members. At first, they were not very warmly received. But they regarded this as part of their Buddhist practice and initiated their activities with sincerity and tenacity.

Shin'ichi Yamamoto visited the area at the beginning

of November. He wanted to dispel clouds of doubt from the members' hearts and bring instead a light of hope born from the sun of faith. He also wanted to encourage them because they had fought so hard through their recent struggles. He visited the new community center and talked about what it means to be a Soka Gakkai leader.

"There are people who appear to be doing their utmost for the Soka Gakkai but are really only thinking of ways to exploit it," he said. "Their faith has the basest of motives. There have been such people in the past, and in the end they caused trouble for the Soka Gakkai and betrayed their fellow members. All of them now seriously regret what they have done. This is the strictness of the Buddhist law of cause and effect.

"There are many leaders in our organization, and in the future there will likely be others, who use the Soka Gakkai for their own profit and end up discarding their faith because of lust for fame and fortune. That must not happen to you. All of your efforts in faith will have been meaningless if you end up suffering in the depths of misery.

"I hope you will put faith before all else. No matter what happens, please live in accord with Nichiren Daishonin's teachings, maintaining pure and single-minded faith, and thereby attain Buddhahood in this lifetime."

Shin'ichi also met with several of the women's leaders who had done activities with Mieko. He explained to them at length that faith must always be centered on the Buddhist Law and spoke of the importance of working for kosen-rufu in accord with the guidelines of the Soka

Gakkai. He also stressed that they must not make a mistake in whom they choose to follow.

Shin'ichi wished he could visit the neighborhood in which the Numayamas lived and speak individually with each member there, but his schedule was already packed and would be difficult to change. At the airport on his way back to Tokyo, he sent a telegram to the members. It read: "I promise I will be back soon to give you my support. Please advance in friendship and with vitality and become truly happy."

The local members engraved these words in their hearts and vowed together to make a fresh start.

THE INCIDENT involving the Numayamas brought home to Shin'ichi just how great the influence a wife has over her husband. Hearing the report of the leaders who investigated the matter, it was clear that while on the surface it seemed that Koji was the cause of the problem, in actuality Mieko was the force manipulating him. It is no exaggeration to say that a wife's faith, attitude toward life and way of thinking are a powerful and even decisive influence on her husband's life. For that reason, Shin'ichi felt it was important to take every opportunity to offer guidance to women.

On November 10, Shin'ichi attended the inaugural meeting for the Hokkaido No. 2 Headquarters in Hakodate, Hokkaido. This was his first visit to Hakodate since becoming president. At this meeting, too, Shin'ichi touched on the influence of a wife. He spoke softly, as if he were at an informal gathering of friends: "Today, I have something I want to say to wives. Your strength and power are extremely important factors in how much effort your husbands put into working for kosen-rufu and how well they do at their jobs.

"The Daishonin has compared a husband to an arrow and a wife to a bow (see WND, 656), meaning that a wife's faith has a strong effect on her husband. The wife, in essence, makes the husband who he is. During World War II, the Soka Gakkai challenged the military government and was harshly persecuted for it. Nearly twenty leaders were imprisoned along with Soka Gakkai presidents Tsunesaburo Makiguchi and Josei Toda. At first, all of them were determined to uphold their faith and stand up for justice, but then one by one they gave in and abandoned their faith altogether. Only presidents Makiguchi and Toda were left fighting to the very end.

"What was the reason that those top leaders discarded their faith? It was because their wives quit first, and then urged them to do the same, so that they would be released from jail and return home."

Shin'ichi's voice then grew stronger: "Recently, in a certain region of Japan, a couple who held leadership positions were expelled from the Soka Gakkai. They cheated their fellow members out of huge sums of money, causing a great deal of trouble to many people.

"When the matter was carefully investigated, it turned out that the wife was very fond of luxuries and bought a lot of expensive clothes. She drove her husband to borrow from members to support her extravagant lifestyle. She manipulated him. You may not be aware of it, but that's how powerful an influence a woman has over her husband."

THE WOMEN continued listening carefully to President Yamamoto's guidance. "To put it plainly," he went on, "it is entirely up to you, in your capacities as wives and mothers, whether your husbands or children turn out good or bad. What would happen if the woman of the house became spiteful and consumed by vanity? Or what if she started behaving like the Mother of Demon Children, who doted on her own children but devoured those of others?

"In the end, her husband, children, and those around her would all be unhappy. I therefore hope that each of you will put faith first and strive to achieve your human revolution, so that your husbands may play active roles in the Soka Gakkai and in society, and that your children may grow into fine adults.

"It is also important that you warmly encourage your family members. If your husband becomes negligent in his practice or begins to act in a way that goes against the Soka Gakkai spirit, you can come right out and say to him, 'Honey, what do you think you're doing?' In most cases he will reply meekly, 'I am sorry. I do not know what I was thinking.'"

The audience burst into laughter.

Shin'ichi continued: "Women are the shining suns of faith and happiness in their families. That is why it is vital that they have strong faith. I hope all of you will be reliable, modest and judicious, steering clear of vanity and ostentation, which can destroy your lives. I also hope that you will manage your daily lives wisely and economically, being careful not to be wasteful.

"If, for example, your husband wants to go to Tokyo

to attend a Soka Gakkai meeting but does not have the money, it would be nice if you could hand it to him and say, 'Here honey, I have saved this for you.'

"That is not to put ideas into the heads of the husbands out there! It is just an example."

Again, the audience erupted in laughter.

"No matter what happens, it is important that you do not fall into the muddy swamp of suffering, complaining all the time and feeling envious of others. Please be vibrant and energetic like the sun, boldly following the path of your life each day.

"I hope you will be people who encourage others going through hardship while at the same time taking care of your own families, and who shed the light of hope in your local communities. I am praying wholeheartedly for the success of the tremendous efforts of the women's division members of Hokkaido."

Shin'ichi wanted to sound a warning for the sake of the future.

SHIN'ICHI could not stop thinking about the members in the region where the Numayama incident had occurred. He continuously prayed that they would advance with fresh resolve and become happy.

In mid-January of the following year, 1964, Shin'ichi visited the region again and attended a leaders meeting in the area where the Numayamas had been responsible. He was carrying out the promise he had made in his telegram two months earlier.

The members displayed remarkable growth.

A leader who abandons faith is a manifestation of the

devilish functions that attempt to obstruct the faith of believers. However, when we face such iniquity head on and fight against it to the very end, kosen-rufu accelerates tremendously. A flag needs the opposing force of wind to fly. Similarly, obstacles present us with an opportunity to forge ourselves and deepen our faith. They give us a chance to make wonderful progress in our lives. If we have courage and prayer behind us and actively challenge our personal limitations, we can move everything in a positive direction.

The faces of the members shone brilliantly from having surmounted a great obstacle. Filled with fresh determination to start anew, they were now solidly united as one.

Shin'ichi said to the leaders who came to welcome him: "Congratulations! You have all fought so hard. This region will grow tremendously from now on. As long as there is a pure source of faith flowing like a spring of clear water, there is nothing to fear. Some may try to contaminate such beauty, but a pure stream washes all away.

"I hope you will keep that pure stream of faith running throughout your lives."

Since the time Shin'ichi became the third president of the Soka Gakkai, the tide of the kosen-rufu movement had risen. The number of leaders also increased. With that growth, there were bound to be some who, ambitious for fame and profit, joined the Soka Gakkai and even became leaders with the intention to exploit the organization for their own benefit. No matter how mighty a river the Soka Gakkai becomes, it must always remain an organization of pure, unsullied faith.

In these recent struggles, Shin'ichi could see before him a new issue he would have to face in the future.

It was a beautiful day, with blue skies stretching wide overhead. The sun shone brightly. Shin'ichi felt the arrival of a season of hope.

So what became of Koji and Mieko, the pair who had caused such trouble for the Soka Gakkai, an organization of noble children of the Buddha?

ONE DAY, more than ten years after the Numayama incident, two men turned up at Soka Gakkai Headquarters. One of them was in his sixties and looked pale and depressed. It was Koji Numayama. The man accompanying him was a relative who had been supporting him. Vice President Hisao Seki met with them.

Numayama's appearance was pitiful in the extreme. As if summoning his courage to speak, he said: "My life has gone completely downhill since I was expelled from the Soka Gakkai. It has been a living hell. My family has fallen apart. I am here today to apologize and ask to be taken back into the Soka Gakkai."

The relative cut in: "The Soka Gakkai made use of Mr. Numayama when things were going well, but as soon as things got rough for him, you got rid of him. Is that fair?"

"He was expelled because he did something terrible and caused the Soka Gakkai a lot of trouble! Isn't that right, Mr. Numayama?" Seki responded.

"Yes, that's right," Numayama replied.

Hearing this, the relative turned to him and said angrily, "You didn't tell me that!"

Though Numayama claimed to be sorry for his actions, he had distorted the truth in his favor when telling the story to his relatives. This was another example of his dishonest nature. He was, after all, the same person who, while refusing to admit his own fault, struck the vice general director investigating the incident.

Numayama, however, must have experienced indescribable suffering to have brought himself to the Soka Gakkai Headquarters to apologize. It was a clear testimony to Nichiren Daishonin's teaching that "people who despise the votaries of the Lotus Sutra seem to be free from punishment at first, but eventually they are all doomed to fall" (WND, 997). Seeing Numayama like this drove home to Seki once again the severity of the Buddhist law of cause and effect.

Mieko, on the other hand, later appeared in a number of tabloid magazines, where she broadcast completely fabricated stories about Shin'ichi Yamamoto. She portrayed herself as some kind of victim of the Soka Gakkai, making slanderous statements and outrageous allegations. She even destroyed her Gohonzon, the very foundation of faith.

The powers bent on obstructing the advance of the Soka Gakkai, an organization paving the way for an age of the people, took aim at the linchpin of the Soka Gakkai's unity, Shin'ichi, and tried to bring him down. To those powers, Mieko's accusations, no matter what a tissue of lies they might be, were a valuable weapon with which to attack the Soka Gakkai. They made clever use of her.

THE FORCES that wished to block the rise of the power of the people were willing to use any and every method to crush the Soka Gakkai. That is why kosen-rufu is such a fierce struggle.

Those who abandoned their faith and left the Soka Gakkai after stirring up trouble and causing serious problems always ended up holding a grudge and viciously attacking the Soka Gakkai. One of the reasons for their anger and resentment was their failure to exploit the organization for their own purposes. It was also no doubt a psychological need of these people to overcome the feelings of guilt and inferiority stemming from their deplorable actions. The only way to do that was to try and justify their misdeeds. They painted the Soka Gakkai and Shin'ichi as "great evils" and themselves as the sacrificial victims battling for truth and justice.

This kind of backward thinking is what happens when "evil demons take possession of others." Often, however, the charges made by such people against the Soka Gakkai resembled the very offenses they had committed themselves. For example, those who instigated scandals involving money or sex accused the Soka Gakkai of being a hotbed of such wrongs, and Shin'ichi its leading offender.

An old Japanese expression goes, "A crab digs a hole in the shape of its shell." By the same token, a person's thoughts are a reflection of his or her state of being. There were some who completely accepted these outrageous rumors as the truth, while others saw them for what they were and laughed them off. These reactions, too, were a reflection of those individual's state of being, their character and their views of humanity. People can only judge others and events based on their own experiences and beliefs.

Mieko continued obsessively attacking the Soka Gakkai and Shin'ichi, but she came to a miserable end. In the final years of her life, she called some Soka Gakkai members she had once done activities with and lamented, saying that she wanted to return to the organization. The members were both shocked and angry to hear from her. One woman wanted to shout: "How dare you! After betraying the Soka Gakkai and causing us all so much trouble!"

But she could not bring herself to say it. Mieko's voice was too filled with pain and suffering. The member's pity for her won out.

THEN ONE DAY, Mieko paid a visit to Katsu Kiyohara, the former women's leader. Kiyohara gasped when she saw how Mieko had changed. She was haggard and lifeless, and her face was drawn and pale.

Through labored breaths, Mieko related in a weak voice how she had contracted cancer, and it was spreading. Hanging her head, she said: "I am so sorry that I caused all that trouble for the Soka Gakkai. Please, let me be a member again."

Suffering from illness and facing death, she had been forced to realize the severity of the cause she had made by turning against the Soka Gakkai and betraying the teachings of Buddhism. The offense of inciting discord within the Soka Gakkai, the organization that acts in complete accord with the Buddha's intent and decree, and revolting against it, is extremely profound. As the Daishonin said, "In the Lotus Sutra, it is stipulated that those who bear a grudge against its votary are destined to fall into the Avichi hell" (WND, 892).

Having studied the Daishonin's teachings in the past, Mieko recognized in her illness the limitless depths of her offense. She must have been terrified, feeling like she was in a living hell. What's more, such negative karma passes from one existence to the next.

Seeing Mieko's pitiful state, Ms. Kiyohara felt sorry for her and could not get angry. She was also struck by the severity of the Buddhist law of cause and effect. She said: "Chant daimoku to make amends and eradicate your past misdeeds. As long as you are alive, continue apologizing to the Gohonzon for your actions."

But Mieko died soon after that meeting. It could only be described as a cruel, sad ending to her life.

We can deceive others, but we cannot deceive ourselves. Even if we can, it is impossible to fool the laws of Buddhism. We must be aware that the judgment of the law of cause and effect is absolutely unyielding in its strictness.

The voyage of kosen-rufu is filled with ups and downs. There are strong winds, pounding waves and raging storms. The only way to succeed is to constantly advance with single-minded determination through the wind and waves. Countless friends await us, in this land and that, wandering on the shores of suffering.

Day after day, Shin'ichi held fast to the wheel of the ship of kosen-rufu, steering the way toward the essential phase of the Soka Gakkai's movement. The sails of hope billowing in the breeze, hence, and the whistle of courage piercing the heavens.

Notes

1 Thomas Paine, *Common Sense* (London: Penguin Books, 1986), p. 91.

2 Ibid., p. 100.

3 Ibid., p. 111.

4 Thomas Paine, *Common Sense* (London: Penguin Books, 1986), "Editor's Introduction," p. 29.

5 Ibid.

6 Ibid.

7 Ibid., p. 64.

8 Rajagriha — Capital of the kingdom of Magadha in ancient India, and formerly the center of many new cultural and philosophical movements.

9 Ryokan (1217–1303) — A priest of the Shingon-Ritsu school.

10 Yorimoto — Part of Shijo Kingo's full name.

11 Reverend Hoki — Nikko Shonin's Buddhist name.

12 Koshin region — Area in the central part of Honshu, Japan's main island, encompassing Yamanashi and Nagano prefectures.

13 Hokuriku region — Part of central Honshu that comprises Niigata, Toyama, Ishikawa and Fukui prefectures.

14 Gumma and Tochigi — Neighboring prefectures located in the central part of Honshu, Japan's main island.

15 Yubari Coal Miners Union Incident (1957) — A case of religious discrimination in which miners in Yubari, Hokkaido, were threatened with losing their jobs on account of their belonging to the Soka Gakkai.

16 Cf. Heinrich Heine, "Deutschland Ein Wintermärchen" (Germany, A Winter's Tale) from *Buch der Lieder Deutschland ein Wintermärchen und andere Gedichte* (Munich: Winkler Verlag, 1982), p. 418.

17 Today, with a daily circulation of 5.5 million in Japan, the *Seikyo Shimbun* is operated through a system independent of the Soka Gakkai organization.

Raging Rapids

I N NOVEMBER 1963, a series of tragedies occurred, throwing Japan and the world into turmoil. On November 9, at 3:10 in the afternoon, there was a huge coal-dust explosion at the Mikawa Coal Mine of the Mitsui Miike Mining Station, located in Omuta City, Fukuoka Prefecture, Kyushu. Some four hundred and fifty-eight people were killed and more than eight hundred injured. Even those who managed to survive suffered the painful aftereffects of carbon monoxide poisoning.

At 9:50 that evening, a freight train traveling on the Tokaido Main Line derailed in Tsurumi, Yokohama. A commuter train bound for Tokyo on the Yokosuka Line crashed into it and then collided with another passenger train heading away from Tokyo. Some one hundred and sixty-one passengers were killed, in what came to be known as the Tsurumi Crash.

Outside of Japan, General Duong Van Minh of South Vietnam carried out a military coup d'etat on November 1, and the following day President Ngo Dinh Diem and his brother Ngo Dinh Nhu were executed. Then, before daybreak on November 23, shocking news rocked the globe.

Shin'ichi Yamamoto was awakened by a telephone call shortly before 6:00 A.M. on the morning of the 23. He had arrived in Kagoshima a day earlier to attend the completion ceremony for the Kagoshima Community Center, and was staying at a local hotel.

"Hello. Is this President Yamamoto?" the voice on the other end asked.

It was Vice General Director Kiyoshi Jujo. He sounded tense.

"Mr. Jujo? It's pretty early. Has something happened?"

"Yes. Something awful. I just received a phone call from Headquarters Leader Masaki in America. President John F. Kennedy has been assassinated!"

"What!?"

"It's true. He was visiting Dallas, Texas, and was shot while riding in a motorcade."

"That's terrible. Just terrible!"

Shin'ichi was speechless for a moment, but soon recovered and said: "The first thing to do is send telegrams of condolence to the United States: one to the White

House and another to our members there. I'm sure they're all shocked and saddened."

"Actually," replied Jujo, "a general meeting for Texas District is scheduled for tomorrow, and Mr. Masaki is set to participate."

"Good. Please ask him to encourage the members wholeheartedly. And suggest that they make the meeting a memorial to President Kennedy."

SHIN'ICHI continued: "Also, please express my appreciation to Mr. Masaki for his prompt action in informing us of this tragedy. When conveying important information, speed is of the essence. It's vital to respond swiftly just as he did.

"Thank you, Mr. Jujo."

Shin'ichi hung up and prayed for President Kennedy, chanting daimoku in his heart. Now, he thought, he would never have a chance to meet the president. They had been scheduled to meet in Washington earlier that year in February, but a certain Japanese politician belonging to the ruling party had interfered, and Shin'ichi canceled his plans at the last minute.

Shin'ichi was saddened when he thought of the significant discussions on peace and the future of humanity he would have had with President Kennedy. And he was deeply struck by the uncertainty of human life.

President Kennedy was shot at 12:30 P.M. on November 22, Dallas time, just two-and-a-half hours before Shin'ichi received the call from Jujo. Kennedy had arrived in Dallas that day to speak at a luncheon. He was riding in an open car in a motorcade through the streets of the city. Dallas was a conservative city located in the southern part of the country, and anti-Kennedy feelings were strong among some segments of the populace. Leaflets denouncing the president as a traitor and calling for his arrest had been distributed, and a newspaper advertisement attacked him as a communist sympathizer. His advisors had been concerned about the trip to Dallas, but Kennedy went anyway.

The parade was proceeding according to plan. The governor of Texas, John Connally, and his wife rode in the car with the president and the first lady. The streets along the route were lined with Dallas citizens giving the president's motorcade an enthusiastic welcome.

The car turned onto Elm Street. Suddenly shots rang out. Two bullets struck the president, one in the head. He was rushed to a Dallas hospital, but he died almost instantly. He was only forty-six years old.

When U.S. Secretary of State Dean Rusk, who was on a flight for Japan, heard the news, he said, "God save our nation." The plane was turned around over the Pacific to return to the United States.

With Kennedy's death, Vice President Lyndon Johnson became the new president. Lee Harvey Oswald was arrested as a suspect in the president's assassination, but only two days later was himself gunned down by Jack Ruby. The truth behind this terrible event was thus cloaked in darkness.

AMERICA was terribly shaken by the news of Kennedy's assassination. Many Americans were left speechless. It was as if the sun had disappeared from the sky. Martin Luther King Jr., the leader of the Civil Rights Movement, said to his wife, Coretta: "This is what is going to happen to me also. I keep telling you, this is a sick society."[1]

The tragic event also sent waves of shock and sadness around the world. President Charles De Gaulle of France sent a telegram of condolence in which he conveyed his respect for the president, saying, "President Kennedy died like a soldier under fire, for his duty and in the service of his country."[2] Soviet Premier Nikita Khrushchev, Kennedy's opponent in the Cold War that dominated the world at the time, also sent a telegram immediately expressing his grief and consolation. He wrote: "I am deeply grieved by the news of the tragic death of the out-standing statesman, President John Fitzgerald Kennedy of the United States of America. The death of J. F. Kennedy is a hard blow to all people who cherish the cause of peace and Soviet-American cooperation."[3]

Across the globe flags were flown at half-mast in mourning for Kennedy.

He was elected president in November 1960 after a hard-fought campaign against then Republican Vice President Richard Nixon. In January the following year, at the age of forty-three, he became the thirty-fifth president of the United States.

He had been in office for just over one thousand days when he was killed. But in that short space of time the youthful president had shown strong leadership, endeavoring wholeheartedly to create a better world in the midst of great tumult. When he became president, the Cold War had emerged from a period of relative thaw and was retreating into another harsh winter of opposition between East and West. A little more than six months after Kennedy took office, East–West tensions in Europe increased dramatically. East Germany began construction on the Berlin Wall, which became a long-standing symbol of the Cold War.

Then, in the autumn of 1962, the Cuban Missile Crisis erupted, and humanity was threatened with the possibility of nuclear war. But President Kennedy persisted in opening the path of dialogue with the Soviet Union. With calm, objective judgment and tremendous courage, he was able to defuse the crisis.

Not long after riding out the Cuban Missile Crisis, the president began working in earnest to conclude the Nuclear Test Ban Treaty, which would prohibit nuclear testing. He had directly experienced the madness of the prospect of nuclear war, and was determined to take steps to prevent it. Soviet Premier Khrushchev also showed a positive attitude toward this initiative. President Kennedy had succeeded in turning the threat of war into an opportunity for peace.

NEGOTIATIONS for the Nuclear Test Ban Treaty were complicated, but President Kennedy did not give up hope. In June 1963, he expressed his determination to realize peace in a commencement address to the students of American University in Washington, D.C., "A Strategy of Peace."

"Our problems are man-made, therefore, they can be solved by man,"[4] he declared. He spoke out against the defeatist view that peace was impossible and that humanity was doomed, and stated that human beings possess the wisdom to carve out their own destiny.

The Limited Test Ban Treaty, which prohibited nuclear testing in the atmosphere, in outer space, and under water, was provisionally agreed upon by the United States, the United Kingdom and the Soviet Union on July 25 of that year. The next day, President Kennedy spoke on television, saying, "Yesterday a shaft of light cut into the darkness."[5] This was without a doubt his genuine sentiment, for he believed the treaty to be a first step toward peace.

Theodore Sorensen, President Kennedy's special advisor, described the president as "an idealist without illusions." Sorensen also said, "Kennedy regarded the Test Ban Treaty itself … as more of a beginning than a culmination."[6] The treaty was officially signed in Moscow in August and went into effect in October. It was regarded as the greatest diplomatic achievement of the Kennedy administration.

Of course, the treaty did not amount to a complete ban on nuclear weapons testing and the abolition of nuclear weapons, but the tremendous difficulty in achieving even this limited agreement revealed just how deep the mistrust ran between the Eastern and Western blocs during the Cold War. It was to a large extent Kennedy's personal character that enabled him to melt this wall of icy distrust even slightly. For example, after the Cuban Missile Crisis was resolved, Kennedy gave strict orders that none of his staff make claims of American victory or in any way cause the Soviet Union to feel bested or insulted.

Kennedy could not have achieved what he did without

possessing the flexibility and sensitivity to view things from the standpoint of his negotiation partners. His brother Robert described the president's feelings about the missile crisis, saying, "If it was a triumph, it was a triumph for the next generation and not for any particular government or people."[7]

True to his character, while pursuing the national interest of the United States and establishing policies and strategies to achieve his aims, Kennedy never failed to consider whether his decisions were right and moral.

AS A LEADER, President Kennedy's ultimate weapon was dialogue. In his January 20, 1961, inauguration speech, he said, "Let us never negotiate out of fear. But let us never fear to negotiate."[8] Kennedy regarded no one as an enemy for whom dialogue was impossible, not even if the person were from the opposing communist camp. He always endeavored to keep the lines of communication open. His political stance seemed to signify a new direction that would transcend the Cold War dichotomy of East and West and lead to peaceful coexistence.

Domestically, it was also during Kennedy's term as president that a new social movement gained momentum, one that aimed at combating the racial discrimination and hostility so deeply rooted in American society. This was the rise of the U.S. civil rights movement. Kennedy was very concerned about this issue and seriously grappled with it.

In September 1962, a major event occurred in the civil rights movement when a young black man was refused admission to the University of Mississippi by the university and the state.[9] President Kennedy called the state governor personally to persuade him to comply with federal law and admit the student. But tensions persisted, and in the end some two thousand five hundred protestors stormed the university campus to prevent the young man from registering. Federal troops had to be called in to quell the unrest. Kennedy was not afraid to use confrontational tactics in the name of protecting equality under the law and fighting the deep-seated barriers of racial prejudice.

In 1963, black citizens of Birmingham, Alabama, held large-scale demonstrations against racial discrimination, demanding an end to silence in the face of injustice. In speeches broadcast on television and radio in June, Kennedy spoke of the need for a civil rights law that would guarantee African-Americans equal rights as American citizens: "This nation, for all its hopes and all its boasts, will not be fully free until all its citizens are free,"[10] he declared. Soon afterward, Kennedy presented a comprehensive civil rights bill to Congress.

The year 1963 was the centennial of Abraham Lincoln's Emancipation Proclamation. On August 28, supporters of the civil rights movement from all across the United States gathered in Washington, D.C. More than two hundred and fifty thousand people, the majority black and white, joined hands and marched to the Lincoln Memorial.

THE CIVIL RIGHTS legislation was the fervent wish of all who believed in freedom and equality. Its passage would shine a new ray of hope on human history. At the close of the gathering at the Lincoln Memorial, Martin Luther King Jr. delivered a rousing speech. Turning to the crowd, he cried out, "I have a dream!" The civil rights movement had reached its peak, with its shining dream of a world without discrimination, a world of freedom and equality for all.

President Kennedy, however, was taken from this world without ever seeing his civil rights bill become law. Abraham Lincoln fought against slavery and was assassinated. Kennedy, too, strove to eliminate discrimination, and was felled by an assassin's bullet. To stand up for justice is to live at the edge of death. Without such steadfastness, social change cannot be achieved.

At 6:00 A.M. on November 23, just seventeen-and-a-half hours after President Kennedy was shot, Nagayasu Masaki, chief of the Headquarters in America, and Yuji Nakahara, vice chief of the young men's division North America General Corps, arrived at the Dallas airport. They had flown directly from Los Angeles to attend the general meeting of Colorado Chapter's Texas District.

The sky was scarlet in the dawn, as if reflecting the profound grief and anger of the American people. Some eighty members were present at the general meeting that evening. The president's assassination was a terrible blow to many of them as they greatly loved and respected him.

Soon after the meeting began, there was a telephone call from the Headquarters in Los Angeles communicating the contents of President Shin'ichi Yamamoto's telegram of condolence. Nagayasu Masaki conveyed the message to the members: "All Soka Gakkai members in Japan express deep condolences on the sudden death of the honorable President Kennedy. Sincerely, Yamamoto."

As Masaki read the telegram, his voice shook with emotion. He was so grateful and happy at this indication of President Yamamoto's profound concern for the members in the United States. To many of them, Kennedy's assassination cast a deep and vast pall over the country, the land of freedom and democracy.

Realizing that the future of the country rested on their shoulders, the members renewed their determination to break through that darkness and build true democracy and peace in the United States.

IN JAPAN, news of President Kennedy's assassination dominated television and radio from the morning of November 23. Ironically, it was on this day that the new U.S.-Japan direct satellite television transmission system promoted by President Kennedy was tested for the first time. The first broadcast, which would be sent via U.S. communications satellite beginning at 5:27 and forty-three seconds Japan time, was supposed to commence with an address from the American president to the Japanese people. But Kennedy had been assassinated just two hours earlier, and his prerecorded message was canceled.

The second transmission began at 8:58 A.M. A Japanese special foreign correspondent announced in a somber voice, "People of Japan, we deeply regret that we must begin this exciting test broadcast with tragic news." The news of the assassination was presented briefly, and then the television screen showed images of the life of the president. Next were broadcast scenes of a crestfallen New York City. The picture was extremely clear, almost as sharp as local Japanese broadcasts.

The satellite transmission was a great success. The images it carried, however, conveyed the profound sadness of the people. As Shin'ichi watched the television, he thought deeply about Kennedy the person.

Shin'ichi was fully aware that there were differing opinions about Kennedy's policies as the leader of a major world power. But he was also certain that Kennedy's one thousand days as president had served as a tremendous guidepost for the world and humanity. Shin'ichi regarded the civil rights bill as an especially important achievement, since he was very committed to this cause himself. From his first visit to the United States in October 1960, he had continued to pray for the elimination of racial discrimination there.

Shin'ichi shared many of President Kennedy's ideals. He thought that if he had been in Kennedy's position, he would have done many of the same things. He felt Kennedy's death to be the death of a comrade, and lamented having lost the chance to meet an ally with whom he could have worked to better the world.

SHIN'ICHI considered what he could do in response to the death of his spiritual compatriot, President Kennedy. The answer was clear. He would take Kennedy's aims as his own and work to bring an end to discrimination everywhere. He would build a lasting peace. He vowed that he would not allow the torch of humane ideals that Kennedy had ignited with his very life to burn out.

On November 23, Shin'ichi attended the opening ceremony for the Soka Gakkai Kagoshima Community Center in Kyushu. Kinko Bay stretched out in front of the center, and beyond it the smoke of the volcanic island Sakurajima[11] was visible. For a few moments before the ceremony began, Shin'ichi stood on the second floor of the building, gazing at the magnificent view before him.

As he looked at Sakurajima, he vividly recalled his first visit to Kagoshima. It was in the summer of 1958, five years earlier. He had celebrated the eleventh anniversary of his joining the Soka Gakkai there on August 24. Josei Toda had died on April 2 that year. In the wake of his mentor's death, Shin'ichi had effectively borne complete responsibility for the organization as the sole general administrator.

The year 1958 also marked twenty years since founding Soka Gakkai president Tsunesaburo Makiguchi first visited Kagoshima. It had been the summer of 1938. According to what Shin'ichi heard from President Toda, President Makiguchi had spent some ten days in the city of Kagoshima attending discussion meetings and talking to people about Nichiren Buddhism. These were the first Soka Gakkai discussion meetings to be held in Kyushu.

At that time, even a special express train from Tokyo to the port city of Shimonoseki[12] took eighteen-and-a-half hours, after which one had to board a ferry to cross the Kammon Strait into the port city of Moji on Kyushu. To get to Kagoshima from there required traveling another eight hours by express train.

President Makiguchi was sixty-seven when he made the trip. His efforts to share Buddhism with others never ceased. He would travel to the remotest areas to visit even a single member, offer encouragement, and discuss Buddhism with that person's friends and family. These activities continued until the military authorities arrested him. President Makiguchi struggled right up to the very end. His life was a true example of faith equaling action.

After that first visit, President Makiguchi made three more trips to Kyushu. He once held a meeting under the direct surveillance of the Special Higher Police at which he boldly pointed out the errors of Shinto. Shin'ichi would never forget the day he first set foot in Kagoshima. Thinking of the selfless devotion of President Makiguchi to spreading Nichiren Daishonin's teachings, he had vowed to dedicate his life to carrying on that legacy.

FIVE YEARS had passed, and it was now Shin'ichi Yamamoto's fourth visit to Kagoshima in Kyushu. He knew that the completion of the new community center in Kagoshima would spark a fresh surge in the pace of kosen-rufu there. The Soka Gakkai had become firmly established in Japan. Its activities in other parts of the world, however, were just beginning. Shin'ichi was determined to give himself wholeheartedly throughout his life to spreading Nichiren Daishonin's teachings, until all people everywhere could enjoy peace and absolute happiness. He resolved that this was his mission as a disciple of first Soka Gakkai president Tsunesaburo Makiguchi.

Shin'ichi looked up at the volcano on the island of Sakurajima with that vow in his heart. The plume of smoke rising from the mountain grew thicker and darker before his eyes. He recalled a Japanese poem: "Compared to the burning fire / in my breast / How pale the smoke / of Sakurajima." Hirano Kuniomi, a pro-imperial activist of the last years of the Edo Period, had written it. Shin'ichi felt that the smoke of Sakurajima also paled in comparison to the passion for kosen-rufu burning in his heart.

After the completion ceremony for the Kagoshima Community Center, Shin'ichi went to Fukuoka.[13] On the following day, November 24, he attended back-to-back leaders meetings for the Kyushu region young women's and young men's divisions at the Yahata Public

Auditorium in Kita Kyushu City. Shin'ichi wanted to encourage the members who had lost loved ones in the mining explosion earlier that month, on the 9th. The accident had occurred at the Mitsui Miike Mining Station in Omuta City, Fukuoka Prefecture.

Since first learning of the disaster, Shin'ichi had given various instructions to the central leaders of Kyushu on how to respond. These included personally visiting and offering encouragement to families that had been affected. Spouses and other family members who had lost the family breadwinner were no doubt in deep distress. They may also have been the victims of unfair criticism from people who asked why this tragedy had happened to them if they were practicing Buddhism. Shin'ichi was pained at the thought of their situation.

While in Fukuoka, Shin'ichi heard detailed reports of the circumstances of members who had been struck by the disaster. One of the women's leaders told him the story of a member who had lost her husband. She had been an active Soka Gakkai member from the time she was in the young women's division. She had just married when the accident took her husband's life. Most of the people who had lost family members were overcome with grief, but she remained strong. It was she who comforted the mourners who came to pay their condolences. Everyone was moved by her example.

"That is wonderful," Shin'ichi said.

"Indeed," the leader added. "She reads the Gosho diligently and studies Buddhist doctrine in earnest."

SHIN'ICHI responded: "That is the power of studying the Buddhist teachings, the power of faith. The Gosho answers the fundamental question of life and death. When we read the Gosho and open the eye of Buddhist wisdom, we learn that death is not something to be feared. Chanting daimoku enables us to experience this and be firmly convinced of it.

"It is only natural to grieve the loss of one's dearly loved partner. But to be defeated by that sorrow is another matter. No one can avoid death. At the same time, human beings cannot help but feel powerless when faced with the prospect of death. Buddhism and faith, however, teach us the correct way to cope with death's reality.

"It is the role of a leader to convey that understanding, and impart courage, hope and conviction to each member. I want all our leaders to put themselves in the place of those who are suffering and continue giving them the support and encouragement they need."

Shin'ichi then proposed that the Soka Gakkai hold a memorial service for the victims of the mining explosion, and discussed the plans in detail with the local leaders.

The Soka Gakkai made astonishing progress again in November. A saying goes, "A courageous general has no weak soldiers." Under Shin'ichi's courageous leadership, members around the country united in a valiant effort to spread the Daishonin's teachings. At the Headquarters Leaders Meeting at the end of the month, the results for November were announced. A remarkable 206,794 households had joined the Soka Gakkai. This was a new record, far surpassing the previous record of 160,777 households achieved in February that year. The tide of kosen-rufu was growing stronger month after month, year after year, taking shape as a powerful new people's movement.

April 2 of the following year, 1964, would mark the seventh memorial (sixth anniversary) of second Soka Gakkai president Josei Toda's death. Shin'ichi had set a goal of three million households by that time, but it was clear that membership would go way beyond that figure, reaching even four million.

Many tragic, dark incidents continued to mar Japanese society, but this had in fact given members a greater motivation to share Nichiren Buddhism with others and realize kosen-rufu. Their strong sense of mission had resulted in the amazing increase in the Soka Gakkai's membership in November.

At the Headquarters leaders meeting, Vice General Director Hisao Seki announced three major goals for the organization in 1964: 1) to realize a three-million-member general pilgrimage to the head temple; 2) to solidify discussion meetings and drive home the importance of gongyo to the members; and 3) to foster capable people.

AT THE MEETING, Shin'ichi expressed profound gratitude to the members for their unprecedented achievement of more than two hundred thousand new member households in the month of November.

"When President Toda died," he began, "we adopted 'Unity' as our motto and embarked on the path of advancement. Since that time, we have continued to put unity first. As a result, we have made tremendous progress, surging forward like a great wave. Now, at this new juncture, let us designate the upcoming year the Year of Unity, and with 'Unity' once again our motto, make a start toward the next seven years. What do you think?"

Vigorous applause shook the Taito Gymnasium.

The Soka Gakkai had become a major people's movement. If the members were to forge stronger unity in their efforts, they would surely be able to transform Japan into a land of peace and happiness. When people unite, their power increases exponentially—fivefold, tenfold, a hundredfold.

The Eleventh Young Women's General Meeting and the Twelfth Young Men's Division Meeting were the last main Soka Gakkai events of 1963. Both were held on December 15 at the Nihon University Auditorium in Ryogoku, Tokyo. The meeting for the young women took place in the morning and the one for the young men in the afternoon. At the young men's leaders meeting held on July 1, five months earlier, Shin'ichi had proclaimed that on the seventh memorial of President Toda's death, April 2, 1964, the Soka Gakkai would enter the essential phase of its development. These December meetings were a kick-off to that event.

The youth understood that the essential phase meant a time when they would realize kosen-rufu, not in concept or theory, but in actuality, and they were determined to make that happen. As a practical step toward this goal, both divisions set out to increase their membership to one million each, a figure that Shin'ichi had proposed at the young women's leaders meeting on July 5. The young men were determined to achieve their target by President Toda's seventh memorial, and the young women by their general meeting in autumn the following year. They had therefore been working in earnest to share Buddhism with their friends and increase their membership.

By the general meetings on December 15, the young women's membership, which had been four hundred and thirty thousand in May, grew to more than seven hundred thousand. The young men, meanwhile, had increased from six hundred and forty thousand to nine hundred and ten thousand by the end of November. Amazingly, by December 15 the young men had reached their goal of one million. The December 15 general meetings were victory celebrations in honor of the incredible progress made by the youth toward the start of the essential phase of the Soka Gakkai's movement.

The realization of high ideals does not take place in some far-away, imaginary realm. It is the result of achieving triumph upon triumph through constant, steady efforts.

THE YOUNG women's and young men's general meetings on Dec. 15, both proceeded with high enthusiasm and energy. Shin'ichi was determined to work together with these young people to complete the essential phase and adorn the century with great achievements in kosen-rufu. He congratulated them on their wonderful departure.

At the young women's meeting, Shin'ichi spoke about the struggles and misfortunes women were forced to endure throughout history. He stressed that the only way to change this situation fundamentally was for each of them to transform her destiny through upholding the Mystic Law and accumulating good fortune. He encouraged them to show actual proof of such happiness in their own lives.

At the young men's meeting, Shin'ichi stated that for kosen-rufu to continue into the future would require many talented people. He urged the young men to therefore give their utmost to fostering younger members.

The Soka Gakkai made historic progress in 1963. A wave of propagation spread throughout Japan, and the banner of the people's victory flew high. The new Soka Gakkai Headquarters building was finished and began to function as a citadel of peace and culture. The organization's development overseas was also smoothly proceeding.

But the most conspicuous growth was that of the youth. As he looked out at the faces of the members gathered that day, Shin'ichi knew that there was nothing to worry about as long as the Soka Gakkai youth continued to grow and develop. The sun of glorious victory would surely shine on the future. The sight of these vibrant young people brought Shin'ichi enormous joy and hope. With these general meetings, the Soka Gakkai was fast approaching its essential phase.

At the end of the year, the Soka Gakkai Headquarters compiled statistics of the organization's overall membership. When the results of members' efforts to introduce others to the practice in December were calculated, the total Soka Gakkai membership was nearing four million households. Hearing this, Shin'ichi exclaimed: "Four million households! We are truly blazing a new trail of kosen-rufu of our own. That is wonderful! President Toda is surely rejoicing, and the Daishonin is without a doubt also praising our efforts."

The Soka Gakkai reached three million households in November of the previous year. This meant the membership expanded by one million in just over twelve months. The tide of kosen-rufu grew at an astonishing rate. This was the true power of the Soka Gakkai, the people and their unity. Filled with a tremendous fighting spirit, Shin'ichi cast his thoughts on the prospects for the year ahead.

AT THE BEGINNING of 1964, the "Year of Unity," Shin'ichi Yamamoto composed the following poems for his friends in the four divisions of the Soka Gakkai:

To the young men's division:
The people are waiting
For our departure

Into a new dawn—
Let us break through
The angry waves of obstacles.

To the young women's division:
Today once more
In your noble struggle
To create happiness
You dance forth gracefully
With strength and pride.

To the men's division:
As emissaries
Of the Great Sage
We set forth
To engage earnestly in battle,
Aiming for total victory.

To the women's division:
Again today
As the Buddha's
Proud messengers
You bloom in a realm
Of peace and happiness
Like the pure white lotus.

The leaders who gathered at the Soka Gakkai Headquarters in Shinanomachi for the New Year's gongyo
meeting read these poems with firm resolve, thus com-
mencing the year joyfully together with Shin'ichi.

With the arrival of the seventh memorial (sixth

anniversary) of the death of second Soka Gakkai president Josei Toda (on April 2) this year, the Soka Gakkai would enter the essential phase of its development. When the assembled leaders thought about the new stage of kosen-rufu they were about to embark upon, their eyes shone with even stronger determination.

In April, the Grand Reception Hall at the head temple, which was built through the contributions of Soka Gakkai members, would be completed, and the three-million-member general pilgrimage would commence. Efforts to spread Nichiren Buddhism overseas would also be stepped up. Shin'ichi was scheduled to visit Australia, Ceylon (Sri Lanka) and India in May. In October, he would travel to Eastern and Western Europe.

From Jan. 15, a party that included Soka Gakkai director Minoru Suzumoto and four other leaders was set to visit seven cities in the Republic of South Korea—Seoul, Taegu, Sunch'on, Kwangju, Cheju, Ulsan and Pusan—to meet with members there. At the time, there were more than 1,000 families practicing Nichiren Buddhism in South Korea. Their activities varied widely from region to region, and discussion and study meetings were conducted independently in each city.

Japanese members felt especially strong ties to their Korean comrades in faith. Some of them had been stationed in Korea during World War II, and there were many members of Korean descent living in Japan who were practicing in local organizations in various parts of the country.

SOKA GAKKAI members in Japan considered the visit of Suzumoto and other Soka Gakkai leaders to South Korea to be a fresh step in the advancement of kosen-rufu in Asia. This prospect excited them and gave them hope. Korea had been the victim of Japanese aggression in the past. The Japanese members therefore felt a responsibility to work for the happiness of the Korean people.

Shin'ichi also had high expectations for Suzumoto's visit. Shin'ichi's father had spent time in Seoul prior to World War II, when he was drafted and stationed there. Whenever the topic of Korea came up in conversation, he would express his indignation at the terrible arrogance and cruelty of the Japanese in Korea to Shin'ichi, who was then in elementary school. These discussions left Shin'ichi with a deep concern for Korea.

Shin'ichi believed that Korea was a great cultural benefactor to Japan, and Japan could best repay its debt of gratitude by sharing Nichiren Daishonin's profound philosophy of happiness and peace with the Korean people. He also advocated the importance of exchange between the peoples of Korea and Japan in order to forge lasting ties of friendship for the sake of future generations.

Japan was the beneficiary of countless cultural treasures from the kingdoms of the Korean peninsula. In ancient times, rice cultivation and the creation of bronze and ironware were all transmitted to Japan from these Asian "neighbors." The same was true of civil engineering, irrigation technology, a system of writing, medicine, pharmacology, and the lunar calendar. Also, the cultivation of the Kyoto Basin[14] in the ancient capital of Kyoto, which endured for some one thousand years, owed much to Korean immigrants.

The most significant treasure of all that Japan received from Korea, however, was Buddhism. Buddhism originated in India and passed through Central Asia into China and Korea, finally making its way to Japan. Japan was the terminal point of its eastern transmission, in the middle of the sixth century. Buddhism had entered the Korean peninsula as early as the fourth century, and it is believed that there were many Buddhists among those who immigrated to Japan. In the beginning, it was probably through these immigrants that Buddhism gradually spread in Japan, but it wasn't until later that it was "officially" introduced to the country.

In his writings, the Daishonin often mentions this momentous achievement of Korea in transmitting the spiritual treasure of Buddhism. He says: "During the reign of the thirtieth ruler, Emperor Kimmei, Buddhist sutras, treatises and priests were sent from the state of Paekche [on the Korean Peninsula] to Japan, as well as a gilded bronze statue of Shakyamuni Buddha, the lord of teachings" (WND, 1113). "Buddhism was introduced to Japan ... by King Syongmyong of the kingdom of Paekche to the west of Japan" (WND, 929).

Korea was a culturally developed land. It was from there that the Buddhism of Shakyamuni was introduced to Japan. Now, it was time for the westward transmission of Nichiren Buddhism to begin.

I N ANCIENT TIMES, the Japanese held Korea in high regard. The ancient Japanese chronicle *Nihon Shoki* describes Korea as a land with "gold and silver and bright colors in plenty."[15] Yet elsewhere in the same work are passages that scorn Korea as well. This no doubt reflected the competitive spirit accompanying the nationalistic sentiments of a newly formed and rising island nation. It also, however, expressed feelings of inferiority and envy toward a country to which Japan owed so much. People who feel inferior often try to make themselves look superior by belittling others.

Many centuries later, in the late sixteenth century, Japan invaded the Korean peninsula. Toyotomi Hideyoshi[16] engineered the attack, first sending a large force to Korea in 1592. He justified his actions by claiming he intended to ask Korea to guide his troops into China.

There were two invasions, one in 1592 and one in 1597, over which time a total of three hundred thousand Japanese soldiers descended upon the Korean peninsula.

In the first invasion, Hideyoshi's troops managed to gain control of most of Korea by a surprise attack. The Korean monarch abandoned the capital and fled north. It was a vicious assault, later denounced for its heinous cruelty and barbarism. But due to the valiant struggle of Korean Admiral Yi Sun-sin to save his country and the courageous resistance of the Korean irregulars across the land, Hideyoshi's forces were driven back. Finally, in 1598, the Japanese invasion ended in defeat.

Many ordinary Koreans were killed in the fighting, and fifty to sixty thousand were taken as prisoners to Japan. Furthermore, the Japanese burned a number of Korean cultural treasures and plundered rare artifacts such as woodblock prints and printed books.

Then, in the second half of the nineteenth century, Japan began a new period of modernization, adopting the slogan "Enrich the Country and Strengthen the Military." Wanting to separate from Asia and ally itself with Western powers, Japan initiated a program of invasion against its Asian neighbors. The basic idea was to become strong and then impose upon Asian countries the unfair treatment it had received from the West in the past.[17]

Korea suffered the most under this Japanese policy. In 1875, in the aftermath of the Kanghwa-do Incident,[18] Japan demanded that Korea open itself to foreign trade. The following year, both countries signed the Treaty of Kanghwa.[19]

THE TREATY of Kanghwa recognized Korea as an independent nation and denied Chinese sovereignty over Korea. At the same time, it was highly favorable to Japan in that it granted Japan extraterritorial jurisdiction over Japanese citizens as well as the freedom to survey the coastal waters of the Korean peninsula. Securing Korea was critical to Japan's plans to invade the Asian continent.

In the following decades, Japan engaged China in the Sino-Japanese War (1894–95) and Russia in the Russo-Japanese War (1904–05). It was during that time that the theory of common ancestry between Japan and Korea was spread throughout Japan. This advocated that the peoples of both countries came from the same ancestral stock, making them "siblings," and that it was therefore only natural that they should unite as one. The proponents of this theory, however, identified the Japanese as the "elder" of the two peoples, placing them in a superior position and encouraging the idea that it was the duty of Japan to protect Korea, its "younger brother." This was how Japan justified the invasion and subsequent occupation of Korea.

In reality, if the relationship between the two countries must be likened to that of siblings, in light of Korea's historical role as a great cultural benefactor of Japan, Korea clearly should be referred to as the elder. Despite this fact, Japan went ahead and attacked the country that it owed a huge debt of gratitude.

Though the Sino-Japanese War was between Japan and the Qing dynasty of China, the fighting in fact took place on the Korean peninsula. The Russo-Japanese War was also triggered by a dispute over rights to the peninsula.

Following the Sino-Japanese War, Korea changed its name to the Taehan Empire.[20]

With the outbreak of the Russo-Japanese War in 1904, Japan ignored Korea's proclamations of neutrality and forced it to accept a protocol obliging it to cooperate in the war effort. Japan's aim was to become a political and military protectorate of Korea and thereby gain control over the country. It also sought economic concessions and to establish a base from which to launch its planned invasion of China.

In August 1904, in the midst of the Russo-Japanese War, the first Korean-Japanese Convention[21] was signed. The war ended in September the following year with the signing of the Treaty of Portsmouth, and Japan was granted authority over Korea.

Then, in November 1905, another Korean–Japanese convention was signed. This gave Japan full administrative control over Korea's foreign affairs and established the Office of Resident General. Japan appointed Ito Hirobumi as its first resident general of Korea. The negotiation of this agreement took place under the supervision of Japanese troops sent to the Korean capital to put pressure on the Korean side.

The Japanese also contacted individual members of the Korean government and coerced them into accepting and signing the new treaty. It is clear that, from start to finish, Japan used strong-arm tactics to accomplish its aims. This naturally sparked fierce anti-Japanese demonstrations in regions across the nation. But with the signing of another convention in July 1907, Japan seized complete administrative power over Korean domestic affairs.

IN AUGUST 1910, a treaty annexing Korea to Japan was signed. This shift from "protection" to "annexation" secured Japan's control of Korea. "Annexation" was nothing more than a euphemism for the elimination of Korea as an independent state and its establishment as a Japanese colony. Thus began nearly four decades of Japan's appalling rule over Korea.

When the annexation of Korea was announced, many Japanese accepted it as a matter of course. This was reflected by attitudes in the media as well as the religious world. Nichiren Shoshu, then known as the Fuji branch of Nichiren Shu, published the complete text of the imperial rescript announcing the annexation in the foreword of its publication *White Lotus*. This included a commentary that deferentially praised the treaty, stating, "The permanent annexation of Korea has been gloriously proclaimed by the imperial command and we, as subjects of the Emperor, humbly embrace his sacred will and rejoice at the procurement of our new fellow countrymen...."

Korea continued to be cruelly exploited as the base for Japan's invasion of the continent. As the war with China (1937–45) intensified, the effort to cultivate loyalty to the Japanese emperor was accelerated in the colonialists' campaign to assimilate Korea to Japan. Japanese imperial education became the curriculum at all Korean schools. Under this system, the Korean people were made to memorize the oath of Japanese imperial subjects, to pay obeisance to the Japanese imperial palace, and to study the Japanese language.

They were also denied religious freedom. A state shrine was built on Mount Namsan, positioned as if glaring down at Seoul. Shinto shrines were also erected across the country. The people were forced to pay homage at these shrines, and to worship a talisman that came from the principal Shinto shrine in Japan.

Meanwhile, in Japan, the first and second presidents of the Soka Gakkai, Tsunesaburo Makiguchi and Josei Toda, were imprisoned by the military government for refusing to worship the same talisman and calling out for freedom of religion. After a sixteen-month struggle, the seventy-three-year-old Makiguchi died in prison holding fast to his beliefs to the very end. The iniquitous Peace Preservation Law of 1925 that was used to incarcerate Makiguchi was also applied in Korea. Any movement that advocated Korean independence was condemned as seeking to change Japanese national polity and persecuted far more harshly than any resistance efforts in Japan.

This cruel treatment extended even to a group of scholars who, in an attempt to preserve their national heritage, compiled a dictionary of the Korean language. Japan rejected every aspect of Korean culture, tradition, and spirituality. It went so far as to try to rob the Korean people of their identity by forcing them to adopt Japanese names.

JAPAN'S colonial rule of Korea was a long, bleak chapter in history. But the invincible Korean people endured the inhumane treatment of the Japanese that was tantamount to an annihilation of the spirit. During this period, tens of thousands of courageous heroes ready to die for their cause kept the torch of Korean independence alight. They believed wholeheartedly that the dawn of freedom and hope would someday arrive and illuminate their dark and wretched land.

That day finally came on August 15, 1945. Japan had been defeated and the sun of liberation began to shine on the Korean peninsula. Cheers rang out across the land. Korea at last bade farewell to the darkness of Japanese military rule and was poised to welcome the light of independence.

But the hardship continued. At the end of World War II, Japan's presence in Korea was replaced by Soviet and U.S. forces moving into the country from the north and south. Korea was divided at the thirty-eighth parallel into two occupied zones under separate policies. Soon the Cold War between the United States and the Soviet Union surfaced and, against the fervent wishes of its own people, the division of Korea into north and south was secured.

In May 1948, elections were held in the south under the supervision of the United Nations to establish an independent government. Syngman Rhee was nominated as the first president, and on August 15, the Republic of Korea was born. Then, on September 9, the Democratic People's Republic of Korea was established in the north, with Kim Il Sung as premier. The Korean peninsula was thus divided into two nations.

Two years later, on June 25, 1950, the Korean War broke out, setting off a civil war between north and south. The northern forces advanced swiftly through the thirty-eighth parallel. In just three days, the southern capital, Seoul, had fallen, and the South Korean government was in flight. This triggered a U.N.-sponsored intervention led by the United States.

The U.N. forces took the offensive and advanced beyond the thirty-eighth parallel, reaching as far north as the Yalu River on the Sino-Korea border. A large force of "Chinese People's Volunteers" then launched a massive counterattack, pushing the U.N. troops back once again. The two sides fought on until an eventual truce was signed. At one point, it is said, the United States even considered using nuclear weapons.

The Cold War tensions between Eastern and Western blocs that arose after World War II brought about a fierce and savage conflict that resulted in bloodshed between a once united people. Though Korea had been liberated from Japanese rule, the spring of peace was still far away.

Three years later, in July 1953, an armistice agreement was at last signed, leaving Korea divided by a demilitarized zone along the thirty-eighth parallel. The war had cost more than 1.26 million Korean lives, and the peninsula was completely devastated.

WITH THE START of the Korean War, Japan, which was still under U.S. occupation, became the base camp for U.S. forces in action on the Korean peninsula. Around this time, the National Police Reserve (later the Self Defense Forces) was founded, opening the way for the rearmament of Japan. It was also during this period that the San Francisco Peace Treaty[22] was signed between Japan and most of the Allied Powers, restoring Japan's independence.

Japan also profited economically from the Korean War. Orders for goods and services from the American military poured into the country. These special procurement expenditures helped revive the Japanese economy, which had been laid to waste by World War II. It is fair to say that Japan's subsequent prosperity was also made possible by the sacrifices of the Korean people.

Talks were convened to normalize relations between Japan and South Korea in February 1952, while the Korean War was still going on. Several sessions were held to discuss the basic relations between the two countries and the legal status of Korean residents in Japan, but negotiations soon became deadlocked. Japan insisted that the annexation treaty of 1910 was effective until the conclusion of World War II. The Korean side, however, rejected the legitimacy of the annexation altogether, and sought reparations for the thirty-six years it had endured under Japanese rule.

At the third conference (in October 1953), Japan's chief representative justified his country's stance by asserting that Korea had benefited as a Japanese colony. He pointed to the fact that Japan had built railroads and harbors and developed farmland in Korea, and dismissed the notion that the Korean people were treated as slaves. He also voiced his belief that any declaration of Korean independence made before the San Francisco Peace Treaty was invalid under international law.

The Koreans were incensed by these outrageous remarks. Their anger was directed at Japan's attempt to defend its actions without the slightest hint of an apology. This was just the first of repeated controversial statements

made by Japanese politicians on this subject in the ensu-
ing years. The talks were thus cancelled and would not
resume for another four-and-a-half years.

Forgetting one's past wrongs is shameful, but to distort
and justify those wrongs is an utter disgrace. It is difficult
to know the degree to which the arrogant words and
deeds of Japan's leaders have obstructed the development
of friendly bilateral relations.

In June 1965, talks between the two nations began
again, resulting at last in the conclusion of the Korea-
Japan Treaty of 1965. From that time on, Japan would
offer assistance to Korea, not in the form of reparations,
but as mere economic aid.

SINCE the independence of the Republic of Korea
in August 1948, the first republic was established with
Syngman Rhee as president. Rhee's despotic behavior,
however, eventually lost him the support of the Korean
people.

In April 1960, mass student-led demonstrations broke
out in protest of his attempt to rig the presidential election held a month earlier.

On April 19, more than ten thousand people led by
university students calling out for justice and freedom
marched on the presidential palace. Police trying to stop
the demonstration shot live ammunition at the protestors,
killing and wounding many. This is known as the April
19 Student Revolution. Then on the 26, despite pressure
from the authorities, demonstrators again took to the
streets of the capital, Seoul. Associated Press reports gave
their number as over one hundred thousand. The United

States subsequently withdrew its support of Rhee, and he was forced to step down.

The second republic was also short-lived. In May 1961, it was overthrown when a military coup led by Major-General Park Chung Hee seized power. Park promised to adopt an anticommunist policy, establish economic independence, and to restore government to civilian control. He later retired from active military service to run in the October 1963 presidential elections and won. The third republic began when Park took office on December 17.

The Korean people had been tossed about like leaves scattered upon the raging rapids of their tempestuous history. Those who were so-called residents of Japan had also suffered bitter hardships. In 1911, just after the annexation, the number of Koreans residing in Japan was around two thousand five hundred. But that number suddenly expanded when Japan's control over Korea intensified.

At the end of World War II in 1945, it is estimated that there were more than two million Koreans living in Japan. Among them were people who, having lost their farmland under Japan's colonial policies, had come to Japan in search of work. Many others had been brought to Japan as conscripted laborers when full-scale hostilities broke out between Japan and China in 1937. In order to guarantee a supply of labor, the Japanese government used the National Mobilization Law and the National Service Draft Ordinance to mobilize people from Korea as well.

Koreans brought to Japan were forced to work in

the mines and in construction for wages much lower than those paid to the Japanese. It was extremely strenuous work.

THE SOKA GAKKAI Youth Division Antiwar Publishing Committee compiled the experiences of Koreans living in Japan during World War II in a book titled *Another Memorial to the Victims of the Atomic Bomb*.[23] In it is the story of Chang Bok Soon, a Korean woman who was born in Japan.

"The only jobs available to my father," she relates, "were dangerous ones, such as coal mining, subway and road construction. The wages he received were much lower than his Japanese counterparts. He would often come home from work injured, but we were never given compensation. We were so poor and didn't have enough to eat."

Chang Bok Soon's father had been a farmer in Kyongsangnam Province in South Korea, but he lost his land in the nationwide land survey conducted by the Japanese governor-general and was forced to look for work in Japan in 1931. Chang was born the following year. Almost a decade later, World War II began. When the American air raids against Japan intensified, the family had to evacuate to the countryside. They moved from Osaka to Hiba County in Hiroshima Prefecture to make their way as tenant farmers.

The family experienced discrimination when they arrived in the mountain village that would be their new home. The shelter they were provided with was nothing but the corner of a barn used for raising silkworms, which was partitioned off by straw matting. Furthermore, they had been allotted a muddy parcel of land situated in a shady recess of the mountain that proved difficult to harvest. They were still, however, compelled to meet the government's strict production quotas. After that, all the family had to eat was whatever edible wild plants, nuts and berries they managed to find.

Chang recollects: "I was picked on just because I was Korean. Even in school races, we had to let the Japanese girls beat us. We had to make them look good. Everyone knew that; it was common knowledge. We weren't allowed to stand out or succeed.

"When we were playing with Japanese children, they would suddenly start chanting 'Korea, Korea,' and throw stones at us and say that we stunk. When I told my mother about this, she said: 'It must be all the garlic we eat. That's what makes us smell. It's only natural for them to say that.' And so I started to think that it was only natural for them to pick on me. I decided to eat as little garlic as possible.

"I was very naive. When I thought later about what my parents said to me, I realized it was their way of teaching me to survive in Japanese society. They knew that nothing good could come of resisting or rebelling."

Yet how anguished those parents must have felt having to teach their children to endure discrimination and prejudice.

THEN the atomic bomb was dropped on Hiroshima. About a week after the bombing, Chang went with her mother to Hiroshima City to check on the safety of relatives and friends living there. After a long search, they finally found one of their friends. Though terribly burned, she was holding her son and shooing flies from his wounds. The woman said: "There aren't enough doctors or medicine, and we Koreans are at the bottom of the list, so we aren't being treated. Everyone is dying, one after another. We're just waiting our turn." Chang's mother burst into tears.

Chang recalls: "She completely broke down and wept uncontrollably, screaming: 'We move to a foreign country and are made to work like cattle and horses. Then we are burned to cinders! Why didn't they just kill us? What crime have we committed to be forced to suffer like this, half-burned to death?' As she ranted on in Korean, she beat her fists on the ground in a total rage as if she was mad. Everyone around us was crying, too.

"This was the first time I had ever seen my mother lose control and voice resentment about Japan. Up to then, she had done all she could to get by in Japanese society. She knew she had no choice, so she tried to make the best of it while holding on to her heritage in her heart. But from that moment, I knew her true feelings.

"My father never tried to learn Japanese. His love for his country was the core of his being. He would say: 'Why should I speak the language of our enemy? We're only living this way because we can't die.' We never spoke anything but Korean in the house."

Though the Japanese referred to the Koreans as fellow "imperial subjects," Koreans in fact faced harsh discrimination and oppression. This tragedy continued after the war as well. When Korea was liberated from Japan's colonial rule, most Koreans returned to their homeland, but more than six hundred thousand stayed in Japan.

Then in 1952, the San Francisco Peace Treaty that had been signed the previous year took effect, and the Japanese government stripped all Koreans living in Japan of their Japanese citizenship. Koreans were thus forced to register with the government as aliens, or to apply anew for Japanese citizenship.

THE JAPANESE government's treatment of Korean residents in Japan after the war was extremely cold and cruel. Even harsher, however, was the unchanging and deep-rooted prejudice and discrimination directed at Koreans by the Japanese people. Regardless of the official policy in place, many Japanese companies refused to employ Koreans, and many people would not rent them rooms.

In this climate, second Soka Gakkai president Josei Toda was profoundly concerned about the welfare of the Korean people and he continued to pray for their happiness. Just after he became the second president of the Soka Gakkai in 1951, in the midst of the Korean War, he published an article in the organization's study journal, *Daibyakurenge,* titled "Kosen-rufu and the Korean War."

In it he wrote: "I am deeply grieved at the fact that because of this heinous war, so many have lost husbands and wives, and so many must now search for their missing children or parents.... Many young people have died without knowing what for. And I am sure old women have been murdered as they cried out, 'I've done nothing wrong!'"

President Toda's greatest desire was the happiness of all people. That is the purpose of the Soka Gakkai. The Soka Gakkai does not discriminate. The Nichiren Buddhism practiced by the Soka Gakkai teaches a principle of life by which all human beings, regardless of race, ethnic background, nationality, sex or age can realize absolute happiness without fail. Everyone has the right to become happy. In fact, those who have suffered the most deserve to become the happiest. The Soka Gakkai has always worked for just that.

In the great effort to introduce others to Nichiren Buddhism that took place after Toda became president, the number of Korean residents of Japan who joined the Soka Gakkai also increased. President Toda had always called for the propagation of Nichiren Buddhism throughout Asia, even conveying this fervent wish in a poem:

To the people of Asia
Who pray for a glimpse of the moon
Through the parting clouds
Let us send them, instead,
The light of the sun.

Inspired by President Toda's spirit, the Korean Soka Gakkai members in Japan determined to work for the happiness of their fellow Koreans. Among these members were Shoji Tajima and his wife, Mie.

Shoji was born in Ulsan, Kyongyongnam Province, South Korea, and moved to Japan with his family when he was six years old. His family had lost its farmland under the Japanese colonial administration and was forced to emigrate. His wife Mie was a second-generation Korean born in Tokyo whose family was originally from Taegu in Kyongsangbuk Province. They got married in 1944. When World War II ended the following year, Shoji's family decided to return to Korea. Shoji, however, was working at a medical university while studying to enter the affiliated medical school, so he remained in Japan.

Fulfilling her responsibility as the wife of the eldest son, Mie returned to Korea with Shoji's family, stepping for the first time on the soil of her homeland.

MIE first arrived at Pusan in the south, and it was there that her son was born. But Pusan was crowded with people arriving from and leaving for Japan. In order to escape the confusion, Mie soon moved on to Ulsan, her husband's hometown.

Many of the Koreans returning from Japan had a difficult time adjusting to life in Korea, and some were looked down upon as useless by their compatriots. Children born in Japan sometimes could not speak Korean, and they were called derogatory names and picked on by other Korean children.

Mie wanted to be trusted in her new homeland, so she worked hard as a farmhand, despite her inexperience. She spent each day working in the fields from dawn until dusk, finally washing the mud from her feet under the twinkling stars. Still, she could barely manage to feed her family.

Then the Korean War broke out. Mie went to visit her own family in Taegu and while she was there, the fighting drew near. This made her realize the possibility of her own death and that she had to be ready. During that time, her father passed away from illness. Her homeland was filled with pain and sorrow, and she began to wish she could return to Japan and be with her husband.

In 1952, Mie heard about a boat going to Japan. She made up her mind to go, and one night, leading her young son by the hand, she boarded a small fishing vessel. At the time there were no diplomatic relations between Korea and Japan, and the situation was volatile. This made it difficult to get to Japan by normal means. Lying low in the boat's hold, Mie and her son left Korea, but they were intercepted by the Japanese coast guard and arrested for trying to enter Japan illegally.

Finally, through her husband's tireless efforts, they managed to gain permission to enter Japan. The family thus began a new life in Yokohama. Shoji was running a small hotel, and things were going well. They soon gave birth to a daughter, but at one year of age she contracted tuberculosis and had to be hospitalized. It was at this time that Mie learned of Nichiren Buddhism through a woman who helped her with the housework. In 1954 she joined the Soka Gakkai in the hope that her daughter would be cured.

Her husband also became a member, but in name only, and he was strongly opposed to any participation in Soka Gakkai activities. Mie gradually gave in to him and distanced herself from the Soka Gakkai. In the meantime, Shoji's business collapsed and he had to give up his hotel. They started a grocery store, then a confectionery, but nothing succeeded. The next thing they knew, they were a family of six living in a cramped six-tatami-mat room.

WHEN HER FAMILY'S financial difficulties hit rock bottom, Mie received some encouragement from fellow Soka Gakkai members. This made her deeply aware of her personal karma and she decided to turn it around through faith. Shoji, too, motivated by their dire circumstances, began to practice sincerely. The couple started making regular visits to the Soka Gakkai Headquarters to chant daimoku.

The Tajimas worked very hard. Early each morning

they set up a food cart in front of the local unemployment office. They didn't have a shop or even a stand. Instead, they would load all of their cooking supplies and implements onto a bicycle-drawn cart, pull it up to the building, and cook the food right there. They prepared a nutritious pork and vegetable soup that they served over rice.

They had nothing to rely on but faith. They acutely understood that they had no choice but to trudge through each day with patience and fortitude. At one point, they were able to receive guidance from second Soka Gakkai President Josei Toda. Inspired by his strong conviction in faith, they vowed to change their karma and actively began to share Nichiren Buddhism with others. Every day they would leave the house at the crack of dawn and pull the heavy cart to the unemployment office. After setting up, Shoji would go off to work as a manual laborer. They spent their evenings together, joyfully participating in Soka Gakkai activities.

They had also suffered because of the harsh and unfair attitudes directed at Korean residents by Japanese society. But they found in the Soka Gakkai a realm of warm acceptance. The kind encouragement and support of their fellow members, who treated them better than family, always moved them.

Shoji eventually started a trading company with a friend and then went into business on his own. He later became active in finance and before long was able to lift his family completely out of poverty. "This Buddhism is amazing!" he thought. "It will absolutely bring happiness to anyone. I must do whatever I can to share this

wonderful faith with my compatriots in South Korea!"
Firmly determined to fulfill that desire, the Tajimas took
a trip to their homeland in the autumn of 1959 and
began to talk to friends and relatives about Buddhism.
While they were there, Mie's mother started practicing.
Shoji's parents and Mie's sister-in-law later followed suit.

Then in 1961, Mie was appointed women's leader of
Waseda Chapter in Tokyo. During the interview for the
position, she said to Shin'ichi Yamamoto with tears in
her eyes, "I don't have the ability to fulfill the huge
responsibility of being a women's division chapter
leader." But Shin'ichi replied reassuringly: "You'll do just
fine! I'll support you. Just be confident and do your best!"

PRESIDENT YAMAMOTO'S words gave Mie
great courage. Two years later, she became a general
chapter women's leader, and her husband Shoji was
appointed vice chapter leader. They began visiting South
Korea regularly, making trips to Ulsan, Taegu, and Pusan
to share Buddhism with their friends.

Sumie Oh'i was another Soka Gakkai member of
Korean descent. She was in her mid-forties and had been
born in Seoul but held Japanese citizenship. She had
moved to Japan during World War II and then returned
to Korea after it was over. In 1947, she went to live in Japan
once again. She joined the Soka Gakkai in 1959 and gradually deepened her faith through Soka Gakkai activities.

In 1960, Sumie received a letter from her younger sister in Seoul, Lee Yeon Hee. She was having some health
problems, perhaps related to menopause, and was spending a lot of time in bed. Sumie decided to take a trip

home after thirteen years, and she was determined to help her sister and do something for the sake of her fellow Koreans.

Lee Yeon Hee was surprised to see how happy, energetic and cheerful her sister was after so many years. What surprised her even more was that Sumie sat down each morning and evening and diligently chanted what sounded like a difficult Buddhist scripture. Sumie spoke to her sister in earnest: "If you practice this Buddhism, you will increase your life-force and definitely become happy. You can even overcome your health problems. I came all the way here because I want you to find happiness."

Lee Yeon Hee could feel the tremendous conviction in Sumie's words. Most of all, she felt her sister's deep love for her. As they continued to speak about faith, she was struck by Sumie's sincerity, and decided to try it herself. After Sumie returned to Japan, Lee Yeon Hee became an avid reader of the Soka Gakkai publications *Seikyo Shimbun* and *The Daibyakurenge*, which Sumie sent her. She then began seriously practicing Nichiren Buddhism. Before she knew it, her health improved. She then started visiting other members in South Korea whose addresses she learned from her sister and encouraged them in faith.

At the time, Shin'ichi had just become third president of the Soka Gakkai, and a great wave of worldwide kosen-rufu began to surge. More and more members of Korean descent were returning to their homeland to tell their friends and families about Buddhism. In addition, those people who took up faith in South Korea were making efforts to spread Nichiren Daishonin's teachings throughout their country.

BEFORE LONG, discussion meetings and study meetings on Buddhist doctrine were being held in the major cities of South Korea. Just as the Daishonin predicted when he said that people would appear to spread the teachings as if "emerging from the earth," people with a wondrous mission were springing up all over South Korea.

According to statistics from the Soka Gakkai Headquarters Overseas Department, in October 1963 there was a total of nine hundred and forty-eight member households in South Korea. There were one hundred and seven in the four provinces—Kyonggi, Kangwon, Chungchongbuk, and Chungchongnam—around the capital of Seoul; one hundred and sixty-seven in Taegu and the surrounding region; five hundred and twenty-four in the southern area around Pusan and Ulsan; one hundred and five in Kwangju and the provinces of Chollabuk and Chollanam; and forty-five on Cheju Island.

Since that time, the membership had continued to grow rapidly in Taegu and other locations. However, not much progress had been made in the way of creating an organization, and many members were practicing without the Gohonzon. Their only spiritual sustenance came in the form of Soka Gakkai publications and the letters they received from Japan.

Yet even in these circumstances, the members in South Korea continued enthusiastically to pursue their faith. They had sent hundreds of requests to the Soka Gakkai Headquarters in Japan for guidance and for the dispatch of leaders to South Korea. The headquarters therefore decided to send Minoru Suzumoto, and Shoji and Mie

Tajima, Korean residents of Japan, as well as other leaders. They were scheduled to be there from January 15 through 25, 1964. The purpose of the trip would be to encourage the South Korean members and to deepen Japan-Korea relations on the private level.

When the South Korean members learned that leaders from Japan would be coming they were overjoyed, and eagerly looked forward to their arrival. General meetings were planned in each area, and preparations were made for proper organization.

Suzumoto and the others applied for visas at South Korea's representative office in Japan, but still hadn't received an answer. They made several trips to the office to inquire, but were always told that the South Korean government had not granted permission yet. The departure day was drawing near, and the leaders began to wonder if there was some sort of problem. The closer the day came, the more anxious they grew.

Then, in the first week of the new year, South Korean newspapers began to publish articles critical of the Soka Gakkai.

HEADLINES reading "Mass Production of Japanese-manufactured 'Happiness'" and "Investigation of Soka Gakkai's Internal Affairs Begins" started appearing in South Korean newspapers, creating the impression that the Soka Gakkai was a suspicious religion exported by Japan. The members there were at a loss for what to do. They couldn't understand how such reports could be written when they had done nothing wrong.

Meanwhile, January 15 came and went, and the leaders

who were set to go to Korea still had not received their visas. It turned out that in the midst of the media's attacks, the South Korean Ministry of Education was deciding how it would deal with the Soka Gakkai. In the January 16 morning edition of Japan's *Mainichi Shimbun* newspaper, the foreign correspondent in South Korea reported that the South Korean government decided two days earlier that the Soka Gakkai and South Korea were "incompatible." The headline read "South Korea Restricts Religious Propagation."

The article identified the points on which the government had based its restriction of the Soka Gakkai's activities in South Korea. One was that Soka Gakkai members chanted daimoku and read the scriptures in Japanese, and when they did so they bowed toward Japan in the east where the founder, the Daishonin, was born. The government called this an offense against the feelings of the Korean people.

Another claim made by the government was that the Soka Gakkai-backed Komei-kai had become the third strongest political force in Japan, and it was concerned about handling the same situation should it happen in South Korea. Also, the ministry of education had surmised that there were more than ten thousand Soka Gakkai members in the country.

On January 16, South Korea's representative office in Japan officially informed Soka Gakkai Headquarters that the visa requests were denied. The next day, the Education Ministry convened a council on religion, which concluded: "We have reason to believe that the Soka Gakkai has strong imperialist tendencies and is a nationalistic and exclusionary group. Therefore, regardless of whether or not it is a genuine religious organization or a political organization, at present we must deem it anti-Korean.

"As we do not wish to open our doors to a covert spiritual invasion that would sully our national spirit, we urge the Korean people to unite immediately to prevent the spread of the Soka Gakkai."

On the morning of January 18, the South Korean education minister announced a government ban on the propagation of the Soka Gakkai's teachings because of the organization's "anti-Korean tendencies." The situation had suddenly become dire.

THE CONCLUSION reached on January 17 by the Education Ministry's council on religion and the statement made by the education minister that the Soka Gakkai was acting against the interests of Korea and the Korean people were also reported in Japanese newspapers. Korean residents of Japan who were Soka Gakkai members were shocked when they saw these articles. They could not imagine what had happened and were concerned about the outcome. It was a truly puzzling turn of events.

As soon as this harsh criticism of the Soka Gakkai began to appear in South Korean newspapers, Shin'ichi Yamamoto set out to analyze the situation objectively and accurately. He examined both the newspaper accounts as well as reports on the situation from the members in Korea.

Shin'ichi decided that the controversial issues cited by the newspapers could be divided into five points. First was the fact that Soka Gakkai members faced east during the first prayer of morning gongyo, which meant they were praying to Japan; second, that they recited daimoku and the sutras in Japanese; third, that members were made to worship Tensho Daijin, the Shinto sun goddess, because her name appeared on the Gohonzon; fourth, that the Soka Gakkai was militaristic and possessed the same militant aggressiveness as the Japanese forces that had invaded and occupied Korea; and fifth, that the Soka Gakkai was actually a political group. These reports stated that because the Soka Gakkai had crossed the boundary of religion and become deeply involved in the political domain, it had forfeited the right to freedom of religion guaranteed by the constitution.

Looking at these claims, it was clear that each was based on misconceptions of the Soka Gakkai. In South Korean society, religion was considered something practiced in a temple or a church where followers would gather, pray, and conduct ceremonies. But Soka Gakkai members did gongyo and chanted daimoku in private; it was in the homes of individuals that their religious activities took place. In fact, the attendance at discussion meetings was often so high that not everyone could fit inside. This enthusiastic way of practicing one's religious beliefs challenged conventional Korean notions of religion, and no doubt it appeared strange to onlookers.

Though their faith was still rather young, many South Korean members had already experienced personal victories over sickness, poverty, and family discord, and they spoke passionately of these experiences. Unfortunately, this gave some people the mistaken impression that the

Soka Gakkai was a false religion that promised to heal the sick and make its members wealthy.

IGNORANCE of the true nature of things causes anxiety, which easily turns to fear. It appeared that the greater the Soka Gakkai membership in South Korea became, the more people connected to the government and the religious world grew concerned. It was also a period of strong anti-Japanese sentiment in the country. For that reason, the announcement in the *Seikyo Shimbun* that the Soka Gakkai was sending leaders to South Korea may have seemed to the government like the start of an invasion by Japanese religion. Furthermore, it probably had little information upon which to base a proper understanding of the Soka Gakkai.

Most of the issues in question, however, stemmed from fears connected to the militarism and imperialist policies of Japan during its occupation of South Korea. These impressions of the Soka Gakkai were of course completely mistaken, but they testified to the depth of the scars left by Japan's thirty-six years of colonial rule. During that time, Japan forced Koreans to worship at Japanese Shinto shrines and tried to suppress their religious beliefs, the very foundation of the human spirit. Robbing a people of their freedom of religion can be likened to spiritual genocide. This naturally left the Korean people leery of Japanese religion.

To add insult to injury, the Japanese media at the time frequently accused the Soka Gakkai of being "militaristic." This was simply because the youth division had adopted such titles as corps leader and company leader, titles that had been used by the military in the past. No matter what the truth was, however, the very label "militaristic" was enough to arouse strong fear and hatred among the Korean people, who had suffered tremendously at the hands of the Japanese military.

Certain intellectuals were also claiming that the Soka Gakkai was violating the separation of church and state by forming the Komei-kai political group, which was comprised of Soka Gakkai-backed politicians. In addition, the South Korean government may also have been influenced by the publication of a special feature on the Soka Gakkai by a popular U.S. magazine in September the previous year that alleged that the organization's aim was world domination.

It was unclear exactly what had been the basis of the government's ideas about the Soka Gakkai. But if this was all the information it had to go on, it was hardly surprising that the Soka Gakkai had come to be seen as an extremely dangerous religion.

Shin'ichi concluded that the present situation in South Korea was based solely on misunderstanding. If that could be corrected, he figured, the problem would be resolved.

SHIN'ICHI decided that, in addition to correcting the misunderstandings of the South Korean government and the media, it was also important to make the full truth of the matter known to the Soka Gakkai members of Korean descent living in Japan. He did not want their faith to be needlessly shaken.

At his suggestion, on January 21 the *Seikyo Shimbun* printed an article featuring the current problems faced by the members in South Korea. The article outlined the events that had transpired so far, and explained in detail the misapprehensions of the South Korean government. It also clearly addressed each point.

First, the article explained that facing east during morning gongyo was in no way a worship of Japan. In doing so, members were greeting the sun as the representative of all the protective functions of the universe. This meant that members across the Pacific in the United States also turned to the east when they performed gongyo, not west in the direction of Japan.

Second, rebutting the notion that Soka Gakkai members chanted daimoku and recited the sutra in Japanese, the article stated that the words Nam-myoho-renge-kyo derived from Sanskrit and Chinese, as elucidated by Nichiren Daishonin. The Lotus Sutra, it said, was also written in Chinese. The Daishonin was very proud of the international nature of his teachings and hoped they would remain as a treasure of humanity, transcending all national and ethnic boundaries.

Third, the article asserted that Tensho Daijin, the Japanese sun goddess, was not the object of devotion of the Soka Gakkai. From the Buddhist viewpoint, Tensho Daijin was but one of the forces protecting those who practiced the correct teachings of Buddhism. This was fundamentally different from the situation during World War II when the Japanese military government forced the people of the Korean peninsula to worship Tensho Daijin in order to cultivate loyalty to the emperor. At that time, in Japan, both the first and second presidents of the Soka Gakkai, Tsunesaburo Makiguchi and Josei Toda, boldly refused to accept the talisman representing Tensho Daijin. This led to their imprisonment by the military authorities and Makiguchi's subsequent death.

Fourth, in response to the charge that the Soka Gakkai was militaristic, the article stated that historically, no other group had stood up to militarism as the Soka Gakkai had. The Soka Gakkai, it affirmed, was an organization of peace and culture diametrically opposed to any form of militarism and committed to working for the happiness of all humanity.

Lastly, the article confirmed that the Soka Gakkai was not a political organization, but a purely religious group. In Japan, it had participated in politics out of a spirit of compassion for the Japanese people, whose interests had been forgotten by the corrupt political establishment. It had no intention, however, of engaging in any political activities outside Japan.

INCLUDED IN the *Seikyo Shimbun* article were comments by Soka Gakkai General Director Koichi Harayama. He wrote: "The Soka Gakkai has of late been the subject of controversy in South Korea. The government there has recently made various statements about our organization, most of which unfortunately have been based on misinformation. It is our sincere wish that this problem be cleared up as quickly as possible, and that a correct understanding of the Soka Gakkai be established.

"Religion has no national boundaries. Transcending all distinctions of race and nationality, Christianity and Buddhism alike spread throughout the world. Buddhism, in particular, originated in India and made its way through China and into Korea, eventually being transmitted to Japan via the ancient Korean kingdom of Paekche.

"The reason the Daishonin's Buddhism is now increasingly being embraced by people across ethnic and national boundaries is that it is a genuine religion dedicated to world peace. It is a world religion with a universal philosophy of life that elucidates guiding principles toward the realization of happiness.

"Our greatest hope is that people in Korea will be able to practice the Daishonin's teachings and thereby contribute to the prosperity of their own nation. Moreover, we can all work together in the effort to build happy lives and achieve world peace."

General Director Harayama also addressed the Soka Gakkai's plans to dispatch leaders to South Korea: "We had prepared to send leaders to South Korea in order to strengthen ties of friendship with the Korean people as well as to encourage the local members in their faith and make sure that things were proceeding in a reasonable manner. It is truly unfortunate that our intentions were not sufficiently understood.

"I firmly believe, however, that these recent incidents will stimulate inquiry into the Soka Gakkai that will result in a fair evaluation based on complete understanding and recognition. I hope that the Korean people will come to appreciate just how committed our organization is to realizing happiness and peace in their country."

Regrettably, because the visa requests of the Soka Gakkai leaders were rejected, it was impossible for the Soka Gakkai Headquarters to meet and talk with the South Korean authorities in order to dispel their misconceptions. This especially disappointed those leaders who had scheduled to make the trip.

On January 21, the same day the article appeared in the *Seikyo Shimbun,* the South Korean State Council resolved to "establish policies to control the Soka Gakkai and prevent its expansion."

IN RESPONSE, on January 23 a request was sent from the education minister. It asked the minister of communications and the chief of the National Security Council for cooperation in regulating all Soka Gakkai–related mail. This meant that it would be difficult for any

Soka Gakkai publications or other printed materials to be sent from Japan to South Korea.

Choi Jeong Yeol was a young man in his thirties who ran a dyeing business. He lived in Taegu, Kyongsangbuk Province, the third largest city in South Korea. He had joined the Soka Gakkai about two years earlier and was very active, playing a central role among the members in Taegu. When Choi read in the newspapers about the new policies the government had adopted toward the Soka Gakkai, he knew that he had to do something. Wanting his country to have a correct understanding of the Soka Gakkai, he wrote up a report explaining just what kind of religious group it was, and sent it to the Ministry of Home Affairs.

After about ten days, in early February, Choi received a letter sent by certified mail dated January 31. It was an official reply from the minister of home affairs that read: "I hereby inform you that the Soka Gakkai to which you belong is a Japanese imperialist religion with strong leanings toward exclusionism and ultranationalism. Therefore, at present, the government has deemed the Soka Gakkai an anti-national, anti-Korean organization.

"Consequently, any meetings, correspondence or announcements with the aim of propagation, as well as the import of publications that support such activities and their distribution, acquisition or perusal, are all in violation of national policy. I ask that you fulfill your patriotic duty and cooperate with the government in this matter."

As Choi read the minister's reply, the color drained from his face and he began to shake with anger. "What has led the government to these unfounded conclusions?"

he wondered. "What has the Soka Gakkai ever done to deserve such treatment? From the start, we've been unfairly branded a dangerous organization. But all we've done is work sincerely for the happiness of our fellow Koreans and to create a peaceful society. What could possibly be wrong with that?"

He chanted daimoku, thinking about what he should do next. As he chanted, he realized that this was the appearance of the three obstacles and four devils that function to impede the progress of kosen-rufu, just as Buddhism taught. A fierce determination to win this struggle thus began to surge inside his heart.

SOON AFTER Choi had received the government's official response, he and six or seven other core members of the Taegu region met in one of their homes. Choi began by reading the letter to everyone. The members looked anxious as they listened. They realized that to continue practicing Nichiren Daishonin's Buddhism could well lead to their arrest and imprisonment. In fact, it was not unusual for their discussion meetings to be conducted under police surveillance.

Choi started to speak, as if to encourage himself: "This document labels the Soka Gakkai as an anti-Korean, unpatriotic organization. It outlaws any meeting or correspondence for purposes of propagation, as well as any attempt to import, distribute or obtain Soka Gakkai publications that may promote our beliefs.

"But the South Korean constitution guarantees the freedom of religion. We haven't done anything to violate the law, have we? I believe that this problem has arisen simply from our government's mistaken perceptions of the Soka Gakkai. We really have nothing to be afraid of."

Choi's voice grew stronger as he spoke. "If we look at this situation in light of the Daishonin's writings, we are clearly being confronted by the three obstacles and four devils that try to prevent people from practicing. In other words, our faith is being tested.

"Given the circumstances, we must of course take into consideration the social implications of our actions. But I also feel that now is the time for us to speak out boldly on behalf of Nichiren Buddhism and the Soka Gakkai, without retreating a single step. What will happen if we allow ourselves to be defeated by this obstacle and let the flame of our faith die out? We will never be able to show our compatriots, who have already suffered terribly, the way to genuine happiness.

"I'm determined to stand up and carry out my faith until the very end, no matter what happens. Please stand up with me! Let's vow that no one will stop practicing and do everything we can to support our fellow members and give them courage."

The members still were all relatively new in their faith. But as they listened to Choi's sincere plea, their eyes gradually began to shine with resolve.

Another meeting was held on February 8. About twenty members attended, including the original group. Together, they solidified their determination to win. Amid the harsh wind of persecution, the flame of the Taegu members' faith burned brightly.

THE SITUATION in Seoul was also dire. Sumie Oh'i had returned to South Korea the previous year (1963), and was staying at the home of her sister Lee Yeon Hee. She had been preparing for the arrival of the Soka Gakkai leaders from Japan. But from early January, when the articles against the Soka Gakkai began to appear in South Korean newspapers, the police started dropping by her sister's home to check up on the family's activities. They were questioned again and again.

Sumie knew she had done nothing wrong. Hoping to dispel the mistaken views of the authorities, she did her best to explain the history of the Soka Gakkai and its true nature to them. She was firmly determined to succeed, believing that if she didn't, the seed of the Mystic Law that had just begun to sprout in Seoul would be wiped out.

The situation grew worse each day. Sumie felt that she was experiencing the passage "If you propagate it [the Mystic Law], devils will arise without fail. If they did not, there would be no way of knowing that this is the correct teaching" (WND, 501). She realized she must encourage the other members in Seoul not to be defeated, no matter what happened.

During this stormy time, the Seoul members gathered in a local Chinese restaurant to discuss the situation. The authorities were watching them, and it would have been dangerous to meet in someone's home. The members' faces were clouded with apprehension. Sumie said to them: "The Daishonin tells us, 'Those who believe in the Lotus Sutra are as if in winter' (WND, 536). That is our position right now. However, the passage continues, 'but winter always turns to spring.'

"As long as we carry out our faith diligently, spring will certainly come. The season of hope will arrive. I hope that you will support and encourage one another and advance together in unity. Please!" Sumie spoke in all sincerity. Her fellow members nodded as they listened, tears shining in their eyes.

A storm of persecution was trying to wash away the young shoots of the Mystic Law that had sprung forth from South Korean soil. But the members clung to the earth with all their might, determined to sink deeply the roots of faith.

In Taegu, Choi Jeong Yeol, having received official notice from the minister of home affairs restricting the Soka Gakkai's activities, was racking his brain to find a way out of the dilemma. What he found so hard to reconcile was that the constitution of the Republic of South Korea guaranteed freedom of religion as one of the basic human rights of all citizens. Choi thought that to prohibit the import, distribution, acquisition or perusal of Soka Gakkai publications must surely be a violation of that basic human right.

AFTER CAREFUL deliberation, Choi met with the central members in Taegu and shared his thoughts: "The response from the Ministry of Home Affairs is presented as a request for cooperation with government policy, but clearly its aim is to prohibit the Soka Gakkai's activities. If we sit back and allow this to happen, the constitutional principle of religious freedom will be compromised and we will be robbed of one of our basic rights as citizens of this country. Since the letter is a governmental order, however, I am thinking of demanding that it be retracted."

In the latter part of February, Choi sent a petition to the home affairs minister asking him to revoke the ministry's request on the grounds that it was in violation of the constitution. At the beginning of March, the minister rejected Choi's petition. Choi then took his case to the Seoul High Court, filing a suit against the minister demanding that the government's policies toward the Soka Gakkai be rescinded.

Soon it was April. Choi was under serious pressure, both direct and indirect, and the situation eventually worsened to the point that he was unable to keep his dyeing business afloat. Nevertheless, the flame of his faith continued to burn. He also received tremendous support from his brother-in-law and other Soka Gakkai members.

A year later, in February 1965, the Seoul High Court handed down its verdict on Choi's case. The defendant had argued that the letter in question was only an explanation of government policy and a request for cooperation in that regard, not an executive action. The minister further stated that if there had been confiscation of any Soka Gakkai-related publications sent through the mail, it had been done, not by governmental order, but under the provisional mail control law. This allowed the government to stop or confiscate any mail deemed a threat to national security or public safety.

The court, however, handed down a decision in Choi's favor. The government was ordered to rescind the measures instituted on January 31, 1964, that prohibited any gatherings or correspondence aimed at promoting the teachings of the Soka Gakkai, as well as the import, distribution, acquisition and perusal of the organization's printed materials. But the Ministry of Home Affairs refused to accept the decision and appealed the case to the Supreme Court.

Six months passed, and Choi was now working on a farm in a suburb of Seoul. One day, the police turned up out of the blue and arrested him, throwing him into the Seodaemoon Detention House in Seoul. He was charged with violating the foreign exchange law, and by extension, the Soka Gakkai fell under suspicion of financial misdeeds.

THE SOKA GAKKAI Headquarters neither sent money to support the activities of the members in South Korea nor collected donations from those members for use in Japan. In other words, there were no financial dealings between the Soka Gakkai Headquarters and the members in South Korea, which meant there was no way they could have violated the foreign exchange law.

While Choi was in police custody, he was forced to listen to criticism of the Soka Gakkai by the official in charge of the investigation. He was told that if he quit the organization he would be released. But Choi held fast to his beliefs, like a great boulder that sits impervious to the raging rapids around it.

After twenty-nine days, Choi was let go without being charged. Other members in Taegu were also subject to various kinds of persecution because of their faith. They were also increasingly given the cold shoulder by society in general. Many were attacked for practicing what was perceived to be a Japanese religion. Some were cut off by their friends who feared being associated with the group, and others even lost their jobs.

Members in other parts of South Korea also faced severe trials. Their discussion meetings were conducted under police surveillance, and the authorities went so far as to confiscate the Gohonzon and Soka Gakkai publications, claiming they were necessary for the investigation.

The members, however, took this situation as an opportunity to summon forth genuine faith. They continued to brave the storm of persecution, speaking out boldly for the Soka Gakkai and Nichiren Buddhism. They chanted daimoku in earnest. Not even the fierce winds of adversity could extinguish the flame of their faith. Through these efforts, the members experienced great benefits one after another, deepening their faith even further. Seeing this, more and more people began practicing Nichiren Daishonin's teachings.

The Supreme Court reached a verdict in October of the following year, 1966, overturning the decision of the Seoul High Court. The verdict stated that Choi's case was based on a misunderstanding of the letter from the Ministry of Home Affairs. Legally, the letter was no more than a "notification of opinion," and not an administrative measure by the governmental authority. The court therefore deemed Choi's demand that the government rescind its order unnecessary and dismissed his claim altogether.

In other words, the ministry's reply was merely a statement of the government's opinion of Nichiren Shoshu

and the Soka Gakkai, and not an executive decision
against religion.

THE SOUTH KOREAN members were not
satisfied with the Supreme Court's decision. The
fact was that in South Korea members were being
arrested arbitrarily, and many had their Gohonzon and
Soka Gakkai publications taken away from them.

They could not help but think that this treatment,
which caused them great suffering and fear, was directly
related to the Ministry of Home Affairs labeling the Soka
Gakkai anti-Korean and unpatriotic. They felt that the
Supreme Court's decision was abstract, for it hid behind
empty legalism while ignoring the reality of the Korean
members' situation. The decision was significant, however, in that it confirmed that the South Korean constitution guaranteed freedom of religion. This was, in a way,
a ray of light piercing the darkness.

Still, there was no change in the attitude that the Soka
Gakkai was acting against the interests of South Korea
and its people, nor did the government alter its line that
the organization's religious activities were a violation of
national policy. Even if the members could hold activities,
it would have been very difficult for Soka Gakkai Headquarters in Japan to send leaders to the country to encourage the members there. Under the circumstances, the only
alternative for the South Korean members was to band
together and uphold the torch of faith on their own. There
was still no sign of an end to their winter of hardship.

The members in South Korea hungrily read the books
and other publications that had been sent to them before

the ban, and studied Nichiren Buddhism. Through learning about such doctrines as the Ten Worlds, the oneness of life and its environment, and three thousand realms in a single moment of life, they came to understand the principles of human revolution and changing one's karma. In this way, their conviction and faith in Buddhism deepened.

As they studied the guidance of Soka Gakkai president Shin'ichi Yamamoto, they learned that Nichiren Buddhism was a religion dedicated to the happiness of all humanity and the realization of world peace. Thus, they renewed their determination to work for the well-being of their fellow citizens.

Nothing can stop a strong determination. Filled with love for their country these courageous members fought onward, never giving in to frustration or despair. It is said that the tree with the deepest roots withstands the drought. The passionate commitment of the South Korean members to bring happiness to their compatriots triumphed over their harsh circumstances, and gradually the circle of members in South Korea grew. By 1969, there were some thirty thousand member households, and flowers of benefit and joy blossomed across the land.

The members established chapters and districts by their own initiative, and advanced their activities with tremendous energy.

A STRONG determination can move the universe. Therefore, no matter how difficult the social circumstances may be, they can definitely change.

Soka Gakkai members in South Korea firmly believed that the day would come when they could hold their heads high in society and freely carry out their activities. Each member worked hard to become a model citizen and continued steadily to pursue his or her faith.

In the mid-1970s, the South Korean government adopted a wait-and-see position whereby it would allow Soka Gakkai activities to take place as long as they abided by the law. This was a considerable change from the days when all activities aimed at sharing the Daishonin's teachings with others were treated as a violation of national policy.

During this time, more and more people began to practice, but no move was made officially to organize the membership. Each area was developing in its own way and becoming organized around the relationships developed between members and the people they introduced to the practice. Consequently, their activities were conducted independently.

At one point, after a series of conferences a central figure and vice leader had been selected to head the South Korean organization, but this did not result in a unification of the membership. In addition, some leaders were acting according to their own whims despite an agreement that the organization would be run in line with the guidelines of the Soka Gakkai Headquarters in Japan. The members thus remained split into several groups.

The members themselves were pure-hearted and had a strong seeking spirit. But in one group, an ambitious leader took advantage of their sincerity and began collecting donations from them for his personal use. This leader later left the Soka Gakkai.

Around 1973–74, the members in South Korea were divided roughly into three groups. On January 26, 1975, the inaugural meeting of the SGI took place on Guam with members from fifty-one countries and territories around the world in attendance. It was a new beginning in the global movement to realize happiness and peace for all humanity. South Korea, however, was not represented because its leaders were still unable to work together. Some of them were practicing as they pleased and had consequently become self-centered.

That is why it is crucial to have firm guiding principles and a strictly impartial leader who works for kosen-rufu in exact accord with the Buddhist Law.

SHIN'ICHI was deeply disappointed that the South Korean organization had not managed to delegate representatives to attend the inaugural meeting of the SGI. He also felt sorry for the members who had endured long years of difficulty and hardship fighting on the front lines of the kosen-rufu movement in South Korea. He therefore decided to establish a section at the Soka Gakkai Headquarters in Japan that would serve to provide encouragement and guidance to the South Korean members. Its ultimate aim would be to help them establish harmonious unity and advance together in mutual respect as disciples of the Buddha who possess a noble mission. Soka Gakkai General Director Kiyoshi Jujo, Vice President Hiroshi Izumida, and other leaders were put in charge.

After a number of discussions, in May 1976 the members in South Korea held a national conference in Seoul to inaugurate the Korean Buddhist Association as the official Soka Gakkai organization. At the meeting, nine steering committee members were chosen, and from among them three were elected as chairpersons. Though it was a tripartite leadership, at last an organization that would unite all of South Korea was born.

Still, the members had many storms to weather. Certain individuals went against the correct teachings and splintered off to form their own groups. Corrupt Nichiren Shoshu priests and people who turned their backs on the Soka Gakkai in Japan went to South Korea and furtively caused trouble in the organization there. But such disturbances only strengthened the purity of the members' faith. As a result, those who wished to exploit the organization for their personal benefit and leaders who cared only about themselves were weeded out. In this way, the group developed into what is now the SGI of Korea, a mighty river of like-minded individuals working together for the peace and prosperity of their homeland.

South Korean society, however, continued to treat the Soka Gakkai harshly. Newspapers still frequently wrote of the organization as a nationalistic, Japanese religion which would threaten the cultural identity of South Korea. Nichiren Buddhism, however, is fundamentally a religion for all humanity that transcends the boundaries of Japan. As the Daishonin said, "The Lotus Sutra is the teaching that enables all living beings to attain the Buddha way" (WND, 59). The Mystic Law is for the happiness of all people without exception.

The Daishonin also referred to the highest political authorities of his time as "the rulers of this little island country" (WND, 765). As this indicates, Nichiren Buddhism does not embrace any form of Japanese nationalism. Furthermore, Buddhism expounds the concept of propagating the teaching according to the locality. This means respecting the culture, spirituality and customs of all nations, peoples and regions, as long as they do not oppose the basic principles of Buddhism.

NICHIREN DAISHONIN writes, "A person of wisdom is not one who practices Buddhism apart from worldly affairs but, rather, one who thoroughly understands the principles by which the world is governed" (WND, 1121). In other words, to practice Buddhism means to value society; it means to contribute to and work for society's benefit. One who does so is a "person of wisdom."

The members in South Korea were determined to demonstrate the truth and validity of Nichiren Buddhism and the Soka Gakkai. If they allowed misunderstanding to pass unchallenged, the truth would be lost. Failing to correct mistaken ideas spells the death of truth and justice.

"Everything depends on how great a difference we can make in society," the members thought. "That is how we can show the integrity of the Soka Gakkai." With this in mind, members all over the country began voluntarily working for the betterment of their communities.

In the 1970s, the South Korean government initiated

a series of programs aimed at rural modernization called the New Village Movement. Seeking to improve the standard of living for all citizens, the movement gradually spread from the villages to the cities, where it promoted increased community awareness, environmental beautification and tree planting.

The South Korea members took active part in planning various social programs for the government initiative. In one campaign to aid farming villages, they helped plant and harvest rice. They also instituted environmental protection activities. Later in the 1990s, they inaugurated a large-scale nationwide clean-up campaign. Much energy was also put into education and social welfare, with the promotion of book donation drives for local schools and efforts to help the underprivileged.

Based on Buddhist humanism, these practical, grassroots endeavors gained trust in society for the organization. In December 1979, it was highly praised for contributing to an increase in food production and crop damage prevention, and the members received a commendation from the Minister of Agriculture, Forestry and Fisheries. This was the first time for the group to be honored by South Korea.

In January 1984, South Korean president Chun Doo Hwan recognized the organization for its contributions to boosting the income of farming and fishing communities. In June 1996, the director of the Office of Environmental Control hailed the group for its work in the cause of environmental protection. It also received numerous citations from regional government agencies across the nation.

All of this was proof that the Korean Buddhist Association had become an organization of hope, indispensable to society. The members' tenacious efforts had broken through the thick wall of misunderstanding that had once prevailed.

SHIN'ICHI YAMAMOTO chanted daimoku every day for the happiness and success of his noble fellow members in South Korea, praying that they would be showered with benefit. Whenever he heard that members from South Korea were arriving in Japan, he would be the first on hand to greet them. He would pour his whole life into offering them encouragement, as if taking each of them in a warm embrace.

Shin'ichi had also worked hard to build an eternal bridge of friendship and trust between South Korea and Japan through the promotion of cultural and educational exchange. As a result of his efforts, in the autumn of 1990 arrangements were completed for the Tokyo Fuji Art Museum's "Masterpieces of European Oil Paintings" exhibit to travel to Seoul. As founder of the museum, Shin'ichi attended the opening ceremonies for the exhibit, at last fulfilling his long-held wish of visiting Korea.

In May 1998, Shin'ichi made another trip to South Korea. He had been invited by the distinguished Kyung Hee University in his capacity as the founder of Soka University and was bestowed an honorary doctorate in philosophy. The doctorate recognized Shin'ichi's "tireless efforts for world peace" and his "enormous contributions to South Korea-Japan friendship based on a deep understanding of Korean culture and history." During the trip, on May 18, he visited the SGI-Korea Headquarters for the first time.

The early summer breeze was refreshing. Members were waiting for Shin'ichi to arrive. Since fierce storms of tribulation had blown in 1964, the members in South Korea had dreamed of, prayed for, and eagerly looked forward to this day. So had Shin'ichi.

He called out to these great champions of faith with deep emotion: "You have shown magnificent proof to all that your presence assures certain victory! You have triumphed!" Joyous applause erupted.

"You are contributing to the welfare of society and promoting humanism," he went on. "The Buddhist Renaissance of the twenty-first century is beginning now from South Korea. Nothing delights me more. The whole world commends you!"

He poured his entire being into each and every word. "Please, lead lives of happiness, lives of meaning, lives of victory!" he said.

Not a single eye remained dry. Everyone was filled with tremendous joy. They burned with a passionate vow to advance anew.

The tree that has withstood the storm glistens with a brilliant fresh green crown of glory. A golden sun that would illuminate the twenty-first century shone in the hearts of the South Korean members, who had endured and overcome incredible hardship.

NOTES

1 Coretta Scott King, *My Life with Martin Luther King Jr.* (New York: Avon Publishers, 1969), p. 248.

2 *Asahi Evening News*, Saturday, 23 Nov. 1963, International section.

3 *New York Times*, Sunday, 24 Nov. 1963, p. 6.

4 Speech delivered on June 10, 1963.

5 From a radio and television address to the American people on the Nuclear Test Ban Treaty.

6 Theodore C. Sorensen, *Kennedy* (New York: Harper & Row, Publishers, 1965), p. 740.

7 Robert Kennedy, *Thirteen Days: A Memoir of the Cuban Missile Crisis* (New York: W. W. Norton & Company, Inc., 1969), p. 128.

8 From President Kennedy's inaugural address, January 20, 1961.

9 In 1962, Mississippi state officials refused to abide by a U.S. Supreme Court ruling that ordered the admission of a black student, James Meredith, to the University of Mississippi. After a night of rioting during which two people were killed, Meredith was finally admitted.

10 From a radio and television report to the American people on civil rights on June 11, 1963.

11 Sakurajima —Volcanic island connected to the Osumi Peninsula in southern Kyushu.

12 Shimonoseki — Port city located on the southernmost tip of Honshu, the Japanese mainland.

13 Fukuoka — A prefecture on Kyushu island.

14 Kyoto Basin — Located in southern Kyoto Prefecture, central Honshu, Japan's main island. At the basin's north end lays the city of Kyoto.

15 *Nihongi: Chronicles of Japan from the Earliest Times to A.D. 697,* trans. W.G. Aston, C.M.G. (Rutland, VT: Charles E. Tuttle Company, 1972), p. 221.

16 Toyotomi Hideyoshi (1537-98) — Warlord who in 1590 completed the work of national reunification.

17 In the 1850s and 60s Japan was forced into a number of so-called unequal treaties with the Western powers that granted the West a number of privileges, including extraterritoriality, and deprived Japan of tariff autonomy.

18 Kanghwa-do Incident — In September 1875, a Japanese warship purportedly taking a survey of the Korean coast was fired upon by a Korean battery on Kanghwa Island when it entered the mouth of the Han River, the main waterway leading to Seoul. This led to the signing of the Treaty of Kanghwa.

19 Treaty of Kanghwa — First modern treaty between Korea and Japan that was signed on Kanghwa Island in February 1876. It provided for the opening of three Korean ports, a Japanese consul appointed to each that had extraterritorial jurisdiction over Japanese nationals and exemption from custom duties.

20 Taehan Empire (Taehan Cheguk) — Replaced Choson as the official name of Korea in October 1897 and was used until Japan's annexation of Korea in 1910. The name was intended to symbolize Korea's independence from all foreign powers.

21 Korean-Japanese Convention of 1904 — Gave Japan the right to install advisors to the Korean government on financial and diplomatic affairs and required Korea to seek Japanese approval of all important diplomatic dealings.

22 San Francisco Peace Treaty — Signed by Japan and 48 other nations in San Francisco on September 8, 1951 and formally implemented on April 28, 1952.

23 All of the quotes from this book are translated from Japanese. *Mou Hitotsu no Hibaku Hi: Zainichi Kankokujin Hibaku Taiken*

no Kiroku (Another Memorial to the Victims of the Atomic Bomb: A Record of the Experiences of Koreans Living in Japan Who Were Victims of the Atomic Bomb) (Tokyo: Daisan Bunmeisha, 1985), pp. 17–27.

Index

More on Nichiren Buddhism and Its Application to Daily Life

The following six titles can be purchased from your local or on-line bookseller, or go to the Middleway Press Web site (www.middlewaypress.org).

The Way of Youth: Buddhist Common Sense for Handling Life's Questions, by Daisaku Ikeda
"[This book] shows the reader how to flourish as a young person in the world today; how to build confidence and character in modern society; learn to live with respect for oneself and others; how to contribute to a positive, free and peaceful society; and find true personal happiness."
—Midwest Book Review (14.95, Middleway Press, ISBN 0-9674697-0-8)

For the Sake of Peace: Seven Paths to Global Harmony, A Buddhist Perspective, by Daisaku Ikeda
"[Ikeda] is a true citizen of the world and peace leader. In *For the Sake of Peace,* he describes a path to peace through individual commitment and self-control, dialogue and

the creation of cultures of peace. Recognizing the considerable obstacles to creating a peaceful world, he inspires hope that such a world is possible."
— David Krieger, President, Nuclear Age Peace Foundation (25.95, Middleway Press, ISBN 0-9674697-2-4)

Soka Education: A Buddhist Vision for Teachers, Students and Parents, by Daisaku Ikeda

From the Japanese word meaning "to create value," this book presents a fresh spiritual perspective to question the ultimate purpose of education. Mixing American pragmatism with Buddhist philosophy, the goal of Soka education is the lifelong happiness of the learner. Rather than offering practical classroom techniques, this book speaks to the emotional heart of both the teacher and student. (25.95, Middleway Press, ISBN 0-9674697-4-0)

The Living Buddha, An Interpretive Biography, by Daisaku Ikeda

This is a biography with a double focus. It is at once a vivid historical narrative based on what is known or can be reasonably surmised about Shakyamuni Buddha's life and times, and an inspiring account of a heroic life dedicated to helping all people free themselves from suffering. (12.95, Weatherhill, ISBN 0-8348-0322-4)

The Buddha in Your Mirror: Practical Buddhism and the Search for Self, by Woody Hochswender, Greg Martin and Ted Morino
"Like the Buddha, this book offers practical guidelines to overcome difficulties in everyday life and to be helpful to others. The authors have done a great service in bringing the profound practices of Asian Buddhism into American idioms. Readers will find these pages are like a helpful and supportive friend."
— Dr. David Chappell, Editor, *Buddhist Peacework: Creating Cultures of Peace* (23.95, Middleway Press, hardcover, ISBN 0-9674697-1-6; 14.00 softcover, ISBN 0-9674697-8-3)

Choose Hope: Your Role in Waging Peace in the Nuclear Age, by David Krieger and Daisaku Ikeda
"This book gives us all hope because it reminds us that in addition to the gift of life, we are each also given the gift of choice. We each can choose to reject the bomb, the bullet, and all the techniques of violence. We can choose to live fully alive in each moment, refusing to hurt or kill our brothers and sisters, who make up the human family. We can, above all, as Daisaku Ikeda and David Krieger remind us in this inspirational book, choose hope."
—Mairead Corrigan Maguire, Nobel Peace Prize laureate (23.95 USA/35.95 CAN, Middleway Press, ISBN 0-9674697-6-7)

The following titles can be purchased at SGI-USA bookstores nationwide or through the mail order center: call 800-626-1313 or e-mail mailorder@sgi-usa.org.

My Dear Friends in America, by Daisaku Ikeda
This volume brings together for the first time all of the SGI president's speeches to U.S. members in the 1990s. (19.95, World Tribune Press, mail order #4104)

The Wisdom of the Lotus Sutra, vols. 1–4,
by Daisaku Ikeda, Katsuji Saito, Takanori Endo and Haruo Suda
A captivating dialogue on the 28-chapter Lotus Sutra that brings this ancient writing's important messages into practical application for daily life and for realizing a peaceful world.
Volume 1 (9.95, World Tribune Press, mail order #4281)
Volume 2 (9.95, World Tribune Press, mail order #4282)
Volume 3 (10.95, World Tribune Press, mail order #4283)
Volume 4 (10.95, World Tribune Press, mail order #4284)

The Winning Life:
An Introduction to Buddhist Practice
Using plain language, this booklet gives a quick-yet-detailed introduction to a winning way of life based on Nichiren Daishonin's teachings. A perfect tool for introducing other to the benefits of practice.
(1.00; World Tribune Press, mail order #4105 [English], 4106 [Spanish], 4107 [Chinese], 4113 [Korean])

Faith into Action: Thoughts on Selected Topics,
by Daisaku Ikeda
A collection of inspirational excerpts arranged by subject. Perfect for finding just the right quote to encourage yourself or a friend or when preparing for a meeting.
(12.95, World Tribune Press, mail order #4135)

For Today and Tomorrow: Daily Encouragement,
by Daisaku Ikeda
Daily words of encouragement that are sure to inspire, comfort and even challenge you in your practice of faith. Great for the newest member and seasoned practitioners.
(16.95, World Tribune Press, mail order #4100)

A Youthful Diary: One Man's Journey
From the Beginning of Faith to Worldwide
Leadership for Peace,
by Daisaku Ikeda
Youthful inspiration for people of all ages. Through the tale of the ever-deepening relationship between the young Daisaku Ikeda and his mentor-in-life, Josei Toda, *A Youthful Diary* is a compelling account of both triumphs and setbacks on the road to establishing the foundation of today's Soka Gakkai.
(23.95, World Tribune Press, mail order #4101)